*Independent Newspapers*

# INDEPENDENT
# NEWSPAPERS
*A History*

Mark O'Brien & Kevin Rafter

EDITORS

FOUR COURTS PRESS

Set in 11.5 pt on 13.5 pt Centaur for
FOUR COURTS PRESS LTD
7 Malpas Street, Dublin 8, Ireland
www.fourcourtspress.ie
and in North America for
FOUR COURTS PRESS
c/o ISBS, 920 N.E. 58th Avenue, Suite 300, Portland, OR 97213.

A catalogue record for this title
is available from the British Library.

ISBN 978-1-84682-360-2

# Contents

# Illustrations

# Contributors

JOE BREEN is a former managing editor at the *Irish Times.* He attended St Vincent's CBS, worked as a copyboy and became a sub-editor at the *Irish Times.* He stayed with the newspaper for 36 years where he worked as chief sub-editor, systems editor, op-ed editor, online editor and duty editor. Since leaving the newspaper he has completed a master's degree in media and international conflict at University College Dublin and is now a freelance editor, lecturer and consultant.

GAVIN ELLIS is a former editor-in-chief of New Zealand's largest newspapers – the *New Zealand Herald* and *Weekend Herald* – that were acquired by Independent News and Media in 1995. He retired in 2005 after a 40-year career in journalism and media management and now lectures on media ownership and on propaganda at the University of Auckland. His current research projects include trustee media ownership, effects of news agency closure, and the relationship between politicians and the press gallery.

JOHN HORGAN is the press ombudsman for Ireland. After careers in journalism and politics, he joined the academic staff of Dublin City University in 1982 as lecturer in journalism, and was later appointed as Ireland's first professor of journalism. He is the author of a number of books on media, including *Irish media: a critical history since 1922* (London, 2001) and *Broadcasting and public life* (Dublin, 2004), as well as several political biographies.

IAN KENNEALLY is a historian and writer. He completed a master's degree in Irish history at University College Cork and is currently an IRCHSS Government of Ireland scholar, undertaking a PhD in history at NUI Galway. He has contributed to numerous publications and is the author of three books including *The paper wall: newspapers and propaganda in Ireland, 1919–1921* (Cork, 2008) and *Courage and conflict: forgotten stories of the Irish at war* (Cork, 2009). His most recent book is *From the earth, a cry* (Cork, 2011), a study of the nineteenth-century journalist, John Boyle O'Reilly.

COLUM KENNY is professor of communications at Dublin City University. A member of the Broadcasting Authority of Ireland and a director of the EU Media Desk in Ireland, he is a regular contributor to the *Sunday Independent.*

His most recent books are *Irish patriot, publisher and advertising agent: Kevin J. Kenny, 1881–1954* (Bray, Co. Wicklow, 2011) and *The power of silence: silent communication in daily life* (London, 2011).

FELIX M. LARKIN is a freelance historian and writer, having retired from the Irish public service in 2009. He is currently chairman of the Newspaper and Periodical History Forum of Ireland and vice-chairman of the National Library of Ireland Society, for which he edited *Librarians, poets and scholars: a festschrift for Dónall Ó Luanaigh* (Dublin, 2007). He has published numerous essays about the history of the press in Ireland, especially about the *Freeman's Journal* – and is the author of *Terror and discord: the Shemus cartoons in the* Freeman's Journal, *1920–24* (Dublin, 2009).

PATRICK MAUME is a researcher for the ongoing 'Dictionary of Irish Biography' published in book form and online by the Royal Irish Academy. He is a graduate of University College Cork and Queen's University Belfast. His publications include *Life that is exile: Daniel Corkery and the search for Irish Ireland* (Belfast, 1993), *D.P. Moran* (Dundalk, 1995) and *The long gestation: Irish nationalist political culture, 1891–1918* (Dublin, 1999). From 1998 to 2001 he undertook research on the history of the *Irish Independent* with the support of Independent News and Media, and he has published several articles on the *Irish Independent* and on other aspects of Irish newspaper and print culture history.

IDA MILNE was employed by Independent Newspapers in various editorial and administrative capacities from 1979 to 2000. She was awarded a PhD in history by Trinity College Dublin for her research on social, political, economic and medical aspects of the 1918–19 influenza epidemic in Ireland. She is a founding member of the Oral History Network of Ireland and a contributor to journals and books on oral, local and sports history and the history of medicine.

GARY MURPHY is associate professor of government in the school of law and government at Dublin City University. He has written extensively on post-war Irish politics. Recent publications include *In search of the promised land: politics in postwar Ireland* (Cork, 2009), *Continuity, change and crisis in contemporary Ireland* (London, 2010) co-edited with Brian Girvin, and *Regulating lobbying: a global comparison* (Manchester, 2010) with Raj Chari and John Hogan. He was visiting Fulbright professor of politics at the University of North Carolina, Chapel Hill in 2011–12.

MARK O'BRIEN is a lecturer in media and journalism history at Dublin City University and the author of *The Irish Times: a history* (Dublin, 2008) and *De Valera, Fianna Fáil and the Irish Press: the truth in the news* (Dublin, 2001). He is co-editor (with Mary P. Corcoran) of *Political censorship and the democratic state: the Irish broad-casting ban* (Dublin, 2005). He was historical advisor on the RTÉ produced *Family Fortune: De Valera's Irish Press* (2004). He is currently secretary of the Newspaper and Periodical History Forum of Ireland and chairman of the media history collection advisory board, Dublin City University.

DONAL Ó DRISCEOIL lectures in the school of history at University College Cork. His publications include *Censorship in Ireland, 1939-45: neutrality, politics and society* (Cork, 1996) and *Peadar O'Donnell* (Cork, 2001) and as co-editor, *Politics and the Irish working class, 1930-1945* (London, 2005). With Diarmuid Ó Drisceoil he has co-edited *The Murphy's story: the history of Lady's Well Brewery, Cork* (Cork, 1997), *Serving a city: the story of Cork's English Market* (Cork, 2005), and *Fifty years have flown: the history of Cork Airport* (Cork, 2011). He is currently completing a biography of Irish revolutionary and journalist Tadhg Barry, and a history of media and literary censorship in twentieth century Ireland.

KEVIN RAFTER is senior lecturer in political communication and journalism at Dublin City University. He worked previously as a political journalist with the *Irish Times*, the *Sunday Times* and the *Sunday Tribune.* A former editor of *Magill* magazine he also presented RTÉ's *This Week* radio programme and worked as a correspondent with *Prime Time*. He has published widely on media and politics. Recent publications include *Democratic Left: the life and death of an Irish political party* (Dublin, 2011) and *Road to power: how Fine Gael made history* (Dublin, 2011). He is also editor of *Irish journalism before independence: more a disease than a profession* (Manchester, 2011).

AOIFE WHELAN is an IRCHSS Government of Ireland scholar in the school of Irish, Celtic studies, Irish folklore and linguistics at University College Dublin. She is currently working on a doctoral thesis on the portrayal of the 'Irish-Ireland' ideology in the *Irish Independent* newspaper using both Irish and English sources. She has previously analyzed a selection of Breandán Ó hEithir's Irish language material from the *Irish Times* in an article in the Irish language journal, *Comhar*.

PADRAIG YEATES has written extensively on industrial relations and Irish history. His publications include *A city in wartime: Dublin 1914–18* (Dublin, 2011), *Lockout: Dublin 1913* (Dublin, 2000), and (with Tim Hastings and Brian Sheehan) *Saving the future* (Dublin, 2007). He is currently project manager for SIPTU on the 1913 Centenary. He is former industry and employment correspondent with the *Irish Times*.

# Preface

January 1905, March 1973 and April 2012 – three key dates in the history of Independent Newspapers (now Independent News and Media). The first edition of William Martin Murphy's *Irish Independent* appeared on 2 January 1905. With the sale of the business to Tony O'Reilly in March 1973 the long-time Murphy family ownership concluded while thirty-nine years later in April 2012 the O'Reilly family's operational control itself effectively came to an end.

When news emerged on 19 April 2012 that Gavin O'Reilly was to step down as INM chief executive, the story led radio and television news bulletins. In subsequent days the machinations in the company's boardroom featured prominently across all media. The public policy implications of businessman Denis O'Brien being the largest – and dominant – INM shareholder drew comment from leading political figures. The debates – regardless of their end results – showed that in a democratic society the media matters. In this respect it is, therefore, important to understand the various forces that make up a media organization, that shape its development and influence its place in wider society.

For over a century Independent Newspapers has been at the centre of public life in Ireland, often in controversial circumstances. Yet, unlike its two leading national competitors – the *Irish Times* and the Press Group – no single-authored history of Independent Newspapers has yet appeared. This book does not claim to fill that void but it does seek to chart the history of Independent Newspapers and will hopefully open the way for further academic research.

Born out of the 'newspaper war' that erupted amid the tempestuous split in the Irish Parliamentary Party, the pro-Parnell *Irish Daily Independent* was first published on 18 December 1891, some two months after Parnell's death. Re-titled the *Irish Independent and Nation* in September 1900 following its acquisition by ardent anti-Parnellite, William Martin Murphy, it was re-launched as the *Irish Independent* on 2 January 1905. The paper and its sister titles, the *Evening Herald* (1891) and the *Sunday Independent* (1905), have played influential roles in the development of the print media and journalism in Ireland and it is this history, or at least its main aspects, that this book seeks to record.

As Patrick Maume's chapter illustrates, the daily title had a precarious existence prior to its purchase by William Martin Murphy. Despite keeping the flame of Parnellism alive, the newspaper was beset by numerous problems including undercapitalization and allegations that it was anti-clerical. Already a controversial and successful entrepreneur, the *Irish Independent* played a central role in bolstering Murphy's business interests, most particularly, as Padraig Yeates demonstrates in his chapter, during the Great Lockout of 1913. But Murphy did not have everything his own way: Felix Larkin's chapter examines Murphy's ownership through the prism of his relationship with long-time *Irish Independent* editor, T.R. Harrington, who was determined that the newspaper cease being the political plaything of the anti-Parnell faction of the Irish Parliamentary Party. Larkin credits Harrington with carrying out a revolution in Irish journalism. Other revolutions were also occurring and Ian Kenneally's chapter chronicles the challenges faced by Harrington and the *Independent* in the aftermath of the 1916 Rising and the subsequent war of independence and civil war.

That the newspapers survived, despite having their printing presses destroyed, was remarkable; and they prospered and grew in circulation as the 1920s unfolded. This success was due in no small part to the endeavours of the company's advertising manager, Tom Grehan, whose life and career are examined by Colum Kenny. The *Irish Independent* was, as Kenny points out, one of the first newspapers in Europe to publish audited circulation figures as a promotional tactic. The support given by the daily title to the Irish language and its early Irish-language columnists are examined by Aoife Whelan while the subsequent chapter looks at the career of Frank Geary, who steered the *Independent* through the turbulent 1930s when the dominance of the title was challenged by de Valera's *Irish Press*. Geary also features in Donal Ó Drisceoil's chapter, which looks at the effects that wartime censorship had on all three Independent titles and the reactions of all three editors to the strictures of the censorship regime that hampered journalism between 1939 and 1945.

The reactions of the Independent titles to major political and economic events from 1945 to 1963 are considered by Gary Murphy. Among the events considered are the Mother and Child Crisis, the publication of T.K. Whitaker's *Economic development*, and Ireland's application for entry to the European Economic Community. Another major event of that period, the repeal of the External Relations Act, features in the subsequent chapter that focuses on the career of Hector Legge, who, as editor of the *Sunday Independent*, scooped everyone else with his exclusive story about the government's intention to declare a republic.

The 1960s was a decade of profound change: it was also, as John Horgan illustrates, a period of change and expansion at Independent Newspapers. Appointed *Irish Independent* editor in 1968, Louis McRedmond sought to bring the title upmarket but was sacked before any substantial change could take place. At the *Sunday Independent*, another new editor, Conor O'Brien, oversaw the publication of an *exposé* on the Sweepstakes that ultimately prompted the Murphy family to sell Independent Newspapers to one Tony O'Reilly. But newspapers are more than editors and owners and are the product of many hands. In her chapter, Ida Milne interviews journalists, administrators and printers and sheds light on what it was like to work for Independent Newspapers from the 1950s to 2004. In his chapter, Joe Breen considers the impact of Tony O'Reilly's arrival on the newspaper group through the prism of the career of Vincent Doyle who edited the *Irish Independent* between 1981 and 2005.

The subsequent chapter chronicles the takeover of the group by Tony O'Reilly, its expansion in Ireland and its oft-time controversial relationship with Irish politics. Taking a wider view, in his chapter Gavin Ellis examines the transformation of Independent Newspapers into Independent News and Media, and its emergence as a international media organization. With media interests in South Africa, India, Australia and New Zealand, the company became a global player but, as Ellis found, much of the expansion involved the assumption of heavy debt that ultimately brought the O'Reilly era to a close in 2012. The final chapter examines the place of proprietors in the life of the company and considers the future for the group and its titles.

Many of the controversies and personalities associated with the Independent titles are woven through the pages of this volume. There are other chapters the editors would have liked to have included – the emergence of tabloid publications such as the *Sunday World* and the *Irish Daily Star*, the relationship of the Independent titles to the Catholic church, and the more recent editorial stance and commercial success of the *Sunday Independent* – but on this occasion contributors undertaking such academic research were not available. The history of the media in Ireland offers a rich vein for scholarly study and hopefully this volume will encourage more work in this important area.

\*\*\*

The editors would like to thank each of the chapter contributors who kept to tight deadlines to ensure this book was published in 2012. Without downplaying any of the other contributors we particularly wish to thank Prof. John Horgan whose knowledge and advice has guided not just this project but also much other work in the development of media and journalism study in Ireland. Thanks are also due to Martin Fanning and his colleagues at Four Courts Press who guided this project from idea to publication in a thoroughly professional manner.

We would like to acknowledge support for this publication from the Social Science Publication Fund at Dublin City University and to INM for providing photographs for this publication. These images vividly show the changing nature of newspaper production and are in themselves an important record of the history of the Independent titles. Particular thanks to Joe Webb, Michael Hinch and in particular Ann Marie Kilfeather whose work in locating certain photographs is very much appreciated.

*Mark O'Brien and Kevin Rafter*

# 1 / Parnellite politics and the origins of Independent Newspapers

## PATRICK MAUME

The present-day *Irish Independent* was launched on 2 January 1905 as a mass-circulation commercial newspaper, politically unaffiliated though associated with middle-class conservatism. The title, however, had a prehistory. From the appearance of the *Irish Daily Independent* in December 1891 until its acquisition (with its sister titles) by William Martin Murphy in August 1900, it had been the official organ of the Parnellite party. The 'Independent' in the title referred to the description that Parnellites ascribed to themselves – that of 'independent nationalists'. This chapter surveys the short life of the Parnellite *Independent* drawing on the newspaper, and particularly its domestic political coverage, as its primary source. While such an approach may involve over-reliance on public rhetoric and underestimate backstage intrigues, it nonetheless offers a valuable insight into *fin de siècle* nationalism.

### IRISH NATIONALIST NEWSPAPERS BEFORE THE PARNELL SPLIT

In the third quarter of the nineteenth century Ireland's most prominent Catholic/nationalist newspaper was the *Freeman's Journal*, owned by the Gray family and associated with conservative-nationalist politics. Its principal nationalist rival was the weekly *Nation*, owned by T.D. and A.M. Sullivan. Through his establishment of the weekly *United Ireland* in 1881, Charles Stewart Parnell had effectively forced the *Freeman's Journal* to support him as leader of the Irish Parliamentary Party. The threat of *United Ireland*, edited by William O'Brien, going daily was enough to secure the *Freeman's* support. The principal loser of this manoeuvring was the *Nation*, which was sold to a syndicate led by William F. Dennehy that transformed it into the *Irish Catholic*. When the O'Shea divorce scandal split the Irish Party, the *Freeman* initially stood by Parnell. In response, the staunch anti-Parnell faction led by Tim Healy christened the *Freeman* 'The Fallen Journal' and established a new daily newspaper to advance their views. The *National Press* was built around the *Irish Catholic*, was funded by Healy's ally William Martin Murphy, and was staffed by *Freeman* defectors and other anti-

Parnellite journalists. Given the circumstances of Parnell's fall from grace, the *National Press* was promoted fiercely by priests. Following Parnellite electoral set-backs, boycotts and financial losses, in September 1891 the *Freeman* switched its support to the moderate anti-Parnellites led by John Dillon.[1] Now it was the turn of Parnellites to excoriate 'The Fallen Journal'. Parnell's own weekly news-paper, *United Ireland*, run by Parnellite chief organizer and Dublin MP, Timothy C. Harrington, was itself crippled by the loss of rural readers who had turned predominantly anti-Parnellite.

## 'PARNELL'S PAPER ... THE PEOPLE'S PAPER'

Faced with the hostility of both the *Freeman* and the *National Press*, in the last weeks of his life Parnell planned a new daily newspaper to bolster his position. Offices were leased in Trinity Street in Dublin city centre[2] and the *Irish Daily Independent* first appeared on 18 December 1891, edited by former *Freeman* editor Edward Byrne. Its deputy editor was John Wyse Power, a former *United Ireland* journalist.[3] The *Evening Herald* followed on 19 December under another *Freeman* veteran, Thomas Moore. Among the *Independent's* early correspondents were John O'Callaghan, a *Boston Globe* journalist and political activist, and Mary Barry O'Delany, a journalist associate of Maud Gonne, who was the paper's Paris cor-respondent. The board of directors combined Parnellite MPs such as John Redmond and Dr Joseph Kenny with Catholic entrepreneurs involved in Dublin municipal politics. These included Joseph Meade (building contractor, lord mayor 1891–3), Daniel Tallon (spokesman for the Dublin licensed trade, lord mayor 1897–9), Alderman Michael Kernan (director of the Dublin Gas Company), William Field, Blackrock-based butcher and organizer of the Dublin meat tradesmen and cattle exporters, and Edward Wholohan, Bray businessman and town commissioner.

The *Independent* claimed to be both 'Parnell's paper' and 'the people's paper' speaking for the country as a whole rather than a proprietor. Its editor, Edward Byrne, joined the board to emphasize that journalists would share control of the newspaper[4] and efforts were made to transform Parnellite political support into capital. Working men formed share clubs,[5] reassured that the company was 'the property of the people ... the people will secure for themselves a property which will not only satisfy for them all the requisites of great newspapers, but

1 F. Callanan, *The Parnell split, 1890–91* (Cork, 1992).   2 Located between Andrew St. and Dame St., Dublin.   3 *Irish Daily Independent*, 18 Dec. 1891 & 21 Mar. 1892. (Hereinafter the *Irish Daily Independent* is abbreviated to IDI.)   4 IDI, 18 Dec. 1891 & 21 Mar. 1892.   5 IDI, 16 Jan. & 7 Mar. 1892.

will pay to them a substantial dividend even in its infancy'.[6] It was a newspaper with a cause: orators declared that even if all Parnellite MPs were unseated the *Independent* papers would ensure the survival of Parnellism.[7] Company director William Field proclaimed 'When all those [anti-Parnellite] periodicals that appeared and disappeared like the signs of the zodiac passed away from the memory of man, the *Independent* newspapers of Ireland would be known, honoured and respected and handed down from father to son as preserving the history and traditions of this political period'.[8]

The *Independent* employed union labour and attacked the Healyite *Irish Catholic* and *Nation* for maintaining a 'rat' (non-union) house.[9] Edward Byrne was prominent in the Irish branch of the Institute of Journalists and the *Independent* echoed trade union advocacy of Irish labour and materials, though it used imported paper because the only Irish paper mill (at Ballyclare, Co. Antrim) could not meet its requirements.[10] In June 1893 the *Weekly Independent* appeared, edited by the Waterford-born journalist M.A. Manning. Like other weekly papers it was aimed at farmers who came to town weekly on market day and emigrants seeking home news. It provided summarized weekly news, serialized stories, a front-page political cartoon, and, on special occasions, a large coloured political cartoon.[11] The weekly paper cost 3*d.*, while the daily, like the *Freeman's Journal*, cost 1*d.*

To keep the spirit of Parnellism alive, each year Parnellites reasserted their identity through commemorative events, dominated by a great procession through Dublin on the anniversary of Parnell's death, recalling his vast funeral of 1891. On that occasion every year several pages of the *Independent* were filled with the names of participating individuals and organizations and editorials declared that the turn-out showed that Parnell's principles lived on.[12] *Independent* journalists marched as a body, laying their own ornate wreath. The Parnellite commemorative calendar also included an annual dinner for journalists and leading Parnellites on the anniversary of the *Independent*'s appearance, accompanied by a tour of the offices as the next day's edition was being produced.[13]

## BUSINESS PROBLEMS

Parnell's *Independent* soon faced financial difficulties. The founders were advised that £50,000 initial capital was required; the newspaper's hasty appearance when just under half this amount had been subscribed was triggered by John Redmond's candidacy in the vital Waterford City by-election of 23 December

6 IDI, 25 Aug. 1893.  7 IDI, 4 May 1892.  8 IDI, 21 Sept. 1892.  9 IDI, 4 Jan. 1892.  10 *Irish Weekly Independent*, 16 Oct. 1893.  11 Ibid., 1 June 1893.  12 IDI, 8, 10 & 11 Oct. 1892.  13 IDI, 18 & 20 Dec. 1892, 19 Dec. 1893, 31 Dec. 1894 & 23 Dec. 1895.

1891.[14] Supplementary share issues brought total capital to £40,000 by
September 1893 and further appeals for funds were made in 1894.[15] Other problems also beset the fledgling title. Many copies of the early issues were spoiled
because of the hasty installation of Hoe printing machines. This resulted in a
lawsuit (settled out of court) against the manufacturers.[16] Clerically organized
boycotts excluded the Parnellite papers from many parts of the country; many
reading-rooms were run directly by the Catholic church and even overwhelm-
ingly Parnellite Dublin societies found spiritual directors using their veto to
exclude the titles.[17]

Amid the bitter political atmosphere of the time, the *Independent* recorded
physical assaults on its reporters by anti-Parnellites[18] and reckless insults
exchanged by the party factions caused an epidemic of libel suits. Republication
of allegations that an anti-Parnellite MP was drunk at a council meeting led to
a libel case, damages, and heavy legal costs against the *Herald* and the *Independent*.
Former *United Ireland* editor Matthias McDonnell Bodkin, who had turned anti-
Parnell, was excoriated by the *Independent* because of his connection to the
*National Press* and his narrow defeat of J.J. O'Kelly as MP for North Roscommon
in 1892 amidst widespread intimidation. He was christened 'Handy Andy, MP',
and described as illiterate and ignorant, with two left feet and a noxious odour.
Bodkin eventually sued when the *Independent* falsely claimed he had been expelled
from the Institute of Journalists. He claimed £2,000 damages but received £20;
the *Independent* endorsed this valuation of his reputation.[19]

The newspaper's resources were further drained because, at this time, MPs
did not receive salaries. Parnellite MPs and leading activists were subsidised
by managerial jobs on the newspaper or sinecure journalistic positions. For
example, the London correspondent was the ex-*New York Herald* journalist,
former Parnellite MP and ex-Fenian J.J. O'Kelly, but most of the work was done
by J. Keppel Hopkins, a London-based journalist. O'Kelly, however, contributed
signed articles on foreign affairs after returning to Parliament in 1895. A separatist later complained: 'while the staff were making up over £1,500 a year out
of their wages to keep the papers going, the directors were paying £1,300 a
year to their own little crowd!'[20]

The business interests of the company's directors also caused tension.
Thomas Moore departed as *Herald* editor in 1894 after being criticized for using
the newspaper to support a hotel scheme under consideration by Dublin
Corporation. Moore sued the *Independent* company, claiming he had received
insufficient notice and compensation. He alleged the *Independent* titles promoted

14 IDI, 9 Feb. & 23 Dec. 1892.   15 IDI, 28 Apr. & 10 May 1894.   16 IDI, 13, 14 & 16 Jan. 1893.   17 IDI, 9 Mar. & 31
Oct. 1892, 11 Oct. 1893 & 11 Sept. 1895.   18 IDI, 1 & 2 Aug. 1892 & 24 Nov. 1894.   19 IDI, 14 Jan., 19 June & 4 July
1895.   20 *United Irishman*, 5 Aug. 1899.

the interests of one of its directors, Alderman Joseph Meade, whose business rivals, including his successor as lord mayor, Edward Shanks, were involved in the hotel scheme. Moore argued he should have been allowed to follow his own judgment rather than coordinating editorial policies with the *Independent*'s directors. He also claimed the management told theatre critics which performers to praise or denounce. Moore failed to prove his allegations, and the case was settled out of court.[21]

## THE *INDEPENDENT* AND POLITICS

In November 1892 the Parnellites launched a new organization, 'Ireland's Army of Independence / Independents', after the general election had reduced Parnellite representation to nine seats. Its defiant martial imagery gestured towards separatists who formed an important section of Parnellite support; the *Independent*'s Dublin office doubled as the headquarters of the Irish Republican Brotherhood (IRB), with many physical-force men on the staff and leading IRB activist Frederick J. Allan employed as office manager. When two IRB hitmen were tried for murdering an alleged informer the *Independent* proclaimed their innocence and when the prosecution collapsed after witnesses withdrew, the *Independent* praised Allan for saving the prisoners from penal servitude.[22] Allan subsequently employed them on the *Independent*.[23]

Whatever about the IRB, given the hierarchy's call for the removal of Parnell as leader of the Irish Party in the wake of the O'Shea divorce case, the *Independent* had an uneasy relationship with the Catholic church. In particular it locked horns with Thomas Nulty, bishop of Meath, who had nominated anti-Parnellite Michael Davitt to stand in the 1892 general election for North Meath and who had warned in his famous pastoral that no Parnellite could 'remain a Catholic'. Parnellites successfully petitioned the courts to have Davitt's election, and that of his South Meath colleague, Patrick Fulham, annulled on the grounds of 'undue clerical influence'. The *Independent* devoted significant space to these hearings.[24] Similarly, during the 1895 general election, the *Independent* publicized clerical intimidation of Parnellites, declaring that certain anti-Parnellite MPs represented only the priests of their constituencies.[25] When, in that election, Parnell's brother, John Howard Parnell, won a seat in South Meath a *Weekly*

---

21 IDI, 29 Nov. 1894, 2, 23, 25 & 26 Feb. 1895. John Wyse Power succeeded Moore as editor of the *Herald*. 22 IDI, 13 & 26 Jan. 1894. 23 L. O Broin, *Revolutionary underground: the story of the Irish Republican Brotherhood, 1858–1924* (Dublin, 1976), pp 56–7. For Allan's role see also D. Meleady, *Redmond: the Parnellite* (Cork, 2008), pp 231–2 & 288–91. 24 For a fuller account of Nulty's activities, see D. Lawlor, *Divine right? The Parnell split in Meath* (Cork, 2007). Although fresh elections were held, anti-Parnellite candidates again, narrowly, won the seats. 25 IDI, 26 July 1895.

*Independent* advertisement proclaimed 'Clericalism the Enemy – Bishop Nulty Knocked Out'. As Nulty inaugurated a diocesan 'Star Chamber' where priests suspected of insufficient anti-Parnellite zeal were interrogated and threatened with suspension, the *Independent* suggested he was insane.[26]

The sometimes salacious content of the newspapers concerned Parnellite priests such as Fr Nicholas Murphy of Kilnamanagh, Co. Kilkenny. In 1894 he warned that over-zealous denunciations of clerical misconduct were being taken up by Protestant proselytizers such as the ex-priest Thomas Connellan and his monthly publication *The Catholic*. Connellan's citations of Parnellite publications were then, in turn, being presented by anti-Parnellites as proof that Parnellism endangered faith and morals.[27] For example, the *Herald*'s publication of a news report about a priest who had eloped to America with a woman and then murdered her, scandalized both Parnellite and anti-Parnellite readers and was eagerly seized on by the 'Connellan cesspool'.

But the Independent titles denied any wish to exclude priests from politics. They argued that corrupt and hypocritical anti-Parnellites would betray the bishops in time. When Michael Davitt and some other anti-Parnellites supported Liberal opponents of denominational education in British school board elections, the *Independent* proclaimed that the Liberal alliance encouraged secularism.[28] Davitt, 'this baseborn peasant', was a particular target because of his longstanding hostility to Parnell.[29] The *Independent* also highlighted the anti-clericalism and prurience of London Radical journalism, exemplified by the *Sun*, published by anti-Parnellite MP and London journalist T.P. O'Connor and condemned from Catholic pulpits for publishing articles by freethinkers and the memoirs of birth-control advocate turned-theosophist Annie Besant.[30] A comment by the bishop of Limerick, Edward O'Dwyer, that if Ireland possessed a clerical party, a Catholic party, or even a Christian party, T.P. O'Connor would be ineligible, was quoted with glee.[31] However, the *Independent*'s boasts of purifying the press from moral corruption did not prevent it titillating readers with murder and divorce cases.[32] On one occasion the *Independent* denounced the public's 'morbid interest' in a murderer whose arrest, trial and crimes it reported on in detail.[33]

The 1892 general election had resulted in a Liberal minority government dependent on anti-Parnellite MPs. It was a government that constantly incurred the wrath of the *Independent*. When a new home rule bill appeared the newspaper complained it did not go far enough. It seized on William Gladstone's suggestion that he might exclude part of Ulster from home rule if unionist

26 IDI, Oct. & 3 Dec. 1896.  27 IDI, 10 Oct. 1894.  28 IDI, 7 Mar. 1892 & 16, 31 Oct. & 6 Nov. 1894.  29 IDI, 1 & 6 Sept. 1892.  30 IDI, 15 Aug. 1893 & 13 Nov. 1894.  31 IDI, 20 Sept. 1892.  32 IDI, 31 Jan. & 9 Nov. 1894.  33 IDI, 3 May 1892.

MPs requested it; it predicted that after sacrificing so much else the anti-Parnellites would now 'segregate a portion of Ulster as a British colony planted in Ireland'. The *Independent* also emphasized the sufferings of evicted 'plan of campaign' tenants formerly assured by William O'Brien and John Dillon that a Liberal government would reinstate them. *Independent* reporters recorded the suffering of what it called 'O'Brien's victims'.[34]

While the high-profile campaign by the *Independent* for John Twiss (hanged in 1893 for an agrarian murder in Co. Kerry) rested on genuine uncertainties about police conduct and trial procedures, it also embarrassed anti-Parnellites and implied Liberals had not changed since the 'Spencer terror' of 1882–5.[35] (The *Independent* compared Twiss to Myles Joyce, believed innocent of the Maamtrasna murders for which he was executed in December 1882.)[36] The *Independent* also publicized Amnesty Association campaigns to release Irish-American dynamiters jailed in the 1880s. Frederick Allan and Maud Gonne highlighted the draconian treatment of the prisoners, with men who had gone mad accused of 'shamming' (i.e., faking their mental illness). This was another stick with which to beat the Liberal Alliance, since home secretary Herbert Asquith vetoed releases and later criticized his Conservative successor for releasing dynamiters on humanitarian grounds.[37]

The *Independent*'s accusation that chief secretary John Morley obstructed teaching of Irish history in schools to extinguish Irish nationality led to a long correspondence (contributors included Michael Cusack, founder of the GAA). Morley was denounced as 'an agnostic bigot' for refusing to give full state funding to Christian Brothers' schools or appoint Christian Brothers as teachers in industrial schools.[38] As the Liberals were routed in the 1895 general election, the *Independent* declared that by betraying Parnell, anti-Parnellites had allowed the Liberals to splinter over fads rather than uniting on home rule.[39]

Meanwhile, significant change had occurred in the newspaper market. In March 1892 the Greys had disposed of the *Freeman* to the anti-Parnellite MPs in a merger with Healy's and Murphy's *National Press*. A bitter struggle for control of the new entity between Tim Healy and John Dillon, both MPs and also directors of the merged company, ensued. The Healyites had expected their *National Press* shareholding would ensure their control but the return of Alderman Michael Kernan to the board to safeguard the residual value of his large shareholding had given the Dillonites control. A shareholders' meeting – described by the *Independent* as 'The Kilkenny cats' final clawing match – The obscene fishwives' orgy in the dead-house of the deceased *Fallen Journal*'[40] resulted

---

34 IDI, 20 Sept. 1892. 35 IDI, 31 Oct. &, 4 Nov. 1893, 12 Jan., 8 and 11 Feb. 1895. 36 IDI, 8 Feb. 1895. 37 Meleady, *Redmond*, pp 254–5. 38 IDI, 30 May & 11 June 1894 & 7 Feb. 1895. See also Meleady, *Redmond*, p. 375, n24. 39 IDI, 31 July 1895. 40 IDI, 30 Mar. 1894.

in the Dillonite faction gaining control and ejecting the Healyite directors. *Freeman* shares, formerly blue-chip investments before the Parnell split, plummeted in value.[41] The Healyites retreated to the *Irish Catholic* and in 1897 they revived the *Nation* as a daily newspaper. Edited by William Dennehy, William Martin Murphy provided its financial mainstay.[42] However, it lacked a nation-wide promotional organization despite support from some militant clergy.

## FIGHTING FOR SHADOWS: FACTIONALISM AFTER 1895

After the 1895 general election, faction-fighting convulsed the anti-Parnellite organization. One Dillonite declared the *Irish Catholic* worse than the *Independent*:[43] Longford Healyites resolved they would sooner read the *Independent* than the *Freeman*.[44] Dillonites tried to exclude reporters from meetings, but Healyites leaked information to the *Independent*.[45] The newspaper declared that this chaos was the inevitable result of replacing Parnell's clear-sighted leadership and denounced any talk of reconciliation with the 'seceders'. The only acceptable reunification would involve submission of the anti-Parnellite rank and file to Parnellism and permanent retirement of anti-Parnellite leaders. Reunion with proven renegades would, the *Independent* believed, be shaking hands over the grave of Parnell.[46] Parnellites would, it observed, as soon unite with Choctaw Indians as with anti-Parnellites.[47]

This ignored the fact that Parnellism remained a decided minority, and that the political debacle was affecting the newspaper. At successive AGMs of the Independent company John Redmond had declared that annual losses were steadily being reduced and the company was on the verge of breaking into profit. If there was any truth in these statements, the decline in political excitement after 1895 and the consequent fall-off in newspaper readership dealt them a death-blow; it soon seemed that the titles might drag the whole party down.[48]

In January 1897 the Parnellite divisions became public when Timothy C. Harrington advocated reunion, accusing *Independent* editorial staff of fuelling the split to preserve their jobs. Harrington pointed out that Parnellites faced apathy and shortage of funds, the Avondale estate was bankrupt and Parnell's mother lived in poverty.[49] When Harrington appealed to the clergy for support, received John Dillon's endorsement and appeared with William O'Brien on a public platform, the *Independent* reminisced about Harrington's former anti-clerical utterances and his new-found associates' attacks on Parnell. The Wicklow

41 IDI, 14 Mar. 1893.   42 IDI, 29 Mar. & 10 July 1894.   43 IDI, 29 May 1895.   44 IDI, 27 Nov. 1895.   45 IDI, 14 Nov. 1895.   46 IDI, 23 Jan. 1896.   47 IDI, 3 July 1896.   48 Meleady, *Redmond*, pp 236–7 & 287–8.   49 IDI, 24 Feb. 1897.

MP W.J. Corbet refused to attend the 1897 Parnell procession because Harrington participated; in response Harrington accused Corbet of political inactivity and rackrenting tenants.[50] *United Ireland* served as a mouthpiece for Harrington's new departure until it succumbed to its accumulated debts in 1898.

DECLINE AND FALL: THE END OF THE PARNELLITE *INDEPENDENT*

In the battle for readers the *Freeman's Journal*, longer-established and backed by the majority faction, was better-placed to secure support. In 1896 police reports estimated the *Independent*'s circulation at 16,000 with the *Freeman* at 28,000. The *Freeman* continued to pay dividends; the *Independent* had never done so. In addition, Edward Byrne proved a problematic editor. After accompanying John Redmond on a fundraising tour of America, Byrne went bankrupt and retired in 1897 to his native Tuam, where he died in 1899.[51] William O'Brien's *Irish People* claimed Byrne was 'evicted from the *Independent* under circumstances … familiar to all acquainted with Dublin journalistic life … he died a victim of political ingratitude'.[52]

Byrne's successor, James O'Donovan, was a forceful individual willing to criticize unaccountable clerical power in such areas as school management. (The police suspected him of IRB membership.)[53] O'Donovan highlighted arbitrary dismissals of schoolteachers by Protestant and Catholic clerics. In letters the *Daily Nation* thought too libellous to print, the Healyite land campaigner Fr David Humphreys accused the *Independent* of conspiring against Catholic education; the *Independent* published them in the name of free speech. O'Donovan also accused industrial schools run by religious orders of inefficient training and profiteering. When the anti-Parnellite dailies accused him of anti-clericalism he replied that he merely criticised abuses, accused the *Freeman* and the *Daily Nation* of servile opportunism, and added that honest critics were more loyal to the church. There were limits however: when a Liberal Unionist said home rule required an educational system enabling Irishmen to think for themselves, an *Independent* editorial noted that Irish people objected to pupils 'being taught … in a way that will naturally cause them to become freethinkers of the type so common in France and Germany'.[54]

By 1897 the newspaper was seeking a business partner. According to widespread reports (which the company denied) the Irish-born Harmsworth broth-

---

50 IDI, 13 & 14 Oct. 1897.   51 F. Callanan (ed.), *Parnell: a memoir by Edward Byrne* (Dublin, 1991). Byrne's memoir of Parnell appeared in the *Weekly Independent*.   52 *Irish People*, 24 Oct. 1899.   53 O Broin, *Revolutionary underground*, p. 85 (O Broin mis-transcribes name as 'T. O'Donovan').   54 IDI, 12 Dec. 1899.

ers refused investment after inspecting the company's books. (The detective John
Mallon believed the Harmsworths had a lien on the business, its extent known
only to Redmond, and their representative had proposed savings of £3,000 a
year.)[55] A syndicate centred on the London-based Linotype Company took on
the business side and left editorial policy to the Parnellite management. New capital was subscribed by the Dublin Parnellite MP and former proprietor of the
*Leinster Leader*, James L. Carew (£2,000), Louis Chanler, a wealthy American sym-
pathizer who joined the board in 1898 (£1,000), Joseph Meade, P.H. Meade and
other leading Parnellites, possibly including Cecil Rhodes' associate Rochfort
Maguire (a Parnellite MP, 1892–5).[56] Carew dominated the newspaper thereafter.
The Trinity Street offices were extended and an ultra-modern Goss printing
machine, capable of colour printing and producing a larger print run was
imported from Chicago, the first outside America.[57] Claims were made of vastly
increased circulation, probably reflecting copies printed rather than sold.

Handset type was replaced by Linotype machines hired from the London-
based company, which received £1,500 in Independent Company debentures in
return. Over a hundred men were dismissed, including Frederick Allan who was
replaced in March 1899 by J.F. Hosker, an English manager nominated by the
Linotype Company. Henry Dixon, Dublin solicitor, separatist and *Independent*
shareholder, protested against these developments. In Arthur Griffith's newly
founded weekly *United Irishman*; Dixon declared that 'The syndicate or its representative can dismiss any of the editors to-day … the directors have most effec-
tually sold the independence of the never-to-be-again Independent papers'. Dixon
accused Hosker of recruiting boy labour and 'sweating' employees; he also noted
the Linotype Company was 'in eternal wars with trades-unionism'.[58]

The appearance of the *United Irishman* in March 1899 marked the dissocia-
tion of a separatist hard core from the crumbling Parnellite movement. Griffith
denounced the *Independent* as 'the Anglo-Jew organ',[59] contaminated by 'the British
Institute of Journalists'.[60] Relations deteriorated further when the Parnellite
leadership announced plans for a Parnell monument. The *Independent* denounced
the *Freeman's Journal* for calling this a dodge to bolster Parnellite support and
boost the 1899 procession (at which the foundation stone was laid). Griffith
alleged the Parnell monument, devised to distract attention from John
Redmond's disastrous handling of the *Independent*, was supported only by 'cos-
mopolitan employees of the St Andrew-street establishment'.[61] When separatists
protested at a Parnell Statue meeting, the *Independent* denounced this 'small knot
of youths' as dupes of the *Freeman*. Griffith called this account 'one huge lie

---

55 O Broin, *Revolutionary underground*, p. 99.  56 Meleady, *Redmond*, pp 288–9. For more on Chanler see L. Thomas,
*A pride of lions: the Chanler chronicle* (Wisconsin, 1974), especially p. 224.  57 IDI, 24 Aug. 1898.  58 *United Irishman*, 20
May 1899.  59 *United Irishman*, 14 Oct. 1899 & 24 Mar. 1900.  60 Ibid., 17 Nov. 1900.  61 Ibid., 15 & 22 July 1900.

… One of our countrymen … still retained on the staff of our Anglo-Jewish contemporary, informs us it was written by one of the foreign vermin'.[62]

The reinvigorated *Irish Daily Independent* acquired the subtitle *The People's Paper* in green ink and advertisements appeared in red and black for emphasis. From 1895 the *Independent* was illustrated by line-block engravings drawn from photographs.[63] The *Independent* proclaimed itself 'the only fully illustrated daily paper in Dublin'. The *Weekly Independent* published front-page cartoons in red or blue ink and by the early months of the Boer War the *Daily* contained three-tone pictures of battle scenes. Other innovations, such as sub-headings within stories, signed humorous essays, and distinctive mastheads for such features as the 'London Letter', brightened the format. While an editorial noted the *Skibbereen Eagle*'s declaration that the *Independent* had raised printing to a fine art, Griffith scornfully compared the newspapers to the popular Harmsworth journal *Tit-Bits*.[64] Some Harmsworthian news techniques, such as compressing reported speeches, were precluded by the newspaper's role as the party journal of record. The Parnellite party was virtually insolvent, and investors in the reorganization acted more from political motives or hope of minimizing losses than long-term hope. In 1899 James O'Donovan resigned as editor to edit the *Cork Daily Herald*; he was succeeded by the Kerry journalist Maurice P. Ryle.

After repeated denials that the *Independent* was insolvent, the directors announced restructuring 'to secure the paper's future'. A libel suit against the *Daily Nation* for asserting that the *Independent* was insolvent was settled by consent. The *Freeman* sued for a similar case to be dismissed since its allegations had been vindicated; the *Independent* claimed the allegations had caused the insolvency. Creditors' meetings in London and Dublin revealed the *Independent* owed £27,000 and that only £44,000 of its projected £60,000 capital had been subscribed. The London manager, Arthur J. Wall (appointed 1898), later recalled that advertising revenue for the last two years of the old paper was less than for one month in 1923.[65]

In August 1900 the *Independent* entered receivership. William Martin Murphy later claimed that John Redmond visited him, predicting devastating political consequences if the newspaper failed to find a buyer and the Irish Party leader was forced into personal insolvency. A bid for the newspaper from the *Freeman's Journal* was rejected by Redmond who did not relish domination by the Dillonite *Freeman*. Murphy supplied £500 for immediate expenses, and the paper was bought for £16,000 by Daniel Tallon, ostensibly for the debenture-holders, the most prominent of whom, was Murphy. The Dillonite MP Michael Austin

---

62 Ibid., 14 Oct. 1899.   63 The half-tone process allowing direct reproduction of photographs was invented in the 1880s but not widely used until the twentieth century.   64 *United Irishman*, 5 Aug. 1899.   65 *Irish Weekly Independent*, 9 June 1923. See also Meleady, *Redmond*, p. 330.

denounced Murphy's 'grabbing the *Independent*' as a Healyite conspiracy. The *Freeman* excoriated Murphy, which the *Independent* attributed to pique at the lost chance of monopoly. Litigation continued unabated; in 1903 a lawsuit by the Cork Parnellite businessman and former director P.H. Meade against Carew claimed he (Carew) had managed the 1898–9 restructuring to benefit himself and his associates. Carew retorted that he had lost more than all other directors combined, and won the case.[66] When Carew died the *Independent* proclaimed that 'owing to his sacrifices ... the inestimable boon of a free and independent Press was secured to the Irish people, and the frenzied efforts ... to create a monopoly for the *Freeman's Journal* frustrated'.[67]

## A LEGACY

The Parnellite *Independent* ended with the appearance of the merged *Independent and Nation* (1 September 1900). Arthur Griffith protested that Parnell's *Independent* had been destroyed by 'Parliamentarian vultures', and declared his *United Irishman* was the true heir to the Parnellite journalistic tradition. The 'Citizen' in James Joyce's *Ulysses* (set in 1904) denounces '*The Irish Independent* ... founded by Parnell to be the workingman's friend ... How's that for a national press?' – a sarcastic suggestion that the *Independent and Nation* bore more resemblance to the original Healyite daily than to the Parnellite organ.[68]

Griffith glossed over the extent to which the Harmsworthian features he deplored reflected extended newspaper audiences, improved communications and appetites for diversion and curiosities. Nevertheless much of Griffith's indictment was unanswerable; the shareholders lost their money, the employees *were* cheated out of their wages, and the company collapsed. The story of the Parnellite *Independent* highlights the costs of the factional warfare that pervaded nationalist politics in the 1890s, and whose memory continued to taint the Irish Party after its reunification under John Redmond. Ironically, the accusations of corruption and servility to the Liberals made against the anti-Parnellites in the 1890s would be turned against Redmond by the Murphy *Independent* and other dissident nationalists after the Liberals returned to power in 1906. The fate of the Parnellite Independent company helps to explain the scepticism frequently expressed by Murphy about the ability of the Redmondite leadership to administer home rule finance.

The merged newspaper was co-edited by Maurice Ryle and William Dennehy until Ryle left in September 1902 to found the *Kerry People*. Despite

66 Ibid., 21 Feb. 1903.  67 *Irish Weekly Independent*, 5 Sept. 1903.  68 H.W. Gabler (ed.), *Ulysses: the corrected text* (London, 1986), p. 245.

some features intended to appeal to residual Parnellite readers (notably coverage of the dwindling annual Dublin procession, now shunned by Redmond), it was essentially a political vehicle for Tim Healy, underwritten at considerable loss by Murphy. From 1902 it became more critical of the united Irish Party, and after the 1903 Land Conference it was openly supportive of the conciliatory policies of chief secretary George Wyndham, and promoted what would become the 1907 International Exhibition as a symbol of the era of good feelings (and incidentally of Murphy's leadership of the Dublin business community). In 1904, having considered selling the newspaper, Murphy realized there was a gap in the Irish market for a cheap commercially-driven title. Dennehy returned to editing the *Irish Catholic* and the *Independent* was prepared for a relaunch, from new premises in Abbey Street, under a new editor, Timothy R. Harrington.

# 2 / The life and career of William Martin Murphy

## PADRAIG YEATES

Without William Martin Murphy there would have been no *Irish Independent*, *Sunday Independent* or *Evening Herald*. The newspaper group he founded, almost as a diversion from his main business enterprises and as a consolation for a blighted political career, became his most enduring monument. It has been a major influence on Irish life since 1905. The Parnell split, in which he played a crucial role, has been relegated to history and literature. The tramways that bound the city together have left a ghostly trail in the numbers of the older Dublin Bus routes and Luas vehicles are no more than soulless imitations of Murphy's stately ships of the suburbs.

The other Murphy legacy is intangible. It is the memory of the 1913 Lockout, of which he was the undisputed architect and victor. It is ironic that a man who created so much employment, was generally regarded as a good employer, and who had acted in his time as an arbitrator in major trade disputes should be remembered for imposing 'a Carthaginian peace' on the city's workers. Another of history's ironies is that this committed Irish nationalist should be remembered for the *Irish Independent's* editorial calling for the executions of Seán MacDermott and James Connolly, while Murphy's subsequent facilitation of Sinn Féin's rise is forgotten.

Murphy's achievements can be ascribed to his intelligence, tenacity of purpose and willingness to speculate in order to accumulate – but always after a most careful reconnaissance. The success of his newspapers owed much to the fact that they reflected Murphy's own core values and aspirations, which he shared with the burgeoning southern middle classes. Like him they were by turns intensely Catholic, nationalist and conservative. The veneer of cosmopolitanism acquired by the Independent Group in recent years would have been quite alien to both.

The *Irish Independent* began life as a vehicle to promote the views of John Redmond but Murphy quickly became disillusioned with the leader of the reunited home rule movement, once the latter refused to back him in an unsuccessful bid to resurrect his own political career against strong opposition from the Irish Party's deputy leader John Dillon and the Cork rural radical William O'Brien.[1] Murphy read Redmond's proclivity for reconciliation and compro-

1 T. Morrissey, *William Martin Murphy* (Dundalk, 1997), pp 28–30.

mise as weakness, and he was proven correct in the political environment of the day, which rewarded combative political strategies. His newspapers certainly proved more adept at attuning themselves to the public mood after the 1916 Rising than Redmond and they played a crucial role in the establishment and legitimization of the Irish Free State. Murphy may have died in 1919 but, as in all things he did, he had laid the foundations well.

## MASTER OF A DEFT 'BACK-HANDER'

Perhaps it was in the blood. His father Denis William Murphy was a builder in West Cork where William Martin Murphy was born on 6 January 1845. He was an only son. His mother Mary Anne (née Martin) Murphy died when he was five years of age and his paternal grandmother took her place until she too died in 1854. Murphy's biographer, Tom Morrissey, attributed his subject's later sense of self sufficiency and 'aloneness that found fulfilment in hard work' to a relatively solitary childhood.[2] The consequences of the Famine barely needed retelling, as Murphy grew up in its immediate aftermath. His view of the catastrophe was mediated in large part through his father and the latter's close friends, the Sullivan clan. A.M., T.D. and D.B. Sullivan were among the leading journalists and constitutional nationalists of the day and formed the core of what became known as the 'Bantry Band', to which William Martin Murphy and his close associate T.M. Healy were recruits. The Sullivans took over the management and editing of *The Nation* newspaper from conservative Young Irelander Gavan Duffy for much of the late nineteenth century. Their politics were in the same romantic nationalist tradition as Gavan Duffy and eschewed anything smacking of social or political radicalism.

It was A.M. Sullivan who persuaded Denis Murphy to send his son to Dublin to study with the Sullivan brood under the Jesuits at Belvedere College. The trip to Dublin at the age of 13 was his 'earliest recollection of being thrown on my own resources'. Even at that tender age he showed independence of spirit when he refused to give up his place on the box seat of the coach, from Bantry to Cork, to a Captain Walker. 'I am afraid I did not show much respect for the age and rank of the "Captain", who had to take "a back seat" on that occasion', he wrote many years later. Clearly neither rank not threats impressed the young scholar, a characteristic that reasserted itself on many occasions with figures as diverse as Parnell, Edward VII and Jim Larkin. The next person to test his independence was an aspiring school bully on his arrival at Belvedere. He dealt

2 Ibid., p. 4.

the offender 'a back hander across the face'. The Rector, the Revd Frank Murphy, who witnessed the incident, told Murphy the other boy had got what he deserved.[3]

Murphy proved an outstanding scholar and excelled in English, chemistry and experimental sciences. Lodging with the Sullivan boys, he had plenty of free time, but already showed signs of the iron discipline that marked his adult life. 'I worked hard, very hard, to hold the head of my class, which whenever I became slack in my studies I had to yield to a rival'.[4] On finishing his studies at Belvedere he entered the offices of John J. Lyons, an architect, and attended classes at the Catholic University. Lyons was also editor of the *Irish Builder* and the young Murphy spent his spare time helping Lyons with the magazine, as well as in the offices of the *Nation* writing notes and articles, even doing 'quite a good amount of sub-editing'. The fascination with journalism and particularly with its potential for expressing ideas and moulding opinion stayed with him. As his oldest surviving son William Lombard Murphy told the staff of the *Irish Independent* many years later, his father could claim the title of 'working journalist, although the work was but a part-time occupation and, one supposes, strictly honorary'.[5] It is possible that he might have dabbled further but for the sudden death of his father in 1863. Once more the Sullivans rallied around; A.M. Sullivan in particular. Years later Murphy wrote to Sullivan's widow that, 'I often think that my success in life was largely due to the happy inspiration of A.M. in getting my father to send me as a school boy to Dublin and I have never forgotten A.M.'s night journey to Bantry the day after my father was buried, when as a forlorn boy, he gave me counsel and encouragement at the most critical period of my life'.[6]

Taking over the family business at 19 years of age was an enormous challenge, but young William Martin was the heir to a thriving sawmilling and building business worth £4,000; an enormous sum at the time. By 1867 the young Murphy had outgrown the narrow commercial confines of west Cork and moved to Cork City. Even at the tender age of 19, Murphy took his religious faith seriously. He was a member of the Society of Saint Vincent de Paul (SVP) in Bantry and one of his first acts on arriving in Cork City was to join a local SVP conference. His deep religiosity would be lauded by friends and certainly enhanced his relations with senior Catholic prelates such as Dr William Walsh, archbishop of Dublin and Dr Patrick O'Donnell of Raphoe (later the Irish Primate). But it enraged opponents, who contrasted it with his often ruthless business and political strategies. As P.A. Chance, a friend and in-law, put

---

3 *The Belvederian*, 2:2 (summer 1910). 4 Morrissey, *Murphy*, p. 6. 5 Address by Dr William Lombard Murphy, 29 June 1941, William Martin papers. 6 William Martin Murphy papers.

it, Murphy carried a copy of the Companies Act in one hand and *The Imitation of Christ* in the other.[7]

Nor did Murphy lose time becoming acquainted with polite society in Cork. In 1870 he married Mary Julia Lombard, the only daughter of James Fitzgerald Lombard, one of the city's leading merchants, who also had extensive business interests in Dublin. By 1875 Murphy had moved to the capital with his young wife. He was already prosperous enough to buy a house in Terenure, where he founded a new conference of the SVP. The family later moved to Dartry, on the banks of the Dodder, where he developed an interest in horticulture and arboriculture in the extensive grounds.[8] It must have been an ideal setting for children, although it is hard to know how much freedom they would have had to enjoy it.[9] Murphy's extreme reserve, 'his devotion to his religion' and his intense self-discipline appear to have made him a distant father figure – a not uncommon role then, or now. His son William Lombard, although clearly devoted to his father's memory, noted, 'He did not make a parade of his kindness and thoughtfulness for others, but his family, when children, received many a sharp rebuke for leaving, for instance, a room in an untidy condition and thus causing unnecessary trouble to servants'. His son remembered him as having a prodigious memory and as an omnivorous reader, assets he put to good use in mastering civil engineering, electrical engineering and contract law. 'He was wary of entrance to a quarrel, but being in he bore himself "that the opposed might beware of him"', his son added. 'In his personal habits he was by no means ascetic but habitually frugal. He never smoked or drank alcoholic liquor during the day, but he smoked a pipe or two of old Rooney's mixture and drank a glass of whisky and water before going to bed'.[10]

## BUSINESS, POLITICS AND STRANGE BEDFELLOWS

Indeed, Murphy needed all of his strength, courage and intelligence in his first great business venture, building light railways across the south and west of the country from Wexford and Rosslare to Baltimore and Clare. It is another of history's ironies that a man often hailed as one of Ireland's great entrepreneurs owed much of his early success to British subsidies to develop a transport infrastructure for the most under-developed areas of Ireland. Indeed politics and business were deeply entwined in late nineteenth- and early twentieth-century Ireland. Murphy had no scruples about using his influence within the home rule movement, including his period as an MP for Dublin between 1885 and 1892, to advance his own commercial interests.

7 Morrissey, *Murphy*, p. 32.　8 *The Belvederian*, 1:3 (summer 1908).　9 Memorandum from Gerry Murphy, William Martin Murphy papers.　10 Ibid.

If Murphy had a weak spot in his political armour it was that he was a poor public speaker. This was a crippling shortcoming in an era when reputations were made on the hustings and at Westminster. Nevertheless, his business acumen, organizational ability and capacity to grasp issues quickly and explain them simply might still have secured him a promising political career had it not been for the Parnell split. Like most of the 'Bantry Band', Murphy appears to have resented the leadership of the home rule movement falling into the hands of a Protestant ascendancy landlord. Certainly, when the O'Shea divorce case broke, Murphy regarded 'the whole thing as an interposition of divine providence'.[11] He brought his enormous financial resources and organizational expertise to the anti-Parnellite cause. Fellow Bantry man T.M. Healy was his principal ally. Even by Irish Party standards the pair was noted for their vicious infighting skills. Erstwhile ally, William O'Brien of Cork, described them as 'Messrs Healy, Murphy & Co., Moral Assassins'. It was a business in which 'Mr Murphy bought the knives and Mr Healy did the stabbing'.[12] Murphy paid a high price politically for the leading role he played in Parnell's overthrow, losing his seat to Parnellite William Field in the 1892 election. He never secured re-election to Westminster again.

Like many of Parnell's opponents he failed to realize how crucial the Chief's role had been, not alone in keeping the party united, but in keeping his lieutenants from each others' throats. Murphy and Healy soon found themselves at daggers drawn not alone with William O'Brien but, more crucially, John Dillon. This quarrel arose over control of the anti-Parnellite press, which Murphy had created from scratch. In 1890 he financed the *National Press* to counteract the *Freeman's Journal*, which had continued to support Parnell. When the *Freeman* came over to the anti-Parnellite camp Murphy and Healy were made members of the new board only to be deposed by O'Brien and Dillon. The latter went on to become party chairman in 1896. Murphy never forgave his treatment after investing so much energy and money in Parnell's defeat. He took over the *Nation* in 1897 and then, largely at the behest of the Parnellites' leader, John Redmond, bought their struggling title, the *Irish Daily Independent*, from the liquidator in 1900. He soon became as disillusioned with Redmond as he had been with Dillon and Parnell.

From soon after the Parnell split of 1890–1, Murphy was increasingly drawn to the world of the tram. If light rail had facilitated his initial route to wealth, the profits and cash streams paled in comparison to those available from the tramways. His father-in-law, James Lombard, provided an easy entree to the industry in Dublin, which hosted three tramway companies by the early 1880s.

11 F. Callanan, *T.M. Healy* (Cork, 1996), p. 363.   12 Ibid., p. 363 and pp 464–89.

Characteristically, Murphy travelled to the home of the electrified tram, the United States, in 1895, immersed himself in the subject and returned home 'an expert electrical engineer, capable of passing any examination which could be set in that subject'. By 1899 he had engineered a buy-out of Imperial Tramways and created the Dublin United Tramway Company (DUTC), of which he became chairman in 1899; a position he held until his death. He was equally successful in building and running tramways in Belfast and throughout Britain.[13]

The success that eluded him in politics continued to bless his commercial endeavours at home, where he diversified into prestigious enterprises such as Clery's department store and the Imperial Hotel, both on Dublin's Sackville (now O'Connell) Street. In the process he became the most important nationalist businessman in Ireland. In 1904 he took a further important step towards acceptance by the still predominantly Protestant and unionist business establishment when he proposed a Dublin International Exhibition along the lines of William Dargan's 1852 Exhibition. Nationalist critics carped that he was after a knighthood. The Exhibition proved an enormous success when it opened in 1907 and was crowned, quite literally, by a visit from Edward VII. William Martin Murphy and one of his daughters were the only Catholic commoners to dine with the king.[14] Nevertheless Murphy was sufficiently stung by nationalist criticism of hobnobbing with royalty to refuse a knighthood for his role in organizing the event.

The Exhibition set the seal of approval on his business career, preparing the way for his admission to the board of the Great Southern and Western Railway Company (GW&SR) and the presidency of the Dublin Chamber of Commerce. Whatever other nationalists thought, political compromise was inevitable as his business interests expanded, especially in sectors such as transport and utilities, where enterprises were often dependent on acts of parliament to progress. This could create strange bedfellows, as when Murphy sought to capitalize on the capacity of the DUTC power station by promoting a City of Dublin Electric Lighting Bill. The Corporation already had legislative approval to generate its own electrical power but it was proceeding at its usual tortuous pace. If successful, Murphy's bill would have vastly increased the value of the DUTC, taking it to an altogether higher business plane. Inevitably it was opposed by his many enemies in the Irish Party. Ulster Unionists, on the other hand, supported him and relished the prospect of deflating Dublin's municipal pride. The bill reached its third stage before being defeated 'and Mr Murphy

13 A. Bielenberg, 'Entrepreneurship, power and public opinion in Ireland: the career of William Martin Murphy' in *Chronicon*, 2:6 (1998), 1–35; *The Belvederian*, 1:3 (summer 1908); Address by Dr William Lombard Murphy, 29 June 1941, William Martin Murphy papers; and Morrissey, *Murphy*, pp 31–2. 14 B. Siggins, *The great white fair: the Herbert Park exhibition of 1907* (Dublin, 2007), p. 88.

and his company remained without the enormous addition to their power and income', Irish Party MP T.P. O'Connor could still write with obvious pleasure over twenty years later.[15]

Murphy was equally committed to defending the broader economic interests of the country as he saw them. Even at the height of the Dublin Lockout he was heavily involved in the campaign to preserve Queenstown (Cobh) as an embarkation point for transatlantic liners when the shipping companies were pressing the Liberal government to allow them to sail direct from Liverpool and Southampton to New York. Of course Murphy had a strong interest in preserving the Cobh stop over, not just as a Cork man, but as a director of the GS&WR that serviced Cobh and the transatlantic traffic.

### LARKIN'S GREATEST CONVERT

As the first Catholic to be admitted to the GS&WR board, Murphy played a leading role, with the chairman, Sir William Goulding, in smashing the 1911 railway strike. The lockout tactics employed provided a prototype for the bigger battle plan required in 1913. In fact the workers were so thoroughly defeated that they failed to join their comrades on the picket lines two years later. Another important role for Murphy was ensuring that what he regarded as the more extravagant aspects of Lloyd George's social and health insurance schemes in Britain were not foisted on Ireland. His concern for the Irish tax and ratepayer helped ensure that Ireland's health and social services limped behind most of Europe for the rest of the century. His ferocious defence of the Dublin ratepayer was shown nowhere more starkly than in his opposition to the Hugh Lane Gallery. His role in the controversy was immortalized by W.B. Yeats in 'September 1913'. Murphy argued, not unreasonably, that the Corporation should not waste money on an art gallery when Dublin desperately needed to re-house the 100,000 people living in its festering tenements. His argument might have carried more credence if he had engaged, like Lord Iveagh, in providing social housing or had not himself been a slum landlord. He remained stoical in the face of criticism, from whatever quarter. By the time Yeats' poem had appeared in the *Irish Times* he had already been subjected to ferocious attacks from trade union platforms in Dublin and throughout Britain, for the Great Lockout had just begun.[16]

Murphy regarded himself as a good employer. He accepted the legitimacy of 'respectable' craft trade unionism. In Dublin, in particular, craft workers were

---

15 T.P. O'Connor, *Memoirs of an old parliamentarian*, 2 vols (New York, 1929), II, pp 55–6.  16 See P. Yeates, *Lockout; Dublin 1913* (Dublin, 2000), pp 142–4.

generally staunch defenders of the status quo, especially when it came to protecting their own privileges. Craft unions were generally supportive of the Irish Party, when they were not enmeshed in Fenian intrigues, and they championed protectionism and home rule because they were seen as the means to promote Irish industry. Such was the commonality of interests that Murphy helped fund the Dublin Trades Council in its early years. He acted as an arbitrator in a number of trade disputes. Most notably, he helped Archbishop William Walsh and Michael Davitt resolve the 1890 builders' labourers strike in Dublin. Murphy was already paying his own employees the rates demanded by the men on strike. Paying decent wages was one of the means by which Murphy kept unions out of his own operations. His principal objection to unions was not the savings that could accrue, important as these were, but a refusal to have any organization contest his absolute authority within his own enterprises.

Unskilled and semi-skilled workers in Britain had been organized in growing numbers for a generation, but attempts to organize them in Dublin had foundered until the advent of Jim Larkin. In 1909, cast off by the National Union of Dock Labourers as too incendiary, Larkin decided to create his own union. By the summer of 1913 the Irish Transport and General Workers Union (ITGWU) had won a series of victories in Dublin forcing up the wages of groups as varied as dockers, carters, confectionary workers and agricultural labourers by between 20 and 25 per cent. Besides his use of the sympathetic strike tactic, more as a threat than in its application, Larkin was an evangelist of revolutionary socialism. He was part of a broad strand in the labour movement stretching from the United States to western and southern Europe known as syndicalism. Larkin's own idiosyncratic variation was soon labelled 'Larkinism'. For Larkin the struggle on the factory floor, at the ballot box and in the streets were merely different aspects of the same fight to establish the socialist commonwealth. It was Larkin, along with James Connolly, who proposed the formation of the Irish Labour Party at the Irish Trade Union Conference (ITUC) in Clonmel in 1912. In line with their syndicalist ideology, it was created initially as an arm of the ITUC, not as a separate entity.

Between February and May 1913 Murphy suffered a bout of prolonged illness and it was during this time that Larkin managed to organize the tramway workers. This was despite a fairly draconian regime of industrial discipline and an extensive network of informers that Murphy had in place to guard against such eventualities. The men were relatively well paid by Dublin standards but the rates were 25 per cent less than in Murphy's tramway concerns in Belfast and in Britain. He acted with his usual decisiveness, summoning all DUTC employees to a meeting at the Antient Concert Rooms in Great Brunswick (now Pearse) Street after midnight on Saturday, 19 July 1913. The timing was to ensure there was no disruption to tram services and the incentive for attendance was a mug of cocoa and a sandwich. Murphy said he had no objection to the men joining 'a legitimate union' but not 'the disreputable organization' run by Larkin.[17] Anyone who did so faced instant dismissal. He was as good as his word, sacking some 600 of the 800 DUTC employees suspected of being in the ITGWU by the end of August. In the last week of the month the remaining union members practically begged Larkin to bring them out. He did so, against his own better judgement.

At 9.40 am on 26 August 1913, the beginning of the Royal Dublin Horse Show, the remaining ITGWU crews stopped their trams. Taking the driver's handle with them in some cases to ensure the vehicle remained immobilized, they joined the strike. The drama of the moment captured the public imagination, but it was actually a sign of weakness. So few unionized crews were left that Larkin had to abandon the conventional plan for mass pickets at the depots and try to immobilize the system by timing the stoppage for the moment when there was the greatest concentration of ITGWU crews near Nelson's Pillar, the node of the system. Within an hour Murphy had the trams running again. The new crews, armed with spare handles where necessary, were accompanied by Dublin Metropolitan Police (DMP) escorts. The city was seething with unrest and, with his usual prescience, Murphy had secured commitments from Dublin Castle that adequate police and military protection would be supplied to face down Larkin. Murphy himself was burned in effigy. In an interview in the following day's *Irish Independent*, Murphy described Larkin's 'so called "strike" ... the feeblest most contemptible attempt that was ever made'.[18]

The strike might well have ended fairly quickly but for police members, many of them the worse for drink, turning their batons on a harmless crowd in O'Connell Street on 31 August 1913. 'Bloody Sunday' was a godsend for Larkin as it happened on the eve of the British TUC conference in Manchester. Delegates, horrified by the pictures in the British press and what they heard from a Dublin Trades Council deputation headed by William Partridge (as Larkin was in prison), pledged unconditional support to the strikers.

The five months of industrial conflict that followed plunged Dublin into unprecedented depths of misery. In his determination to smash Larkinism, the president of the Dublin Chamber of Commerce invoked 'Murphyism'. He promoted the term quite proudly and it could be argued that Murphy was indeed Larkin's greatest convert. For if Larkin had convinced Dublin's unskilled masses that they could defeat the bosses by the application of the sympathetic strike and blacking the tainted goods and services of any employer with whom they

---

17 Yeates, *Lockout*, p. 7.  18 *Irish Independent*, 27 Aug. 1913.

were in dispute, Murphy persuaded over 400 of the city's employers that they could destroy the ITGWU by the sympathetic lockout of union members and members of any other union that supported the ITGWU's right to represent its members. Although Murphy achieved total victory it was a closer run affair than many realized at the time. Only secret subsidies from Lord Iveagh, head of the Guinness dynasty and from the British Shipping Federation kept some of the weaker employers on side.[19] Murphy also introduced imaginative new measures such as the creation of a fund to subsidise the purchase of motorized vehicles by smaller firms to replace their strike-bound horse-drawn carts.

## AN INDEPENDENT VOICE

Another weapon of immense power in Murphy's arsenal was Independent Newspapers. All three titles, the *Irish Independent, Sunday Independent* and *Evening Herald* were recruited to the class war, along with the *Irish Catholic*, which he also owned. In 1904 Murphy had considered selling off the ailing *Independent* but instead followed the advice of Sir Alfred Harmsworth (later Lord Northcliffe) and transformed it into a modern newspaper. It was an enormous risk, trying to turn around a newspaper that had already cost him £100,000. He halved the cover price to a halfpenny, invested in the latest printing equipment, eschewed wordy political diatribes against his many enemies (which must have been difficult), hired an outstanding editor in Timothy R. Harrington, used photographs extensively and peppered the pages with features and serials on a scale never seen before in an Irish publication. Most importantly, the faster presses meant the *Irish Independent* could be delivered to the provinces much earlier than the rival *Freeman's Journal*, the official organ of the Irish Party.

The circulation of the *Independent* rose from 8,000 in 1904 to almost 60,000 by September 1913, passing out the 40,000 circulation of the *Freeman*. The *Weekly* and *Sunday Independent* had over 51,000 readers by 1913 and the *Evening Herald* almost 19,500. In fact the nearest rival to Independent Newspapers within Dublin was Larkin's *Irish Worker*. But its print runs varied enormously depending on finances, libel writs and the whereabouts of the editor. In 1913 Murphy abandoned any pretence of objectivity and the Independent titles traded insult for insult with the *Irish Worker*. If Murphy was denounced as a 'whited sepulchre', 'capitalist sweater' and 'financial octopus', Larkin's followers were described as 'all the foul reserves of the slums, human beings whom life in the most darksome depths of a great city has deprived of most of the characteristics of civilization'.[20]

---

19 Yeates, *Lockout*, p. 376.   20 *Irish Catholic*, 6 Sept. 1913. See Yeates, *Lockout*, pp 129–34.

Circulation of the *Irish Independent* rose rapidly after the Lockout, reaching almost 107,000 by September 1914. While there has been a tendency for Murphy and his fellow employers to be viewed retrospectively as a tiny arrogant capitalist aristocracy imposing their will on the city, the reality is that they had the support of most middle-class Dubliners in their battle with the workers, not to mention churches of all denominations. Unfortunately for Murphy, his victory over the ITGWU proved short lived. The outbreak of war in August 1914 ultimately created the conditions that resulted in the resurgence of the ITGWU, just as they helped destroy the Irish Party. Despite the immense difficulties the war imposed on the Irish newspaper industry, Independent Newspapers continued to prosper. The shortage of newsprint was overcome by cutting the size of editions. Murphy was happy to see coverage of parliamentary speeches and Dublin Corporation proceedings slashed in his publications while, miraculously, his tramway system was not seriously damaged in the 1916 Rising.

The one great blunder that would live in infamy was the *Irish Independent* editorials calling for the execution of MacDermott and Connolly.[21] The call for Connolly's death was seen as vindictive because he had been Larkin's lieutenant in the Lockout. While Murphy sought to exercise tight editorial control over many aspects of the news, particularly political and business coverage, the offending editorials had been written by Timothy R. Harrington. Later Harrington would point out that he had only written what many people were demanding when they went to bed, before changing their minds when they awoke to hear of the executions next morning. Unfortunately, such was Murphy's popular image that many readily believed he did write the editorials.

He received an unexpected opportunity to participate once more in the political life of the nation as a member of the Irish Convention. This was convened by the British government in 1917 as a bid to establish a basis for agreement between nationalist and unionist camps. Now in his seventies, Murphy knew it was his last opportunity to make a direct impact and he put aside business affairs to advocate what was in effect dominion status for a united Ireland. He consistently opposed partition and demanded that the new Irish parliament have full fiscal autonomy. In many ways he anticipated the Treaty settlement, except that the Free State was shorn of what had become Northern Ireland in the meantime. It was far more than either unionists or Whitehall would concede in 1917 or 1918, and far less than the new ascendant force in Irish politics, the radical nationalists of Sinn Féin and the Irish Volunteers would settle for.

By 1918 Murphy had become completely disillusioned with the Irish Party. He regarded Redmond's early surrender on partition, albeit on a temporary

---

21 *Irish Independent*, 10 & 12 May 1916.

basis, as indefensible. The succession of his old nemesis, John Dillon, to the leadership of the party on Redmond's death only aggravated resentment at his treatment by the leaders of constitutional nationalism. If he still found it impossible to support Sinn Féin because of what he regarded as the impracticality of its strategy, he certainly facilitated its rise. The Independent titles gave extensive coverage to Sinn Féin candidates in the snap election of 1918 and the *Irish Independent* ran a series of front page display advertisements in the week before polling that seriously undermined the Irish Party. Even more remarkable was Murphy's support for the general strike against conscription on 23 April 1918. Without a hint of irony, the *Irish Independent* urged trade unionists to show solidarity with each other that day and man the picket lines. Murphy died on 26 July 1919 at his home in Dartry and was buried with his wife in the O'Connell circle at Glasnevin cemetery, Dublin. He left an estate worth £250,000 and a newspaper empire that had already helped shape the course of Irish history and would continue to do so. If he left few close friends to mourn his passing, this one-time politician, successful businessman and newspaper proprietor left a host of enemies.

# 3 / No longer a political side show: T.R. Harrington and the 'new' *Irish Independent*, 1905–31

## FELIX M. LARKIN

When William Martin Murphy was introduced to Bernard Shaw at a lunch party at Kilteragh, Sir Horace Plunkett's house at Foxrock, Co. Dublin, in October 1917, he was astonished to be told that he was the man in all Ireland whom the playwright had been most anxious to meet. He afterwards wrote about their encounter to his son, Dr Lombard Murphy, who was serving with the Royal Army Medical Corps in Salonika:

> [Shaw] has pleasant manners and is not at all the kind of man his books and writings would lead you to believe. For the public he poses and advertises himself, but he does not find this necessary in private life. I expect his anticipation of what I was like was equally unlike the reality. I have no doubt that he expected to find in me a man with an aggressive attitude.[1]

There are many reasons why Shaw should have so wished to meet Murphy. It is clear that Murphy himself thought it was because of his role as the stern and unbending leader of the employers in the great Dublin labour dispute of 1913. However, Murphy had had a long and varied career, any one aspect of which might have been of interest to Shaw. He was then aged 73, and his record of involvement in Irish public life encompassed a wide spectrum of politics and commerce.[2] On the political side, he had been an Irish nationalist MP at Westminster and one of the leaders of the campaign against Parnell after the 'split'; he later became disillusioned with the Irish party, opposed its leadership from 1896 onwards and eventually gave tentative support to Sinn Féin post–1916; and he was a member of the Irish Convention of 1917–18. His extensive

I am grateful to Ian d'Alton, Peter Lacy and Professor Robert P. Schmuhl for their comments on earlier drafts of this chapter. My thanks go also to Patrick Maume for letting me have a copy of 'Commerce, politics and the *Irish Independent*, 1891–1919', his unpublished paper read before the 24th Irish Conference of Historians in 1999.   1 W.M. Murphy to L. Murphy, 14 Oct. 1917, W.M. Murphy papers, in private possession; I am grateful to the late T.V. Murphy for access to these papers.   2 See T. Morrissey, *William Martin Murphy* (Dundalk, 1997). See also A. Bielenberg, 'Entrepreneurship, power and public opinion in Ireland: the career of William Martin Murphy', *Irish Economic and Social History*, 27 (2000), 25–43, and D. McCartney, 'William Martin Murphy: an Irish press baron and the rise of the popular press' in B. Farrell (ed.), *Communications and community in Ireland* (Dublin & Cork, 1984), pp 30–8.

commercial interests included building and contracting, newspapers, retailing, and tramways and railways; and he was the prime mover behind the Industrial Exhibition of 1907, as well as the principal opponent of James Larkin and James Connolly and their trade union. He gained W.B. Yeats' disdain for his refusal to support the proposed gallery in Dublin for the Hugh Lane pictures. The *Irish Independent* was, therefore, only part of his multifarious life, and probably for him not the most important part – though the *Independent* was a notable success and it revolutionized the world of Irish newspapers. Ironically, as we shall see, it was a project that he drifted into almost by accident.

Murphy's indispensible ally in creating the modern *Independent* was its first editor, Timothy R. Harrington – like Murphy himself, a native of Castletown-bere, Co. Cork. Their respective contributions to the success of the *Independent* were aptly described by Harrington's obituarist in the *Sunday Independent* as follows: 'It was William Martin Murphy who planned the revolution in Irish journalism; it was T.R. Harrington, in his editorship of the *Irish Independent*, who carried it out.'[3] Their relationship in this joint endeavour was often turbulent, but it survived and ultimately prospered because of Murphy's respect for Harrington's professionalism. It is wrong, however, to credit them with having founded the *Independent* – as the newspaper today is wont to do. For example, one of its journalists, James Downey, asserts in his 2009 autobiography that 'the *Irish Independent* was founded by William Martin Murphy in 1905'.[4] The real credit for founding the *Independent* belongs to Charles Stewart Parnell, and possibly the reason for the *Independent*'s persistent misrepresentation of its history is that its Parnellite origins do not sit comfortably with its later pro-clerical editorial policy under William Martin Murphy and, afterwards, under his son and grandson – before it was acquired by Tony O'Reilly in 1973.

The *Independent* was, in fact, a product of the newspaper war in Ireland that was unleashed by the Parnell 'split'. The various divisions in the Irish Party precipitated by the 'split' were replicated in the newspaper market. The *Freeman's Journal*, the leading daily nationalist newspaper in the country in 1890, remained loyal to Parnell in the initial months of the 'split' – but eventually switched sides after the majority anti-Parnell faction in the party started a new daily newspaper, the *National Press*, to counter the *Freeman*'s influence. When the *Freeman* abandoned him, Parnell made arrangements for the establishment of a new title – originally known as the *Irish Daily Independent*. It first appeared on 18 December 1891, two months after his death. The name of the paper emphasized that the Parnellites were 'independent' of any alliance with British political parties, whereas their nationalist opponents were tied to Gladstone's Liberal party and

---

3 *Sunday Independent*, 26 Sept. 1937.   4 J. Downey, *In my own time: inside Irish politics and society* (Dublin, 2009), p. 232.

had deposed Parnell as leader at the diktat of the Liberals. The *Independent* survived as the organ of the Parnellite wing of the Irish Party until the party's reunification under John Redmond in 1900, when it was purchased by William Martin Murphy.[5] Meanwhile, the two anti-Parnell newspapers, the *Freeman's Journal* and the *National Press*, amalgamated under the former's more venerable title.

The *National Press* had been established mainly through the efforts of T.M. Healy, with Murphy as its principal financial backer. This was Murphy's first serious venture into the world of newspapers. Murphy was a close associate of Healy, a fellow Corkman; he was one of the so-called 'Bantry Band' of MPs who had roots in west Cork or were otherwise linked to Healy and his influential uncles, A.M and T.D. Sullivan, successively owners of the weekly *Nation* newspaper.[6] The *Nation* had ceased publication in 1891, but was briefly revived as a Healyite organ – again funded by Murphy – in 1896. It continued as the *Daily Nation* from June 1897. The *Daily Nation* was merged with the *Irish Daily Independent* when Murphy acquired the *Independent* in 1900. The *Daily Independent* was then the personal mouthpiece of T.M. Healy until 1905, when it was transformed by Murphy and Harrington into the modern *Irish Independent*.

Harrington became chief reporter of the new *Daily Nation* in 1897, and he went on to hold the same position on the *Irish Daily Independent* after its merger with the *Nation*. Of farming stock, he was born in 1866 and joined the staff of the *Cork Daily Herald* in the mid–1880s, when Alderman John Hooper MP was editor. He was christened plain 'Timothy', but began adding 'Richard' to his name early in his career – perhaps to differentiate himself from the better-known Timothy C. Harrington, journalist and MP, who was also a native of Castletownbere. They were not, however, related. Confusingly, T.C. Harrington was briefly associated with the Parnellite *Independent* in the early 1890s, before becoming manager of the *United Ireland* newspaper in its final years. There is evidence that T.R. Harrington chafed at the very partisan style of both the *Daily Nation* and the *Irish Daily Independent* and that, as chief reporter, he tried to lessen those newspapers' subservience to Healy. Thus, the editor of the *Daily Nation* – and later editor of the merged *Nation* and *Daily Independent* – William F. Dennehy, had occasion to rebuke him formally in an undated letter for failing to consult Healy. He wrote:

> Unless you can see your way to act on such instructions as I must occasionally give you, it will be necessary for me to appoint someone else to

5 For further information about the newspaper war unleashed by the Parnell 'split', see F.M. Larkin, 'Mrs Jellyby's daughter: Caroline Agnes Gray (1848–1927) and the *Freeman's Journal*' in F.M. Larkin (ed.), *Librarians, poets and scholars: a festschrift for Dónall Ó Luanaigh* (Dublin, 2007), pp 121–39 (at pp 134–7). 6 The 'Bantry Band' comprised three Sullivan brothers (A.M., T.D. and Donal), two Healy brothers (T.M. and Maurice), two Harrington brothers (Timothy C. and Edward), John Barry (a distant relation of the Healys), James Gilhooly and William Martin Murphy.

fill the position of chief reporter in your stead. I am simply amazed at
the style and temper of your communication. I have now only to repeat
that it will be necessary for a member of the reporting staff to call
each evening at Mr Healy's, and that I must ask you to see that this is
done.[7]

This unambiguous instruction to Harrington offends against modern notions
of the independence of the press and the profession of journalism. However,
these concepts were only beginning to gain currency in the late nineteenth and
early twentieth centuries. Journalism in Ireland at this time was intensely political and there was nothing unusual about journalists working in concert with
individual politicians or political parties. Newspapers were organs for particular points of view, usually those of their proprietors, and tended to promote in
reportage as well as in the leader columns the views of those who owned or
otherwise controlled the papers. Rather than upholding professional values such
as we might expect journalists today to have, journalists then were actively
engaged in the politics of their day, unashamedly polemical – perhaps aspi-
rant politicians, or politicians manqué.

Tim Pat Coogan, writing in 1966, could reasonably claim that 'more of the
country's newspapers [were] coming to see their role as stimulators of the mind
and not as retailers of received prejudices'.[8] Developments of this kind lay very
far into the future during T.R. Harrington's lifetime. Nevertheless, the restructuring and modernization of the *Independent* by William Martin Murphy in 1905
involved a major advance in professional standards in journalism in Ireland –
to quote the newspaper itself, 'a departure from the traditions of [Irish] journalism'.[9] Nothing symbolized this more than the appointment of Harrington
as editor in place of Dennehy. Harrington's prior experience had been on the
reporting staff of the newspaper, whereas the usual route into an editorial chair
had been through the leader-writing staff – the commentators, not the
reporters, got the job. Given Murphy's deep political involvement and author-
itarian instincts in the commercial sphere, it might be thought that he was a
most unlikely figure to effect such change. However, the *Daily Nation* had
incurred heavy financial losses – and so too did the *Independent* after the merger.
Murphy sought to address this problem, and concluded that a radical transformation of the *Independent* was required. He himself explained his approach
in an article published in 1909, on the fourth anniversary of the launch of the
new *Independent*:

7 W.F. Dennehy to T.R. Harrington, n.d., T.R. Harrington papers, 1052/1/5, National Archives of Ireland.   8 T.P.
Coogan, *Ireland since the Rising* (London, 1966), p. 174.   9 *Irish Independent*, 1 Jan. 1906.

I had proved by experience what I had often heard and indeed knew well enough, that newspapers as a side show to politics were never known to result in anything but a loss. In 1904, I was getting tired of running political side shows on such terms and my personal interest in the issues which had given rise to my journalistic essays had considerably abated. I looked about for a buyer for the *Independent* papers as a going concern and, strange to say, I found a very probable purchaser who employed experts to report on it. The advice these experts gave was to issue the *Independent* as a halfpenny paper and to conduct the undertaking as a business proposition.[10]

Instead of selling up, Murphy decided to revamp the *Independent* along the lines that the potential purchaser of the paper had proposed and to try to make a success of it himself.

The new *Independent*, selling for a halfpenny, cost half the price of its competitors and had a more popular, less partisan style than its rivals. In effect, Murphy copied in Ireland what Lord Northcliffe had done in London in 1896 when he had launched the *Daily Mail*, the first mass circulation newspaper in these islands. Murphy tells us that, before embarking on his enterprise, he first checked with Northcliffe on whether he had any plans to publish a halfpenny newspaper in Dublin that would rival Murphy's. When Northcliffe confirmed that he had none, Murphy asked for and obtained Northcliffe's advice and assistance in restructuring the *Independent* – and Murphy was afterwards happy to acknowledge his debt to Northcliffe. The first edition of the new *Irish Independent* appeared on 2 January 1905. It was an immediate resounding success, and by 1909 Murphy could proclaim that 'the commercial success of the *Independent* papers, as a profit earning property, is now absolutely secured'.[11] Annual profits by 1915 amounted to £15,000, with circulation rising from an initial 25,000 to 100,000 in 1915.[12] Profits and circulation continued to grow thereafter, boosted by the closure of the *Independent*'s main rival, the *Freeman's Journal*, in 1924 – and checked only by the establishment of the *Irish Press* in 1931.[13] It was a period of increasing demand for newspapers in Ireland, as elsewhere. Total sales of daily newspapers in Ireland grew by a factor of seven between the early 1880s and the 1920s – from 75,000 copies per day in the 1880s to over half a million in the 1920s.[14]

---

10 W.M. Murphy, 'The story of a newspaper', *Irish Independent*, 2 Jan. 1909.  11 Ibid.  12 T.M. Healy to M. Healy, 27 Nov. 1915, quoted in F. Callanan, *T.M. Healy* (Cork, 1996), p. 484. The *Independent* claimed a circulation of 110,000 in the *Newspaper press directory* of 1915.  13 Circulation had reached over 143,000 per day by June 1931, two months before the launch of the *Irish Press* (*Booklet published by Independent Newspapers Ltd to mark retirement of Mr T.R. Harrington, 20 Aug. 1931*, Hector Legge papers, in private possession).  14 L.M. Cullen, *Eason & son: a history* (Dublin, 1989), pp

The *Independent*, with up-to-date machinery, was in a position to take advantage of this growth. The *Freeman's Journal* was not. It did not have the printing capacity to expand its circulation and could not afford to upgrade its plant. The newspaper war that followed the Parnell 'split' had left it chronically short of funds for investment – and its management, afraid of losing control, would not raise new capital. It did not have a commercial focus. As the organ of the Irish Party, it remained a political side show – and indeed was described *c*.1916, in an anonymous memorandum in the Redmond papers, as 'a sort of political bulletin, circulating amongst already staunch friends of the Party, and bringing them information and arguments with which they supported the movement and [its] policy'.[15]

In contrast, the *Independent* set out its editorial principles in the first issue following its re-launch in terms that echoed the newspaper's original Parnellite stance of 'independence' – though Murphy's *Independent* eschewed all political alliances, not just alliances with a British political party:

> The *Irish Independent*, under its new editorial and managerial control, will justify its claim to be a national journal in fact as well as in name. It holds itself free to help on every good cause which is for Ireland's benefit. It will place our country's interests above those of party, and it will not work to exploit any section or individual. The extravagances of partisanship will be unknown in its editorial columns ... the *Irish Independent* will be neither offensive nor aggressive in its style of advocacy, and as a newspaper will be found acceptable by every class and creed.[16]

Harrington's contribution to the *Independent*'s success was twofold: to preserve this non-partisan editorial policy and to present the news 'quickly, brightly and crisply, yet accurately and completely ... [to meet] the needs and desires of the busy reader'.[17] Brevity, like objectivity, was not the norm in Irish journalism at that time. As his *Sunday Independent* obituarist noted, Harrington 'killed the ponderous leading article, the page-long, wearisome reports of political meetings and the dull, verbose reports of the doings of public bodies that then formed the stock-in-trade of newspapers'.[18] His approach was evident in the written

77 & 307; I have assumed that about one-third of total sales of newspapers in Ireland were through W.H. Smith, the antecedent of Eason's (see Cullen, *Eason*, p. 355). Raymond Williams likewise calculates a sevenfold increase in aggregate daily newspaper circulation in Britain between 1880 and 1920 (Williams, *The long revolution* (paperback ed., London, 1965), p. 198). **15** John Redmond papers, MS 15,262/1, National Library of Ireland. For a full account of the *Freeman's* decline, see F.M. Larkin, 'Two gentlemen of the *Freeman*: Thomas Sexton, W.H. Brayden and the *Freeman's Journal*, 1892–1916' in C. Breathnach & C. Lawless (eds), *Visual, material and print culture in nineteenth-century Ireland* (Dublin, 2010), pp 210–22. **16** *Irish Independent*, 2 Jan. 1905. **17** Harrington's obituary, *Sunday Independent*, 26 Sept. 1937. **18** Ibid.

instructions given to reporters covering the 1906 general election for the
*Independent*:

1  Reporters are to bear in mind the policy of the *Independent* as an
   impartial newspaper and are to prepare their reports in an unbiased,
   impartial and reliable manner.
2  They are to consider themselves representatives of the paper and not
   as adherents of one party or another and to approach their work with
   a perfectly open mind.
3  Reporters should avoid as far as possible any comments, inferences
   or prophesies in connection with [election] contests and confine
   themselves as a rule to reporting facts or speeches in a fair and impartial way, following our usual practice of not giving things fully [i.e.,
   summarizing, rather than providing verbatim accounts].
4  It is generally advisable that reporters should engage their own cars
   and should come with other pressmen, if possible, and thus be independent of both the opposing parties to a contest.
5  These instructions apply to all contests anywhere in Ireland.[19]

The significance of the last paragraph was that Harrington's instructions
applied to contests in constituencies in which dissident nationalists – most
notably, T.M. Healy – might be opposed by official Irish Party candidates. In
the event, few seats in Ireland were actually contested in 1906; those that were
mostly involved unionist candidates, rather than rival nationalists.

The possibility that Healy would be opposed in his North Louth constituency by an official Irish Party candidate in 1906 gave rise to a serious crisis
in the affairs of the new *Independent* that tested Murphy's resolve that it should
be an impartial newspaper. Healy wrote a letter decrying the threat of a contest in his constituency that Murphy asked Harrington to publish. Murphy also
asked Harrington to publish a sub-leader that Murphy had drafted in support
of Healy.[20] Healy's letter did appear in the *Independent*,[21] but Harrington refused
to publish the sub-leader. He justified his action to Murphy in a letter that sets
out clearly the rationale for the agreement between them on editorial independence:

You remember before I took up the editorship of the paper what the
arrangement was in the event of such a contingency as a contest in North
Louth. I told you I would send two reporters down, one with each party

19 Harrington papers, 1052/3/4.  20 W.M. Murphy to T.R. Harrington, 31 Dec. 1905, Harrington papers, 1052/3/1.
21 *Irish Independent*, 2 Jan. 1906.

in the contest, and that I would give them instructions to report fairly
and impartially, without fear or prejudice, what took place and that we
would publish such reports and take no part editorially in the contest.
You assented definitely to that arrangement in your room in 39 Dame
Street. I believe Mr Healy's letter tonight speaks for itself and that no
editorial notice should be taken of it. I believe further that the sub-leader
you sent to me would, if published, not serve the paper – but would,
on the contrary, do it great injury … In taking this step, I am acting
solely and entirely in the interests of your property, as I am sure you will
admit when the storm of the election has blown away. The present is a
grave crisis for the paper which I believe has a splendid future before it
if only prudence, caution and good judgement are observed. I repeat
again that you should calmly and reasonably weigh the situation before
embarking on a line of policy in the paper which will undoubtedly be
unpopular and which in my strong opinion is bound to greatly militate
against the success of the concern in which so much of your money is
involved … The entire staff agrees with me in the view that it would
be ruinous to the paper in this crisis to support Mr Healy even in the
mildest form.[22]

The proposed sub-leader was never published. Subsequently, when it emerged
that a contest in Healy's constituency had been averted, the *Independent* welcomed
the news with the bland editorial comment that 'we are glad that the electors
of North Louth will be spared the trouble and turmoil of what might have
proved a bitterly contested election'.[23] Murphy conceded, albeit in hindsight,
that Harrington's demurral was 'a very fair one'.[24]

Nearly ten years later, Harrington once again had occasion to defend the
editorial independence of his newspaper. He wrote to Murphy in astonishingly
frank terms seeking reassurance:

that I will be given a free hand as regards the policy of the *Independent*
on political questions and matters, and that you will not persist in forcing your unpopular political views on me with a view to getting them
into the editorial columns of the *Independent*, especially when I tell you,
as I have often done, that I believe such opinions would, if published in
the paper in the form in which you want them, inflict untold injury on
it.[25]

22 T.R. Harrington to W.M. Murphy, 1 Jan. 1906 (draft), Harrington papers, 1052/3/3.   23 *Irish Independent*, 9 Jan.
1906.   24 W.M. Murphy to T.R. Harrington, 12 Jan. 1906, Harrington papers, 1052/3/5.   25 T.R. Harrington to
W.M. Murphy, 28 June 1915, Murphy papers; quoted in Callanan, *Healy*, pp 485–6.

In response to this letter, Murphy denied that he had ever forced Harrington to publish his opinions, but defended his right 'to discuss policy with you or to impress my opinions, whether strong or weak ones'.[26] In fairness, Murphy did generally remain at a distance from day-to-day editorial matters and Harrington accordingly enjoyed an unprecedented degree of editorial autonomy and journalistic independence, which is how they had agreed the newspaper should be run. Not surprisingly, that gave rise to considerable tension between Murphy and Healy. The latter deeply resented no longer having a subservient newspaper at his disposal. He regularly complained to Murphy about 'the blackguard Harrington'[27] who would not give him the publicity to which he felt entitled by virtue of his long association with Murphy. However, Murphy stuck to his guns, once responding to Healy that 'if the new *Independent* was edited as you think it ought to be, and as Dennehy edited the old *Independent*, in which money was poured as into a bottomless pit, you would not have any daily paper existing today that would print even "snippets" from your speeches'. Murphy was determined that the *Independent* should no longer be a political side show.[28]

Harrington's approach in formulating the *Independent*'s editorial policy was to follow public opinion as he perceived it and articulate positions broadly acceptable to his predominantly middle-class, Catholic, nationalist readers – so as not to lose their custom. In the words of Serjeant Sullivan, son of A.M. Sullivan of the *Nation*, 'the editor's job was to ascertain in what direction the mob was moving and to grovel to its decrees'.[29] That strategy generally served the *Independent* well, though not in relation to the 1916 Rising. Like the other mainstream Irish newspapers, the *Independent* condemned the rising unreservedly. Then, when the number of executions started to mount and there arose a widespread demand for clemency, it supported that demand only as regards the rank and file of the rebels and in two notorious leading articles – published on 10 and 12 May – it called for the execution of James Connolly and Seán MacDermott, the only signatories of the 1916 Proclamation not executed by then. In the first of these articles, the *Independent* opined:

> We do not think that extreme severity should be generally applied, nor do we think that there should be extreme leniency all round … When, however, we come to some of the ringleaders, instigators and fomenters not yet dealt with, we must make an exception. If these men are treated with too great leniency, they will take it as an indication of weakness on

---

26 W.M. Murphy to T.R. Harrington, 30 June 1915, Murphy papers.   27 T.M. Healy to W.M. Murphy, 22 May 1916, Murphy papers; quoted in Callanan, *Healy*, p. 486.   28 W.M Murphy to T.M. Healy, 24 May 1916, Murphy papers; quoted in Callanan, *Healy*, p. 486.   29 A.M. (Serjeant) Sullivan, *Old Ireland: reminiscences of an Irish KC* (London, 1927), p. 202.

> the part of the Government … Some of these leaders are more guilty
> and played a more sinister part in the campaign than those who have
> already been punished with severity and it would hardly be fair to treat
> these leniently because the cry for clemency has been raised … Let the
> worst of the ringleaders be singled out and dealt with as they deserve,
> but we hope there will be no holocaust or slaughter. [30]

This obviously referred to Connolly and MacDermott, though not by name.
The *Independent* renewed its call for their execution two days later:

> Certain of the leaders remain undealt with, and the part they played was
> worse than that of some of those who have paid the extreme penalty.
> Are they because of an indiscriminate demand for clemency to get off
> lightly, while others who were no more prominent have been executed?
> … We are no advocates of undue severity, but undue leniency to some
> of the worst of the firebrands would be just as bad … We think in a
> word that no special leniency should be extended to some of the worst
> of the leaders whose cases have not yet been disposed of. After these have
> been dealt with, it would be a mistake to apply severe or drastic pun-
> ishment to the rank and file and those who played but a minor part in
> the Rising. [31]

Connolly and MacDermott were shot early on the morning of 12 May, a few
hours after the second article had gone to press; they were already dead when
most people read it.

   These were truly extraordinary tirades – given that, by 10–12 May 1916, even
moderate nationalist opinion in Ireland had moved decisively against the policy
of executing the leaders of the rising. As early as 9 May, the *Freeman's Journal* –
still the *Independent*'s main competitor – had written that 'sympathy is being
aroused with the victims [i.e. the executed leaders] where nothing but indignant
condemnation of their criminal enterprise previously existed'. Echoing these sen-
timents, John Dillon condemned the severity of the reaction of the authorities
to the rising in a speech in the House of Commons on 11 May. In that speech,
he generously – and controversially – spoke of the 'courage' of the insurgents and
proclaimed that they had 'fought a clean fight, a brave fight, however misguided'. [32]

   Immediately after the first executions on 3 May, John Redmond had privately warned the British prime minister of the adverse consequences of fur-

---

30 *Irish Independent*, 10 May 1916.   31 Ibid., 12 May 1916.   32 F.S.L. Lyons, *John Dillon: a biography* (London, 1968), pp 380–3.

ther executions. So why did the *Independent* publish such bloodthirsty pieces? Many thought that Murphy was seeking revenge for Connolly's role in the 1913 Lockout, but it seems that the articles were written without his knowledge. He was away in London pressing the government for compensation for property destroyed in the rising when the articles appeared and was simply not in a position to try to impose an editorial line on the newspaper at that time – even if he had been so inclined. He afterwards repudiated the articles in private – though never in public, apparently out of loyalty to the *Independent*'s editorial staff.[33] A more likely explanation is that the *Independent* and its editor simply misread the shifting mood of the public. The evidence for this is that Harrington was quoted soon after the rising as saying – somewhat ruefully – that 'the people cried out for vengeance and when they got it, they howled for clemency'.[34] Whatever the explanation, the charge of having sought the deaths of Connolly and MacDermott haunted William Martin Murphy until his death in 1919. It would haunt the *Irish Independent* for much longer.[35]

Despite its response to the rising, the *Independent* under Harrington's editorship had long been critical of the Irish Parliamentary Party – persistently accusing it of jobbery (particularly in local government) and differing with it on, for example, Lloyd George's 1909 budget and the financial provisions of the third home rule bill. William O'Brien characterized the editorial stance adopted by Harrington as 'giving voice to the suppressed wrath of the country' against the party.[36] The *Independent* thus played a significant role in undermining the party's authority – even before the 1916 Rising. T.P. O'Connor wrote that 'of all the many agencies that finally broke down the Irish party, and led to the regime of Sinn Féin and its accompaniments, the *Independent* and William Murphy behind it must be regarded as perhaps the most potent'.[37] Likewise, T.M. Healy described Murphy's revamped newspaper as 'a new portent [that] flamed into the Irish political sky … This revolutionized the situation and ultimately destroyed both the parliamentary party and the *Freeman*.'[38] Under the pressure of competition from the *Independent*, the *Freeman* had begun to incur heavy trading losses from 1908 onwards and only survived until after the 1918 general election through subsidies paid from Irish party funds.[39] In 1919, it was bought by a Dublin wine-

33 Morrissey, *Murphy*, pp 63–4. See also Downey, *In my own time*, p. 233.  34 E.M. Murphy to T.R. Harrington, 29 June 1916, Harrington papers, 1052/5/2. For another interpretation, see 'Appendix II: Press reaction to the Rising in general' in O. Dudley Edwards & F. Pyle (eds), *1916: the Easter Rising* (London, 1968), pp 264–70.  35 Even in 1966, in a leader on the celebration of the fiftieth anniversary of the rising (11 Apr. 1966), the *Irish Independent* attempted to finesse the record: 'In 1916, there were many to revile the Rising – not least this newspaper, as our critics have long taken care to remind us – for the Rising seemed to undermine what parliamentary endeavour had achieved.'  36 W. O'Brien, 'The party': who they are and what they have done (Dublin and London, 1917), p. 31.  37 T.P. O'Connor, *Memoirs of an old parliamentarian*, 2 vols (London, 1929), ii, p. 58.  38 T.M. Healy, *Letters and leaders of my day*, 2 vols (London, 1928), ii, p. 470.  39 See F.M. Larkin, 'Two gentlemen of the *Freeman*' (at pp 219–20).

merchant, Martin Fitzgerald, who gallantly struggled to keep it going until 1924.[40] Piquantly, the last editor of the *Freeman* was Patrick Hooper, son of Harrington's early mentor on the *Cork Daily Herald*, Alderman John Hooper.

After 1916, the *Independent* gave tacit support to Sinn Féin once it was clear that public opinion was moving in that direction. Murphy himself was initially doubtful about the rise of the party, advising Harrington in late 1917 that 'while giving them a fair show, it is not well to identify the paper too much with Sinn Féin'.[41] Murphy lived to see the party's triumph in the 1918 general election, but died shortly afterwards. He was succeeded as chairman of Independent Newspapers by his son, Dr Lombard Murphy – a much less forceful figure than his father, which meant that Harrington was now able to consolidate the editorial independence that he had secured under Murphy *père*. Strongly in favour of the Anglo-Irish Treaty of 1921, the *Independent* was later sympathetic towards the government of the new Irish Free State in the 1920s and – contrary to its founding ethos of avoiding 'extravagances of partisanship' – eventually came to be regarded as the semi-official organ of the government party, Cumann na nGaedheal. The challenge of running a newspaper during the years of the war of independence and the civil war in Ireland was considerable. For example, in December 1922 the editors and proprietors of Dublin newspapers received death threats from the anti-Treaty forces because of hostile reporting of their activities, and as a consequence Harrington actually lived and slept in the *Independent*'s office for several weeks under guard.[42] The strain of those times took its toll on his health and he had a nervous breakdown in 1924. He never fully recovered and his influence over the newspaper was much reduced thereafter, though he remained as editor until 1931 and was a director of the company from 1929 until his death in 1937.[43] Significantly, he retired as editor just as the *Independent* prepared to meet the imminent challenge of de Valera's *Irish Press*, launched on 5 September 1931 to counter the opposition to Fianna Fáil of newspapers such as the *Independent*.[44]

Shakespeare wrote: 'The evil that men do lives after them, / The good is oft interred with their bones'.[45] So it is with William Martin Murphy and T.R. Harrington: the former is remembered chiefly as the implacable foe of the labour movement in 1913, and the reputations of both men are besmirched by the memory of the leading articles published in the *Independent* after the 1916

---

**40** For information on the last years of the *Freeman's Journal*, see F.M. Larkin, 'A great daily organ: the *Freeman's Journal*, 1763–1924', *History Ireland*, 14:3 (May/June 2006), 44–9 (at 48–9). **41** W.M. Murphy to T.R. Harrington, 11 Oct. 1917, Harrington papers, 1052/4/29. **42** See J. Dillon to T.P. O'Connor, 11 Dec. 1922, John Dillon papers, MS 6740–4/906, Trinity College Dublin. **43** Harrington's obituary, *Irish Independent*, 25 Sept. 1937. **44** Harrington's retirement as editor was noted in the London *Times*, 24 August 1931. He was succeeded by his long-time deputy, Timothy Quilty. **45** *Julius Caesar* (1599), III.ii.

Rising. However, as this chapter has shown, they deserve to be fêted as enormously innovative newspapermen who planned and carried out a revolution in Irish journalism – an important milestone in the slow, fitful advance of the freedom of the press in Ireland. It seems that Harrington himself had some sense of the importance of his contribution. Thus, in an address to the *Independent* staff on the occasion of his retirement, he remarked that 'during the twenty-seven years I have filled the editorial chair I have put what is equivalent to more than forty years' work into the paper'.[46] It was a fair boast at the end of a truly remarkable career.

46 *Booklet published by Independent Newspapers Ltd to mark retirement of Mr T.R. Harrington, 20 Aug. 1931*, Legge papers.

# 4 / Nationalist in the broadest sense: the *Irish Independent* and the Irish revolution

## IAN KENNEALLY

The *Irish Independent* has been inextricably associated with the editorials that it published in the weeks after the 1916 Rising. We have seen in the preceding chapter how the newspaper offered a furious denunciation of the 'criminal madness' of those who had planned and carried out the rising.[1] As a result of those editorials the *Irish Independent*, in the popular imagination, is remembered as a reactionary force, an opponent of Irish nationalism throughout the period 1916–23. Yet, in the aftermath of the rising, the newspaper would develop a complex relationship, sometimes fraught but often supportive, with the republican successors of 1916. Despite the violence of the rising, its immediate influence was on political rather than military events. Although the Irish Volunteers would reorganize with figures such as Michael Collins and Richard Mulcahy coming to the fore of the organization, it was the political rise of Sinn Féin as an 'organized separatist party which was capable of winning and holding the loyalties' of most Irish people that was to mark a profound change in Irish society.[2] Over the period from the rising to the inauguration of Dáil Éireann the *Irish Independent* was to display a growing closeness to the Sinn Féin party that was the main beneficiary of the events of Easter 1916.

That party's ascent was in stark contrast to the seemingly inexorable decline of the Irish Parliamentary Party (IPP). In the summer after the Easter Rising, John Redmond and other leaders of the party had engaged with the British government to seek some compromise on home rule. Parallel discussions were held between the British government and unionists. These talks collapsed without any agreement, discredited the party and left the morale of its members in tatters. Throughout the rest of the year the *Independent* rarely missed an opportunity to denounce the IPP. One editorial in December 1916 was typical of the general tone: 'In any other country in the world we know what would be the fate of leaders who were found wanting in every great emergency and flung away opportunities as Mr Redmond and his colleagues have done.'[3] In making its crit-

I would like to thank the Irish Research Council for the Humanities and Social Sciences for its support in the funding of my PhD studies at NUI Galway, and Dr Simon Potter for his comments and advice.  1 *Irish Independent*, 4 May 1916. The *Independent* was out of circulation from Easter Monday (24 Apr.) until 4 May 1916.  2 M. Laffan, 'The unification of Sinn Féin in 1917', *Irish Historical Studies*, 17:67 (1971), 353–79 at 353.  3 *Irish Independent*, 9 Dec.

icisms the *Independent*, or at least its owner, was motivated by personal as well as political reasons. William Martin Murphy had supported the anti-Parnellites during the infamous party split; however, a humiliating series of election defeats saw him turn to newspaper ownership as his means of gaining political influence. Manoeuvrings within the IPP later resulted in Murphy becoming an implacable adversary of John Dillon and also John Redmond. Following its master, the *Independent* became a constant critic of both men and the IPP. The *Irish Times* later said of Murphy that while he 'was certainly not a Sinn Féiner' he 'used every weapon to defeat the old party and all Sinn Féin's attacks on it received full publicity in his newspapers'.[4]

By 1917 the newspaper's view of the IPP coincided with the opinion of much of nationalist Ireland. This would be made very clear with the Sinn Féin triumphs in the by-elections in North Roscommon, South Longford and East Clare that same year. The *Independent* watched with no little glee as the IPP suffered defeat. The paper derided Redmond's performance in Westminster over the previous five years and accused him, and other leaders of the party whom they called 'the old gang of incompetents', of having 'betrayed Ireland'.[5] The result of these by-elections, according to the *Independent*, demonstrated that the Irish public had:

> a profound distrust of British statesmanship, a loss of all confidence in the Irish Parliamentary Party, and an intense antipathy to partition. The days of cant, humbug, and hypocrisy are gone. The people stand for the old nation one and undivided; and to all parties and the Government they say that only a scheme of Dominion Home Rule will satisfy or appease them.[6]

The editorial accused the party, in terms that were mirrored in Sinn Féin election pamphlets, of conspiring with the government in the 'overtaxation of Ireland' and of supporting an 'inadequate and unworkable' home rule bill. Most damningly, the paper accused the IPP of standing idly by as partition became an integral part of the home rule schemes proposed by the British government and while 'Ulster Unionists were allowed to organize armed resistance with absolute impunity'. There could be no doubting the accuracy of the paper's blunt conclusion: 'The leaders of the Party represent to-day only a minority of the Irish people ...'[7]

However, the *Independent* was not motivated only by an animus towards the IPP. William Martin Murphy deplored the idea that partition could play a part in

1916.  **4** *Irish Times*, 3 July 1919 (Murphy's obituary).  **5** *Irish Independent*, 19 July 1917.  **6** Ibid.  **7** Ibid.

any settlement leading to Irish home rule. His aversion to the idea was shared by the *Independent*'s editor, Timothy R. Harrington and the paper's editorials displayed a clear disillusionment with the attitude of the British government towards home rule. By 1918, Murphy, appalled by the fact that partition now seemed a likely outcome of any home rule settlement, had become, according to T.M. Healy, 'astonishingly nationalist in an active way'.[8] Murphy's nationalism may have manifested itself in the *Irish Independent* throughout that year as the paper moved closer to Sinn Féin during the conscription crisis that engulfed Ireland.

The failure of the Irish Convention to reach a settlement by March 1918 and the perilous situation facing the Allied forces on the Western Front resulted in the British government extending conscription to Ireland. Murphy had publicly supported Irish recruitment to the British army earlier in the war but now his newspaper was a leading opponent of the government's decision. It asserted that 'Promise after promise to the Irish people has been broken by the Government, with the result that they have destroyed voluntary recruiting in this country.'[9] It also offered an alternative to conscription: 'Grant the country full self-government', it advised, and then the government 'could withdraw thousands of troops from Ireland for a theatre where they are more needed, and would be more serviceable.'[10] Almost every day during April and May 1918 the *Independent* warned the government that conscription would lead to disaster and, most likely, a widespread nationalist rebellion. The newspaper was part of a grand alliance of various sections of nationalist Ireland; Sinn Féin, the Catholic church, and trade unions that worked together to foil the proposed scheme.

## 'THE ROOT CAUSE OF ALL THE TROUBLE AND DISCONTENT'

William Martin Murphy had always espoused 'a strong independent Home Rule Ireland, which preserved the link with the monarchy and the Empire ...'[11] The *Independent* had followed its owner's lead throughout its existence. Following the 1918 general election, however, the political landscape in Ireland had been utterly changed. While the *Independent* and Sinn Féin had been part of the nationalist consensus that had opposed conscription it remained to be seen how the paper would react to that party's strident republicanism. Sinn Féin put this republicanism into practice in January 1919 when it created a counter-government to British rule in Dublin's Mansion House, the first Dáil Éireann. The *Independent* seemed to take fright at the speed with which Sinn Féin was now pushing forward its agenda. In common with other national dailies the *Independent* was dubi-

8 Quoted in F. Callanan, *T.M. Healy* (Cork, 1996), p. 532.   9 *Irish Independent*, 6 Apr. 1918.   10 Ibid.   11 T. Morrissey, *William Martin Murphy* (Dundalk, 1997), p. 74.

ous that the Dáil would be able to carry through its stated aims, such as the creation of an independent Irish republic and it warned that Sinn Féin's actions
could gravely damage the prospects for full dominion home rule.

Yet, in a continuation of the paper's policy since 1917 its coverage of Sinn
Féin became increasingly positive throughout 1919, with detailed coverage given
to the workings of Dáil Éireann and the pronouncements of its politicians.
Indeed, at the time of the suppression of Arthur Griffith's newspaper *Nationality*
in September 1919, the *Independent* was the mainstream newspaper that provided
Sinn Féin with its most sympathetic coverage. The *Independent's* evolving attitude
towards Sinn Féin had not been changed by the death of William Martin
Murphy in June 1919. His successor as chairman of Independent Newspapers,
his son William Lombard Murphy, assured readers that 'there will be no departure from the policies hitherto pursued in these journals. In the future as in the
past the Independent Newspapers will be nationalist journals in the broadest
sense, detached from parties, independent, outspoken and fair ...'[12]

Other factors also worked to push the *Independent* closer to Sinn Féin. This
development can be seen, in part, as a response to the change in editorial policy
undergone by the *Freeman's Journal*. That newspaper, which had previously been
a semi-official newspaper of the IPP, had been purchased by Martin Fitzgerald
in October 1919. Under its new owner the *Freeman's Journal* abandoned its previous Redmondite loyalties and began to advocate many Dáil Éireann policies.
Fitzgerald also encouraged his journalists to take a confrontational line with
officials in Dublin Castle's Irish administration and in their reporting of the
activities of Crown forces. It seems likely that, at this time, both the *Independent*
and the *Freeman* were following rather than leading public opinion. Both newspapers were competing for the same readership; a readership that had abandoned the IPP for Sinn Féin in the 1918 general election and that was
increasingly repulsed by British rule in Ireland.

The political affiliations of the *Independent's* staff have to be taken into
account. The printers and journalists were not detached from the events they
covered. Dan Breen, for example, wrote in his memoir that 'many of the
[*Independent's*] staff were members of the Irish Republican Army'.[13] Breen was
almost certainly correct in this statement. The paper's chief proof reader,
Martin Pender and drama critic David Sears were both long-time republicans.[14]
A sub-editor, George Gormby, was a member of the IRA.[15] Reporters Ned
Lawler and Michael Knightly both provided information to the IRA. Knightly,

12 *Irish Independent*, 3 July 1919. William Lombard Murphy abandoned a successful career in medicine in order to
take over the leadership of Independent Newspapers.   13 D. Breen, *My fight for Irish freedom* (Dublin, 1981), p. 94.
14 H. Oram, *The newspaper book: a history of newspapers in Ireland, 1649–1983* (Dublin, 1983), p. 140.   15 J. Gleeson, *Bloody
Sunday* (London, 1962), pp 86–7.

who had fought in the 1916 Rising, was heavily implicated in the IRA's assassination of resident magistrate Alan Bell in March 1920. Days before that attack,
Knightly had provided Michael Collins with an up-to-date photograph of the
magistrate. Knightly, in later years, stated how he viewed his role as a reporter.
His job, he said, allowed him to combine 'newspaper work with intelligence
work for the IRA ... Newspaper work also afforded opportunities of helping
the cause in the political field and I was always glad to assist in this way.'[16]
Knightly, following a tip-off given to the police by a journalist in the *Irish Times*,
was arrested in early 1920 and spent seven months in Mountjoy gaol. On his
release he was immediately re-employed by the *Independent*. Clearly, within the
*Independent*, there was no stigma attached to being a known member of the IRA.

Despite the *Independent*'s positive coverage of Dáil Éireann and Sinn Féin, it
remained consistently critical of the violence carried out by the Irish Volunteers
throughout 1919 (throughout the war of independence the *Independent* usually
referred to the IRA as the 'Volunteers' or sometimes, 'the extreme wing of the
popular movement'). Volunteer activities such as attacks on the police, derail-
ing trains and raiding post office vans were habitually described as 'murders',
'outrages' or 'dastardly crimes'. This vein of reporting provoked retaliation from
the IRA. Following a report on the ambush of the Lord Lieutenant, Viscount
French, in December 1919 the IRA attacked the newspaper's offices. The
*Independent* had devoted a large amount of coverage to the 'miraculous escape' of
French. Its editorial called the attack 'a deplorable outrage', while the correspondent covering the event compared the 'thrilling nature of the sensational
occurrence' to the Phoenix Park murders of thirty-seven years before.[17]

The IRA took offence at the fact that the editorial called the ambush 'a
dreadful plan of assassination' and the dead Volunteer, Martin Savage, 'an assas-
sin'.[18] Dan Breen, who had taken part in the ambush, later recalled in his memoir,
that he had been particularly angered by the editorial since: 'This was the very
paper which depended on the support of the people who had voted for the
establishment of an Irish Republic'.[19] The *Independent* reported that the leader
of the 'masked men' (Peadar Clancy) informed the editor, Timothy Harrington,
that his paper was being suppressed for having 'endeavoured to misrepresent the
sympathies and opinions of the Irish people' through its coverage of the
ambush.[20] The men, some of whom, according to Breen, wanted to shoot
Harrington then caused 'enormous destruction' to the printing machinery. Breen
wrote that the intention was to cause so much damage that 'no edition could
appear for some time'.[21] Despite the damage and intimidation the *Independent* was

---

16 Bureau of Military History; Witness Statement number 834: Michael Knightly.   17 *Irish Independent*, 20 Dec. 1919.
18 Ibid.   19 Breen, *Irish freedom*, p. 93.   20 *Irish Independent*, 22 Dec. 1919.   21 Breen, *Irish freedom*, p. 94.

able to publish the following day and Harrington reprinted the offending editorial in its next edition.

The IRA's attack did little to alter the tone and content of the newspaper's reportage over the following months of the conflict. It remained supportive of Dáil Éireann and its work while criticizing the violence of both IRA and Crown forces. Throughout 1920 the *Independent* pushed two great, but related, objectives in its editorials; its support for Irish self-government and its relentless opposition to partition. In addition, it publicly supported Horace Plunkett's framework of an Irish settlement (Plunkett was a founding member of the Irish Dominion League) that proposed that any Irish settlement would have to be based on three basic principles; the unity of Ireland, recognition of Irish nationality and the right of the Irish people to the government they desired.

By 1920 the *Independent* supported many of the positions articulated by the *Freeman's Journal* and ultimately Dáil Éireann. Editorials asked the British government why it refused to grant Ireland her 'just rights' when they had supposedly fought a war for the defence of free nations. Over the following months it printed a series of powerful editorials and reports that accused the British government of preparing for the 're-conquest' of Ireland. These editorials accused the Irish administration of being 'a cruel and inhuman regime' that had to be removed before Ireland would be at peace: 'The one glaring evil; the one outstanding crime in Ireland is British misgovernment. It is the root cause of all the trouble and discontent. Remove that cause and Ireland at once becomes a contented country.'[22] The paper had unfailingly condemned all violence but it now declared that the British government must 'bear full responsibility for the consequences throughout the world' for subjecting Ireland to 'an iron rule of oppression'.[23]

In making such statements the *Independent* could be viewed as following the general contraction of the 'extremists' and 'moderates' of Irish nationalism into a single entity; an entity created by the failure of Dublin Castle and the British government to counter the rise of Dáil Éireann with any policy other than coercion. The new vigour in the *Independent's* reportage was typified by its coverage of the republican hunger strikers imprisoned in Mountjoy gaol during April 1920. Those that had been tried, the newspaper argued, had been convicted of political offences and should not be subjected to 'the rigours of ordinary prison life'.[24] The *Independent* was now making a clear distinction, one that it had not made in 1916, between political and non-political prisoners.

---

22 *Irish Independent*, 18 May 1920.   23 Ibid.   24 Ibid., 12 Apr. 1920.

'THE PAPER WHICH CREATES, FOSTERS AND FOMENTS HATRED'

The *Independent's* large circulation allied to its antipathy towards British rule in Ireland made it a potent critic of the Irish administration and the Crown forces, which it now termed as 'the army of occupation'.[25] During 1920 the *Independent's* circulation rose from 114,967 daily sales in January to a high of 141,751 in July. It ended the year with a circulation of 134,117 per day. These are net daily sales and only include editions bought and paid for.[26] The figures were extremely impressive since the newspaper had a circulation of around 25,000 copies soon after its 1905 re-launch.[27] Circulation continued to climb slowly through 1921 and seems to have been tens of thousands of copies ahead of its rivals the *Freeman's Journal* and the *Irish Times*.[28] The paper's popularity was not welcomed in governmental or police circles. In August 1920 the west Galway RIC County Inspector reported: 'the mainstay of the Sinn Féin movement in this county is the *Irish Independent*. It is this paper which creates, fosters and foments hatred of the English Government from day to day, from week to week, from year to year. It never lets it alone.'[29] By 1921 the *Independent* had become so critical of the government and Crown forces that the general officer commanding of the British army in Ireland, Nevil Macready, accused both it and the *Freeman's Journal* as being 'nothing less than daily propaganda of rebellion'.[30]

Consequent to the *Independent's* belief that the British government was to blame for the violence in Ireland, what also changed over 1920 and 1921 were the newspaper's descriptions of the IRA's attacks on Crown forces. Terms such as 'crime' and 'murder' no longer appeared above or in these reports. Such events were now reported as 'Four policemen killed' or 'Police Inspector shot dead'. 'Appalling Tragedy' was the headline that now replaced 'dastardly crime'. The *Independent's* reaction to the death of Kevin Barry, 'the Boy Martyr', demonstrated how the newspaper's attitude towards those engaged in violence against the Crown forces had altered in the years since 1916. The newspaper sought a recall of the death sentence not only because of Barry's youth but also because it believed that the proposed execution was contrary to the rules of war. This and similar reports throughout late 1920 and through 1921 marked the *Independent's*

---

**25** For a detailed study of the *Irish Independent* during the war of independence see I. Kenneally, *The paper wall: newspapers and propaganda in Ireland, 1919–1921* (Cork, 2008), pp 101–18.   **26** Kenneally, *Paper wall*, p. 205. See also *Irish Independent*, 16 Mar. 1921.   **27** Oram, *Newspaper book*, pp 106–7. L.M. Cullen estimates that total daily newspaper sales in the Irish market were over 500,000 copies. See L.M. Cullen, *Eason & Son: a history* (Dublin, 1989), p. 307.   **28** F.M. Larkin, 'A great daily organ – the *Freeman's Journal*, 1763–1924', *History Ireland*, 14:3 (2006), 44–9. Larkin details how the *Freeman's Journal* had sales of only 35,000 copies per-day during this period. That was the limit of the paper's production capacity due to a combination of a lack of funding and also, probably, as a result of the damage caused to its offices in 1916.   **29** Colonial Office file 904 122 (UCC), Aug. 1920, chief inspector's report for Galway.   **30** Colonial Office file 904 188 (UCC), 7 Mar. 1921, Nevil Macready to John Anderson: see also Anderson reply of same date.

acceptance of the IRA as a legitimate army. Dan Breen claimed that this change in the newspaper's reportage was a direct result of the 'salutary lesson taught to the Independent' by the IRA's attack on the newspaper at the end of 1919.[31] Breen's claims are debatable since the *Independent* continued to condemn violence throughout the war. The change in language began to become apparent from the spring of 1920 and could be seen as a response to both the increasingly vicious coercion doled out by Dublin Castle and the apparent successes of the Dáil counter-state and the IRA.

Also, contrary to Breen's claim, throughout 1920 and 1921 the *Independent* consistently regarded the taking of human life as wrong and repeatedly counselled the 'Volunteers' to be steady and refuse to answer what it termed the 'provocations of the army of occupation'.[32] It questioned the benefit to Ireland of IRA attacks on Crown forces that inevitably resulted in bringing the terror of reprisal and martial law down upon the local community. In the aftermath of the burning of Cork city centre by the Auxiliaries during December 1920 the *Independent* asked: 'What is the mentality of the men who plan or carry out ambushes or take part in the kidnapping of individuals when it is clear to them that appalling consequences flow from these activities.'[33] However, the newspaper refused to blame the 'extreme wing' for events in Ireland as it stated that these men were provoked beyond self-restraint by the iniquities of British rule. This attitude was exemplified by an editorial in June 1921 that asked whether the 'English Government' thought it could break 'the will of our people':

> It may kill, but it will not conquer; it may produce a wilderness by such methods but it cannot contrive a peace … The Irish people has determined that its country is not a province, by that determination it will stand … If English men and women want our friendship they can have it; at the moment it would almost seem that they want – and they are certainly earning – our ceaseless and bitter hatred. Is that the legacy they want to leave to their children and to ours? The English people and ours have more interests in common than they have for rivalries, more reason for friendship than for antipathy. But friendship can be rooted not otherwise than in freedom.[34]

While the violence had continued to grow in intensity the newspaper's editorials displayed little hope that political developments at Westminster would lead to peace. Throughout 1920 and 1921 the *Independent* was obsessed with the pos-

31 Breen, *Irish freedom*, p. 94. 32 For example see *Irish Independent*, 10 May 1920. 33 *Irish Independent*, 14 Dec. 1920. 34 Ibid., 11 June 1921.

sibility that the British government would partition Ireland. It insisted that the government of Ireland bill, the British government's proposed settlement for Ireland that divided the island into two states, was no basis for a durable peace. In attempting to push the bill through parliament the British prime minister, David Lloyd George, was accused by the newspaper of committing himself 'once more to the unconstitutional doctrine that the minority must rule the question at large in Ireland ...'[35]

The *Independent* was certain that any settlement that included partition would soon collapse; either because nationalists in the north would make such an agreement unworkable or because any northern state would be economically unviable. The paper did not believe the passing of the Act at the end of 1920 would make the division of Ireland a permanent feature of Irish life. Similar to many other nationalist papers, there is a sense that the *Independent* missed the importance of the Act, believing it to be a temporary measure since it was so clearly unacceptable to all sections of society bar unionists in the north-east. The Act created the need for a general election on both sides of the new border in May 1921. These elections highlighted the extent to which the *Independent* now viewed Sinn Féin and Dáil Éireann as the legitimate political expression of Irish nationalism. In the twenty-six county elections Sinn Féin ran unopposed for 124 out of 128 of the available seats. In an editorial titled 'The Nation's Verdict', the *Independent* welcomed the success of Sinn Féin: 'Mr De Valera in his proclamation said Sinn Féin would take part in the election in order to give an opportunity to the people of proving once more their loyalty to the principle of Irish Independence ... Today the world will learn that Ireland rejects with scorn the great measure of partition.' Sinn Féin, it concluded, had surpassed Parnell 'at the zenith of his success'.[36]

The truce that ended the conflict came a few weeks later in July 1921. By now the *Independent* had fully accepted the Dáil as the government of Ireland. Its editorials expressed much gratitude towards Eamon de Valera for his 'statesmanship' and recognized him as the leader of the Irish nation: 'In the natural order, belligerent nations having declared a truce, settle down to discuss terms of peace. The real negotiations between Mr Lloyd George's Government and Irish Republican leaders have yet to take place.'[37] De Valera was further acclaimed for challenging Lloyd George to end violence by stating that an end to bloodshed was the 'essential condition' of peace negotiations and the newspaper offered him its full support as he and the 'peacemakers' began their series of meetings with Lloyd George.[38]

35 Ibid., 11 Feb. 1920.  36 Ibid., 14 May 1921.  37 Ibid., 9 July 1921.  38 Ibid., 14 July 1921.

'OBEDIENCE TO ALL LAWFUL ENACTMENTS'

The *Independent*'s support for de Valera would prove to be ephemeral. It fully supported the Anglo-Irish Treaty of 1921 and greeted the news of its signing with a mixture of joy and relief: 'Now that the Treaty has been signed by the Irish plenipotentiaries and accepted with satisfaction by the mass of the citizens, we expect that the pact will be ratified by the people's representatives.'[39] Despite its long-held opposition to partition, the newspaper was happy to leave that issue to a future Boundary Commission as provided for in the Treaty. It was the refusal of many members of the Dáil to ratify the Treaty that was to most concern the *Independent*'s editor, Timothy Harrington. Following the seizure of the Four Courts by the anti-Treaty IRA, the newspaper attacked 'de Valera and his party' for offering the country no alternative than 'civil war and anarchy'.[40]

The *Independent* continued to report in such a manner during the civil war; it acted, albeit in a much more restrained manner than the *Freeman's Journal*, as a supporter of the provisional government. It viewed the Anglo-Irish Treaty as the only means by which to safeguard the future of Ireland and also, it claimed, to bring about the gradual demise of partition.[41] As such, it supported the provisional government's decision to attack the anti-Treaty forces barricaded in the Four Courts:

> It is sad to see brother Irishmen in deadly conflict, but when the right of the Irish nation to decide its own destiny and future was openly challenged, it is difficult to say how the clash could have been avoided. If national liberty is to count for anything it must mean the firm denial of the claim of any individual to over-ride the clearly expressed will of the people.[42]

The civil war, especially during 1922, was a harsh and unforgiving period for Irish newspapers. The economy was damaged by the violence across the country and newspaper revenues, especially from advertising, suffered accordingly. The provisional government maintained a strictly enforced censorship regime with Piaras Béaslaí in the position of chief censor. The censorship became especially strict after the anti-Treaty forces seized the Four Courts and newspapers were required to submit reports, especially those pertaining to military events, to Béaslaí before publication. The anti-Treaty forces took a less subtle approach and attacked newspaper offices across the country. They also intercepted the delivery of newspapers they considered to be hostile and so 'large quantities of newspapers simply never made it to their destination'.[43]

39 Ibid., 8 Dec. 1921. 40 Ibid., 17 Apr. 1922. 41 See, for example, *Irish Independent*, 15 Feb. 1922. 42 *Irish Independent*, 1 July 1922. 43 M. Valiulis, *Portrait of a revolutionary: General Richard Mulcahy and the founding of the Irish Free State* (Dublin,

Having been at the receiving end of IRA violence in the past, Harrington was fearful that the paper he edited would suffer repercussions from anti-Treaty forces. For a time, during 1922, he believed that he would be the subject of an assassination attempt by the anti-Treaty IRA. To evade his enemies Harrington lived in his office on Abbey Street: 'Colleagues remembered him coming to the front door when the coast was clear, a pale-faced man snatching a quick breath of fresh air'.[44] Harrington's had sound reasons for his fear: during the civil war, Liam Lynch, operating as chief-of-staff of the anti-Treaty IRA, had ordered Ernie O'Malley to assassinate the editors of the *Irish Independent* and *Irish Times*.[45] O'Malley never acted upon this order. Another anti-Treaty IRA order claimed that 'the entire press is at present being used as a medium of enemy propaganda'. The order continued to say that 'hostile' papers should be seized and destroyed; the *Independent* was one of a handful of papers listed by name.[46] Despite the *Irish Independent's* antagonism towards the anti-Treaty forces the paper was not merely a pawn of the government; its persistence in offering readers detailed reports on the evolving military situation greatly annoyed the government.[47] It also expressed disapproval of some government policies, as may be seen in its reaction to the government's execution of anti-Treaty soldiers.

Following the executions of Rory O'Connor, Joseph McKelvey, Richard Barrett and Liam Mellows in December 1922 the *Independent* expressed sorrow that the executions had taken place and offered its hopes that there would be no repeat of that event. The four men had been executed as a reprisal for the assassination of pro-Treaty TD Seán Hales a few days earlier. They were executed without having been tried and despite the fact that there was no legal justification for their deaths. The newspaper made it clear that it considered the executions to be wrong, observing that 'we deprecate such a proceeding', although that was as far as the editorial was willing to go.[48] Others were less circumspect. In the Dáil, Labour TD Cathal O'Shannon declared that the executions were 'nothing short of murder' while the Catholic archbishop of Dublin wrote to the government, albeit privately, to protest that the executions were 'entirely unjustifiable from the moral point of view'.[49] It could be argued that the *Independent's* relatively muted response resulted from a fear of antagonizing the government. Since early 1919 an element of self-censorship had been a factor in the *Irish Independent's* reportage and that policy had helped it to avoid the unwanted attention of the provisional government and, before that, the erstwhile British rulers in Dublin Castle. Even so, it had become skilled in pre-

1992), p. 158.   **44** Oram, *Newspaper book*, p. 151.   **45** R. English, *Ernie O'Malley: IRA intellectual* (Oxford, 1998), p. 81. **46** Ernie O'Malley papers UCD, P17/A/16 IRA Operational Order No. 7, 7 Aug. 1922.   **47** See Mulcahy papers UCD, P7/B/244: minutes of the Provisional Government 6–8 July 1922.   **48** *Irish Independent*, 9 Dec 1922.   **49** Quoted in J.P. McCarthy, *Kevin O'Higgins: builder of the Irish State* (Dublin, 2006), p. 94.

senting its message within the parameters imposed by censors, whether British or Irish. Its editorial repeated the newspaper's consistently held view that, while the executions were to be deplored, the government must be supported in its war against the anti-Treaty forces. It reminded readers that 'We have supported the Treaty; we support the Government, and shall continue to support it in its arduous task of consolidating the gains secured in its effort to put an end to anarchy and to restore order and public security.'[50]

This remained the paper's editorial line throughout the rest of the war. During May 1923, as the anti-Treaty IRA dumped its arms across the country and brought the civil war to an end, the *Independent* offered its political vision for the country:

> Once the ballot and not the bullet becomes the weapon with which our political differences are adjusted we know that neither the Government nor the people will seek to place obstacles in the way of the legitimate propaganda of any political party. Like every other democracy, Ireland will even recognize many advantages in the existence of several political parties. They can all contribute their share to the intellectual and indus-trial advancement of Ireland.[51]

The political landscape that was forged in Ireland between 1916 and 1923 proved to be a hostile environment for many newspapers. Chief among these was the *Freeman's Journal*, which had been the *Independent*'s prime competitor, and had seen the destruction of its offices during the Easter Rising. It had then suf-fered the devastating consequences of its outspoken journalism in the years after.[52] During the war of independence it had been targeted by Dublin Castle and the Crown forces, enduring a series of violent attacks, including incendi-ary bombings.[53] It was left to Rory O'Connor's anti-Treaty forces to deal the fatal blow to the *Freeman* in 1922 when they wrecked its printing presses. The *Freeman's* struggles provided the opportunity for Independent Newspapers to take control of the national daily newspaper market. When the *Freeman* finally ceased publication in December 1924 the title was purchased by Independent Newspapers so as 'to prevent others from carrying on the *Freeman* tradition'.[54]

The *Irish Independent* had not only survived the revolutionary period but had emerged to stand as the most successful daily newspaper in Ireland. The com-mercial success of the *Independent* during these years ensured that it would be a

---

50 *Irish Independent*, 9 Dec. 1922.   51 Ibid., 8 May 1923.   52 For an illustration of the type of journalism that so antagonized the Crown forces and then the anti-Treaty IRA see F. Larkin, *Terror and discord: the Shemus cartoons in the Freeman's Journal, 1920–1924* (Dublin, 2009).   53 See Kenneally, *Paper wall*, pp 5–42.   54 Oram, *Newspaper book*, pp 157–8.

prominent fixture in the public life of the Irish Free State. This was ultimately a triumph, albeit posthumously, for William Martin Murphy. The *Independent* had evolved in tandem with the changing character of Irish nationalism and its success was partly due to the fact that Timothy Harrington and the Murphy family had made certain that the newspaper followed the majority of public opinion in the aftermath of the 1918 general election. They also remained cognisant of the opinions of the Catholic hierarchy and the Catholic middle class and the newspaper routinely echoed the views of the bishops.

Yet there is no reason to doubt the newspaper's sincerity in its consistent and firm commitment to one core ideal, that of a free and fully self-governing Ireland. In some instances it had been prescient, or perhaps lucky. It had backed the winners in the great conflicts that shaped the modern Irish state: Sinn Féin over the Irish Parliamentary Party; Dáil Éireann over British rule; and the provisional government over the anti-Treaty forces. In future years the *Independent* would face competition from the *Irish Press* and, later, a re-invigorated *Irish Times* but the events of 1916–23 – and the newspaper's reaction to those events – were crucial in establishing Independent Newspapers as a dominant player in the Irish media with political and social ramifications that continue to the current day.

# 5 / Tom Grehan: advertising pioneer and newspaper man

COLUM KENNY

Towards the close of the nineteenth century, the development and expansion of media in Ireland, as elsewhere, was underpinned by improving levels of literacy, new printing technology, mass manufacturing of commodities and the encouragement of consumption. Opportunities for journalism grew as advertising boosted both the number and size of publications. The role of advertising was central to the success of any newspaper venture, and central to the role of advertising at the *Irish Independent* during the first half of the twentieth century was Tom Grehan, its advertisement manager. He was one of a small number of Irish advertising practitioners whose advanced methods dispel any notion that the business of advertising in Ireland before independence was simply naïve.[1] The fact that he occasionally took to writing in the pages of his own newspaper in order to explain the benefits of advertising gives us an insight into developments that he managed at the *Irish Independent* for twenty-seven years.

Grehan came to be highly regarded in the newspaper world. Following his death in 1943 the *Irish Times* described him as 'a pioneer in the advertising business'.[2] His obituarist in the *Irish Independent* likewise referred to him as 'a pioneer in modern selling methods', and claimed that he had 'initiated in Europe the policy of publishing auditor certified net paid sales — a revolutionary step in newspaper promotion methods in those days'.[3] Grehan's championing of net sales figures and his success in eliciting advertisements from a broad range of Irish firms and services greatly contributed to the success of the *Irish Independent* as a medium of journalism in the twentieth century.

## EARLY LIFE AND CAREER

Thomas à Kempis Grehan was born in Salthill, Co. Galway, and educated at St Ignatius College, Galway. In 1896 he left his native county to take up a position in the advertisement department of the Dunlop Tyre Company in

---

1 For a critique of the development of the advertising industry in Ireland see C. Kenny, 'Not so quaint: reflections on early Irish advertising', *Irish Marketing Journal*, 21:1 and 21:2 (2011). 2 *Irish Times*, 28 Oct. 1943. 3 *Irish Independent*, 28 Oct. 1943.

Coventry. From 1898 to 1902 he was employed on the advertising staff of Lever Bros. in Port Sunlight, across the River Mersey from Liverpool.[4] Grehan subsequently joined the London advertising agency S.H. Benson where he worked for more than six years.[5] He told the Galway Chamber of Commerce in 1926 that:

> For nearly seven years I was in charge of the advertisement writing department of a firm that annually handled at that time – sixteen years ago – over £1,000,000 of publicity per year. The man who founded, guided and controlled that firm would allow no misleading descriptions in any advertisement put out by his organization. I remember one of his clients at the time – he is still a client – whose annual expenditure was over £70,000, threatened to take his business away because my old chief would not allow him to use certain flowers of language that the client said he was entitled to use in his advertisement. He was bluntly told that if he insisted, he could take his account elsewhere. That advertising agency I have referred to is not only still in business but to-day, it stands in the forefront of all organizations of its kind.[6]

During these same years before he moved to Dublin, Grehan joined the London Gaelic League and made the acquaintanceship of Michael MacWhite, its president from 1903 to 1905. MacWhite later became the 'continental correspondent for several European newspapers' and Paris correspondent of the *United Irishman*, and later still served for nearly a decade as the Irish Free State's minister to the USA.[7] Another person involved in the London Gaelic League at that time was Michael Collins.

Grehan may have been the unnamed 'member of a firm of advertising agents' who in 1908 was reported to have presided at a lecture in London by one A.C. Beet on the theory and practice of advertising. This unnamed person pointed out that 'such world-known firms as Beechams and Lever Brothers owed their present position to extensive advertising'. Perhaps it was Grehan himself who wrote the report of the lecture that appeared in the *Irish Independent*.[8] Certainly, while he was employed in London, Grehan met William Martin Murphy who commissioned him to write some articles on advertising. These appeared under the pen name 'John Fergus' in the *Irish Independent* in 1909. 'That', it was later claimed, 'was the first occasion outside America that the subject

4 *Irish Times*, 28 Oct. 1943 and *Connacht Tribune*, 20 Jan. 1926 & 30 Oct. 1943. Port Sunlight was a model village created by William Hesketh Lever in 1888 for his Sunlight soap factory workers.  5 *Irish Times*, 28 Oct. 1943. See also *Irish Independent*, 22 Nov. 1932 & 28 Oct. 1943.  6 *Connacht Tribune*, 6 Feb. 1926.  7 *Irish Independent*, 31 Mar. 1933.  8 Ibid., 20 Oct. 1908.

received its due recognition in the editorial columns of a daily newspaper ...
At the time it was a daring adventure.'[9]

Grehan moved back to Dublin in 1909 when he joined the *Irish Independent* as
'Advertisement Manager', a position that he held until 1938. It was later said
that, 'He was, indeed, the first Advertisement Manager ever appointed in
Ireland.'[10] Arthur J. Wall, who was for decades the London manager of
Independent Newspapers, later 'took pride in having introduced Mr Grehan as
advertisement manager in Dublin'. He added that, 'It was necessary that an
Irishman should fill that position, and Mr Grehan knew all about advertising
not only in Ireland but in England [too]. Mr Grehan was one of the finest
acquisitions made by the Independent newspapers.'[11]

### EYE-CATCHING AND EFFECTIVE

The articles that Grehan wrote in 1909 for the *Irish Independent* set out to persuade conservative Irish business people that they ought to advertise more. In
one article published on 2 April 1909, Grehan (as 'Fergus') noted the large sums
of money being paid to individuals in both Britain and the United States to
plan and present 'interesting, convincing, eye-catching' advertisements. He
observed that he could name at least six successful Irish enterprises that had
paid people 'an impressive salary' to plan and write advertising that produced
'most beneficial results – in one or two cases remarkably beneficial results':

> A successful advertising man need not necessarily be a polished writer
> of language, a 'deep thinker', or a man of abundant culture, but he must
> know how to put his thoughts in a clear, convincing sequence, in a way
> that appeals that goes straight to the heart of the reader. He must know
> his subject, he must feel a genuine enthusiasm for it, and he must know
> how to 'inject' that enthusiasm into his advertisements.[12]

In another of these articles, headed 'Advertising: The Big Part Played by the
Newspaper', Grehan wrote:

> The 'Age of Advertising' has not yet come. Many people are convinced
> that it has. That mysterious, elusive, omnipresent item, 'The Man in
> the Street,' is quite sure that it is very much 'here.' True, we are rapidly
> nearing it, almost, one might say, on the threshold. Yet, the real age of
> advertising has yet to come. When it does come we shall all know about

9 Ibid., 24 May 1933, p. 5.  10 *Connacht Tribune*, 30 Jan. 1926.  11 *Irish Independent*, 6 Oct. 1936.  12 Ibid., 2 Apr. 1909.

it. Then, verily, shall we all be living in an atmosphere of restless push, in an era when all shall make obeisance to the might of the printed word. We shall know it has come by the real fierceness, the calculated exactness, the persistence and surprising universality of the advertising habit. When it comes, and there are any monuments to be erected, any national memorials to be established, any odes to be written and dedicated, let the first to be honoured, be the newspaper.[13]

The picture that he painted of the future of advertising was not one calculated to appeal to those who regarded it as a deplorable activity catering to people's lowest tastes and degrading public life. He explained why newspapers were the superior medium for advertisers, and was glad to note that the way of doing business had changed:

In the days before advertising took on its present mantle of seriousness, in the good old times before the searching, penetrating eye of the expert was brought into play in the diagnosis of newspaper claims, advertising was handed out a good deal on the 'hand-shaking' basis. Even in this land of intense friendships and intenser [sic] prejudices, we are fast getting rid of the idea that the paper that 'me mother and father used to read' is the one the advertisement should go in. In Ireland, as in other countries that have taken up advertising in the modern spirit, the distribution of newspaper advertising is yearly becoming more and more a question of value for money and less and less of political prejudice, tradition or sentiment.

Grehan predicted that 'The days are numbered of the newspaper that refuses to modernize its advertising columns, that maintains old, time-worn motheaten, silly rules and regulations as to positions, rates, and so forth. Nowadays, the businessman regards the buying of newspaper space as he would regard the buying of a piece of land. He wants to know its valuation, and must have that valuation, not in vague generalities or on hearsay, but in black and white.'[14]

Grehan was not alone in promoting the use of advertising. Later in 1909, the proprietor of Kenny's Advertising Agency, Kevin J. Kenny, took the podium at the All-Ireland Industrial Conference in Belfast to advocate modern methods of advertising:

The Irish business men had not, he said, yet realized the vast difference between the slovenly announcement of a decade ago and the inspiriting

13 Ibid., 24 Apr. 1909.  14 Ibid.

man-to-man talks adopted by the more progressive advertisers today . . . Dealing with the advertising of Irish-manufacturer goods, he said that there was no reason whatever why they should continue to sell goods of equal or inferior quality principally by the aid of the 'support Irish manufacture' argument. To ask a man to buy a collar or a cap merely because it was Irish was certainly not business, and yet it was done every day. This could only lead to the inevitable result that the buyer would think he was paying an additional price or getting an inferior-quality for the sentiment that was in him.[15]

Kenny, who founded what came to be regarded as the first full-service advertising agency in Ireland, was to be a close ally of Grehan in subsequent years.[16]

SALESMANSHIP

During 1911, under his own name, Grehan wrote more articles for the *Irish Independent* to encourage Irish business to promote itself effectively. Claiming that the 'science of selling' had been ignored in Ireland, he believed that 'America's bounding prosperity is largely due to the extraordinary attention they give there to every aspect of salesmanship'. He noted that several American universities and colleges taught and gave diplomas in salesmanship and argued passionately that it should be taught at 'Dublin's palatial headquarters for Technical Instruction' that was about to open its doors [in Bolton Street] and that had managed to find room to teach, 'if you please, "Airmanship"':

> Trinity College has added a course of Journalism [short-lived]; the National University is teaching Accountancy. Salesmanship has, so far, never yet been the subject of five minutes' instruction in any school, College or University in Ireland. Why should we go on ignoring so vital a science?[17]

Less than two months later he returned to the need for Irish concerns to promote themselves efficiently, both at home and abroad. In a piece headed 'Up, Ireland!' he was optimistic, believing that Ireland was, commercially, 'pulling herself together, so to speak, and, for the first time in a century, making distinct headway.' For the first time in Ireland's modern history, he wrote, 'our Census reveals what looks like a "turn for the better"'.[18] He rejoiced in the recent success of the Ui Breasail exhibition of manufacturing and trade

15 Ibid., 7 Aug. 1909.  16 Kenny was also the first business manager for D.P. Moran's *The Leader*. See C. Kenny, *Irish patriot, publisher and advertising agent: Kevin J. Kenny, 1881–1954* (Bray, 2011).  17 *Irish Independent*, 31 July 1911.  18 Ibid., 13 Sept. 1911.

held in Ballsbridge, Dublin, and looked forward to a future business exhibition that would display modern business ideas, methods, appliances and equipment.

However, notwithstanding technical advances in printing that had facilitated developments in the design and presentation of advertisements, it remained difficult at times for Grehan and others to persuade Irish businessmen to advertise. It is said that when he addressed the Dublin Chamber of Commerce in 1911 on the subject of advertising, 'half the attendance walked out because they thought that the subject was too vulgar to be worth their interest!'[19] Grehan subsequently advertised free copies of this lecture, entitled 'The Position of Advertising in Modern Commerce'.[20] Filled with enthusiasm by reports from a major advertising congress in Baltimore, Maryland, in 1913, he wrote about it for Irish readers, pointing out that:

> In its unchecked growth within the past twenty years advertising has changed the 'face' and a good deal of the 'inside' of most of our modern newspapers. If you feel doubtful on this point get hold of a copy of a newspaper of even ten years ago. Notice how 'quiet', unexciting, dry-as-dust the advertisement columns are. Then put the paper alongside a copy of the same journal of this morning. You will not take long to see the vast difference. The type dress of the announcements has all been changed, as has the method of grouping, classifying, and setting out the advertisements. If you look deeper into the matter you will find that the change is not merely in the mechanical disposition, but also in the policy. If you trouble to study the phraseology of the advertisements, the ideas they embody, you will find how very much more interesting, more persuasive, more attractive are to-day's advertisements as compared with those of even ten years ago.[21]

Businessmen ignored at their peril the growing influence of Grehan's daily newspaper as it achieved unprecedented national circulation: 'The *Irish Independent* was the first newspaper from Dublin to start arriving for breakfast'.[22] Its success in circulation terms was both a geographic and a numeric achievement and Grehan would make sure that people knew exactly what its growing sales figures were.

## THE ADVERTISING DEPARTMENT

Tom Grehan was not the first person to work in advertising at Independent Newspapers. Amongst the long-serving employees who joined before he did,

**19** H. Oram, *The advertising book* (Dublin, 1986), p. 387.   **20** *Irish Independent*, 18–24 Oct. 1911.   **21** Ibid., 16 June 1913.
**22** Oram, *Advertising book*, p. 390.

and who continued to work alongside the dynamic new advertisement manager, were J.S. Henderson and Edward Hollywood. Henderson had been there from before the launch of the new *Irish Independent*, being presented with 'a very handsome diamond ring' to mark his twenty-five years association with the firm in 1928. Hollywood, whose uncle of the same name had accompanied William Smith O'Brien and Thomas Francis Meagher to Paris in 1843 'to present an address of congratulation to the second French Republican Government', had joined the outdoor advertising section of the old *Irish Daily Independent* from Allen and O'Reilly printers and continued with the new *Irish Independent* as an advertising representative. He is said to have had 'a golden store of racy Dublin lore'.[23]

Grehan himself was a genial man and a keen golfer, 'a powerful exponent of the "get-together" principle in business relations', according to one acquaintance who added that, 'this fraternal outlook carried him smoothly throughout a long and very varied experience in advertising and publicity in England and Ireland.'[24] As befitted a man of his conviviality he was one of the earliest people to join the new Dublin Rotary Club, itself the first such club to meet in Europe. He helped to promote Rotary Club interests in the media while also using it to promote the interests of Independent Newspapers. He was also a founding member of the Publicity Club of Ireland.

Grehan was eager to provide potential advertisers with accurate information on the basis of which they could plan and cost campaigns. His arrival at the *Irish Independent* coincided with a big push to provide not only circulation figures but net sales statistics. On 24 August 1906, the newspaper had observed that, 'It is circulation, not antiquity, that counts in advertising, and up-to-date businessmen are the first to realize this fact.' However, a piece in the paper of 2 February 1910 went further by distinguishing between circulation and sales:

> 'Don't talk to me about "circulation." What I want to get at is your sales. Tell me the number of people that actually buy your paper every time it comes out.' Thus have advertisers spoken to newspaper canvassers for years, yet the only papers in Ireland, England, Scotland, and Wales that have ever published their sales and published them over a chartered accountant's certificate are the 'Irish Independent', the 'Weekly Independent', and the 'Evening Herald' ... Anyone who knows anything about newspapers will quickly appreciate the difference between 'circulation' and 'net sales'. In 'circulation' is included 'free copies', 'spoiled copies', 'returns', as well as sales. In 'net sale' is included – 'net sale' and nothing else.[25]

---

23 *Irish Independent*, 28 July 1928 & 2 Apr. 1929. See also, H. Oram, *The newspaper book: a history of newspapers in Ireland, 1649–1983* (Dublin, 1983), pp 107–8.  24 *Irish Independent*, 28 Oct. 1943.  25 Ibid., 2 Feb. 1910.

A striking example of Grehan's lively approach to promotion, and how it contrasted with that of some older newspapers, is found in the pages of the catalogue published for the Civic Exhibition held in Dublin in 1914, of which major event his acquaintance Kevin J. Kenny was the commercial manager. A full-page advertisement for the *Irish Independent* catches the eye, not least because it sets out clearly the growing readership for the new look newspaper. It boldly proclaims at the outset that net sales 'average 62,798 copies daily', before proceeding to explain in some detail that such audited net sales 'mean the average number of copies per day each month sold and paid for, as periodically certified by the eminent firm of Messrs Craig, Gardner & Company.' It notes that the certified net sale of the paper 'now exceeds by more than 20,000 copies daily the net sales of all the other Dublin morning papers added together'. To emphasis 'the remarkable growth' of the title the advertisement included figures, in bold, for the previous nine years, as shown in the accompanying table:

*Irish Independent* circulation, 1905–13

| Year | 1905 | 1906 | 1907 | 1908 | 1909 | 1910 | 1911 | 1912 | 1913 |
|------|------|------|------|------|------|------|------|------|------|
| Sales | 22,608 | 29,243 | 32,458 | 36,932 | 40,788 | 47,614 | 51,416 | 54,207 | 56,462 |

Reinforcing these growth figures, the advertisement concludes with an assertion that, 'Practically everybody in Ireland who reads a newspaper at all reads the "Irish Independent".' It is worth adding here that the circulation of the *Irish Independent* appears to have almost doubled during the First World War and it continued to rise thereafter.[26] It sells today, in very different circumstances, about 131,000 copies daily (ABC, 2011).

By comparison with the advertisement for the *Irish Independent* in the Civic Exhibition catalogue those for the *Freeman's Journal* and for the Dublin *Daily Express* and Dublin *Evening Mail* were staid and uninteresting. 'Ireland's Great Financial Paper' is all that the *Daily Express* had to say for itself, while the Dublin *Evening Mail* appeared to believe that it was enough to assert itself as 'The leading Irish evening paper'. There is something almost desperate about the full-page appeal by the *Freeman's Journal* that states only, 'The *Freeman's Journal* has been Ireland's national journal for the past 150 years. Support it.'[27]

When Grehan later spoke at a Dublin Rotary luncheon about an international exhibition of advertising that took place in London in 1920, he returned

---

26 P. Maume, 'The *Irish Independent* and the Ulster Crisis, 1912–21' in D.G. Boyce and A. O'Day (eds), *The Ulster crisis, 1885–1921* (Basingstoke, 2006), pp 202–28.   27 Civic Exhibition Executive Committee, *Official Catalogue of the Civic Exhibition, Ireland* (Dublin, 1914), pp 72, 128, & 152.

to the theme of audited sales figures. Noting that, at the exhibition, 'The Irish newspapers, in proportion to their number, were much more strongly represented than those of any other country', he added:

> One of the biggest features was the nett sales campaign organized by the 'Daily Mail'. In the United States and Canada every publication was obliged by law to publish regularly a duly authorized document showing its circulation ... Newspapers in Ireland and Great Britain had been shy in publishing their gross nett sales, but the 'Irish Independent' newspapers had been among the first newspapers in Europe to adopt this policy.[28]

Responding to Grehan, Kevin J. Kenny 'commented upon the unity among the Irish newspapers represented [at the international exhibition], and said that the venture had proved the pulling power of advertising. Ireland had led the way on the question of the nett sales campaign years before the "Daily Mail" had taken the matter up'.[29] Indeed, the *Independent* had beaten the *Daily Mail* by four years in the publication of net sales figures and claimed that it had been 'the first paper outside the USA to give the public these figures'.[30] Despite such innovation, 'certain proprietors of advertising media' remained reluctant to endorse net sales as a measure of their success.[31]

### IRISH ASSOCIATION OF ADVERTISING MEN

The Dublin Civic Exhibition took place just as Europe was consumed by war. The optimism about Ireland's future that Grehan had expressed in his article in September 1911 was to be sorely tested. The island was about to be afflicted by almost a decade of violence. However, admen in general, and the advertisement manager of the *Irish Independent* in particular, continued to do what they could in the face of European turmoil, local rebellion, a struggle for political independence and finally the Irish civil war. Grehan and Kenny were among those elected to the council of a new 'Irish Association of Advertising Men' formed as the First World War ended in 1918. This was to be succeeded by the Publicity Club of Ireland.[32]

During May 1921, when the IRA burnt down the Custom House in Dublin and elections were held for the two planned parliaments of the partitioned

---

28 *Irish Independent*, 18 Jan. 1921.  29 Ibid.  30 Ibid., 12 Sept. 1931.  31 See P. Derrick, 'Newspaper net sales published' in *Irish Independent*, 28 July 1922 & W.S. Crawford, 'Logic of net sales' in *Irish Independent*, 2 Sept. 1922.  32 *Irish Independent*, 4 Oct. 1918, 31 Jan. 1919 & 15 May 1920.

Ireland, in Chicago Rotary International was publishing its monthly magazine. Tom Grehan saw this as a vehicle for advancing the interests of both Rotary in Dublin and of his own newspaper group. Inserting a full-page advertisement into the *Rotarian* of May 1921, he invited 'any other Rotary advertising or news-paper man there, no matter from what part of the two hemispheres he may hail [to] meet me in Edinburgh' at the forthcoming convention of Rotary International. The text that was spread around a small photograph of Grehan informed international Rotarians in respect to the *Irish Independent*, that:

> This is Ireland's great national organ of public opinion. It has a truly wonderful nation-wide sale. An acknowledged, progressive, live-wire, advertising medium, that is to Ireland in the matter of net sales even more than the 'Daily Mail' is to Great Britain. In Ireland, it has been truly said, that almost everyone that buys a newspaper reads the 'Irish Independent'. It's away out on its own on the Irish ground. Only two British Newspapers – outside of London – exceed the IRISH INDE-PENDENT in net sales.[33]

The war of independence had scarcely ended when Ireland found itself facing the possibility of civil war. Undaunted, Grehan's friend Kevin J. Kenny, organized what was described as the 'First Advertising Dance'. It was held on 17 February 1922 in the small ballroom or hall of the DBC on St Stephen's Green. A photograph of about eighty unidentified people who attended survives and these included Tom Grehan. One cannot be certain but others in the photograph may be Arthur Griffith TD, recently elected president of the new Dáil, and Ernest Blythe TD, then minister for trade and commerce, and Harry Boland TD. Four months after this event, civil war erupted.

As the volume of advertising continued to grow internationally, Grehan took the opportunity of a world congress of advertisers in London to reflect on his own career and to protest (perhaps a little too much) that things had changed greatly in relation to public attitudes towards advertising in Ireland. He wrote from Wembley:

> When I returned to Ireland some fifteen years ago, after several years' close association with what was then regarded as the most modern minds on expert advertising, and after a somewhat intensive training in all that then pertained to the science of what we called 'scientific publicity', I was appalled to find that, at that time, advertising was regarded gener-

33 *Rotarian*, 18:5 (May 1921), 267.

ally speaking, as shall we say, bordering on the vulgar? Things have changed very much in Ireland, of course, in the interval – very much, indeed! I was, as a matter of fact, the first advertisement manager any Irish newspaper organization had ever appointed.[34]

Grehan's experience did not go unappreciated by the new Free State government: in 1926 he was appointed to a committee to advise the Minister for Posts and Telegraphs on the establishment of a publicly owned broadcasting service.[35]

## SPREADING THE WORD

In February 1926 Galway Chamber of Commerce warmly welcomed Grehan to one of its meetings, in contrast to his experience in 1911 when members of the Dublin Chamber had apparently expressed their disapproval of his profession by walking out during his speech. This time, in his native city, his long address was to be reproduced in full by the *Connaught Tribune*. He noted that:

> People thought there was something beyond the understanding of the plain man in Advertising. He asked them to discard or rather not be frightened by much of the high-flown writing in text-books about Advertising. Advertising was one of the oldest and one of the simplest arts in the world.

Grehan took the occasion to read a cablegram from New York from James O'Shaughnessy, the eldest son of another Galwayman who had emigrated from Gort to the United States. O'Shaughnessy fared very well in the world of advertising. The advertisement manager of the *Irish Independent* said that he had met O'Shaughnessy two years earlier at an advertising congress in London and had later been one of a few people in Dublin who greeted him during a brief trip to Ireland and who had presented him with a Claddagh Ring. The cablegram that Grehan read from O'Shaughnessy expressed 'My love to Galway, the birthland of my father and wife's father. – Jim'.[36] O'Shaughnessy, one of the highest paid admen of his generation, was the first executive secretary of the American Association of Advertising Agencies. He would be described by *Time* magazine in 1929 as 'the best in the business', and that same year would be guest of honour at a lunch in Dublin organized by founding members of the new Irish Association of Advertising Agencies (later renamed IAPI). Grehan himself

34 *Irish Independent*, 15 July 1924.  35 Wireless Telegraphy Act, 1926, ss. 17, 19 and S. I. no. 31/1927.  36 *Connacht Tribune*, 6 Feb. 1926.

wrote at least one report about the IAAA for readers of the *Irish Independent*.[37] The *Connaught Tribune* was far from being a disinterested bystander when it published Grehan's address in Galway, for it appeared to be irked by the continuing reluctance of some Irish businesses to invest in advertising:

> In this country we are the merest tyros in the matter of advertising. Some of the organizations that represent wealthy trades and industries would weep for a week if they were asked to expend the equivalent of a few subscriptions on publicity matter for their own benefit and profit. They would expect the harassed newspaper publisher (whose business to-day, if it is worth utilizing as an advertising medium, is the most costly in the world to run) to give them free publicity. Such lack of imagination almost makes one despair of the country, which is every day and every week being successfully exploited by British advertisers who sell their own products here by sound and effective advertising.[38]

The writer trusted that Grehan's talk would help to inform people better about the benefits of advertising. Businessmen ignored at their peril the growing influence of his newspapers as they achieved unprecedented national circulation. Advertisements for a wide variety of goods and services were placed in the *Irish Independent*, thus providing the revenue necessary to employ journalists.

It is easy to underestimate the visual impact of the new-look *Irish Independent* during the first decades of the twentieth century. Leafing through back-issues today, it can seem quite staid. The mixture of small ads announcing births, marriages and deaths with bigger ads for department stores and other goods or services that were spread across every front page until and including 1 July 1961 may seem very old fashioned now, but compared to its predecessors the newspaper that Grehan joined was a pioneer of style. When it warned its readers on Saturday 1 July 1961 what to expect the following Monday morning, its editor admitted that by then '... fresh generations have grown up who have come to expect headline news on Page One. Most of the newspapers of the world have already adopted this custom and the *Irish Independent* is happy to present the news in a manner that will meet the needs of the time.' The editor then recalled a story, 'long-remembered', of an American reader who was said to have once congratulated the *Irish Independent* 'on keeping the really important news on the front page – the births, marriages and deaths.'

The means used to promote the *Irish Independent* and its sister titles were both traditional and innovative. In June 1932 the *Irish Independent* produced a special

37 *Irish Independent*, 21 May 1927, 19 Feb. & 7 Sept. 1929; *TIME*, 29 July 1929; 17 Apr. 1933.  38 *Connacht Tribune*, 30 Jan. 1926.

*Eucharistic Congress Souvenir* which 'proved an amazing success'. It was edited by Kevin M. Kenny, who was a son of the advertising agent and an uncle of the present writer. On 23 June 1932, 'while the streets of Dublin were crowded after the Midnight Masses', a special edition of the *Irish Independent* issued at 1.45 a.m., 'giving a full account of the Congress, and also reports of the Midnight masses, illuminations, sky-writing, etc.'[39]

On a distinctly more secular note, when the singer Gracie Fields came to Ireland in September 1932, electricians of the Marconiphone Company erected loudspeakers on the roof of Independent House on Abbey Street so that 'the Lancashire mill girl' could charm Dubliners with her songs. There were 'amazing scenes'. The reviewer J. A. Power wrote that:

> At four p.m. yesterday I looked down from the roof of Independent House upon a Middle Abbey St. that was strange to me – and I have known this street of ours for more years than I care to count. From O'Connell St. practically to Liffey St. it was packed with thousands of people.

Power deemed one fact significant that we might take for granted today: 'Women and girls accounted fully 50 per cent' of the crowd. He added that people also studded surrounding roofs and that 'a roar of greeting went up from the packed throng in the street below'. Grehan presented Fields and her manager with two Irish blackthorns as souvenirs.[40]

It was simple but very effective marketing to use the roof of the relatively new Independent House to promote the newspapers. The company regularly hosted visiting sports teams, dignitaries, singers and bands on the roof of the building and published photographs and reports of same in the *Irish Independent*. In October 1924 the New Zealand 'All Blacks' rugby team was hosted on the roof, while in May 1933 Jack Hylton and his band played on the roof to crowds twenty people deep below in Middle Abbey Street.[41]

This new loudspeaker technology was put to more serious use early in 1933. It must be remembered that the state's single broadcaster provided a very limited radio service. Independent Newspapers caused traffic jams by arranging to transmit election results via Marconiphone loudspeakers erected at both their Abbey Street offices and on Carlisle Building, which housed the commercial department on the quays: 'Thousands lined the south side of O'Connell Bridge to hear the progress of the count' and trams had to be diverted. In addition to audio announcements there was 'screen-flashing' of election results and of adver-

39 *Irish Independent*, 22 & 24 June 1932.  40 Ibid., 9 Sept. 1932.  41 Ibid., 29 Oct. 1924 & 17 May 1933.

tisements, this being 'the first time in the history of advertisement in Ireland that such a thing had taken place'. Later that same year Independent Newspapers relayed live and recorded music in the city centre to mark Irish Week.[42]

## LAST DAYS

In 1931 Grehan became president of the Publicity Club of Ireland. He was still pressing for improvements in education in respect to commerce and advertising.[43] Describing advertising agents as the 'shock troops' of commerce, he wrote that:

> 'Any "damn fool" could write advertisements,' a man still active in trading a few years ago sincerely told me. Perhaps that might have explained the amazing output of 'damn fool' advertisements we used to read in newspapers some years ago. If the Agents did nothing else, they certainly helped towards the speedy interment of the 'damn fool' idea.[44]

Grehan's support for such agents had been greatly appreciated, not only by Kevin Kenny but also by others such as Charlie McConnell who in 1916 established what was to become another of Ireland's leading agencies, namely McConnell's. In 1933 McConnell recalled that, at the time that he had set up his agency, 'there were only three advertising agents in the country, while today there were at least 12 or 14'.[45] He was almost certainly referring to 'advertising agent' not in the sense of one who simply sold space in or on behalf of a newspaper or journal but in the sense of the modern service agency that was prepared to write copy, design advertisements, buy space across various publications and otherwise offer its customers a range of assistance that eventually included market research. He later added that 'when he started his office in Dublin the great question for advertising agencies was to get recognition, and he had found a great friend in those early days in Tom Grehan'.[46]

In 1937 Grehan served as president of the Dublin Rotary Club. One year later, after more than a quarter of a century in charge of advertising at the *Irish Independent*, he retired. To mark the occasion, the Irish Association of Advertising Agents made him a special presentation of a solid silver platter. He was described by P.L. McEvoy of McEvoy's Advertising Agency as 'one of the forerunners of modern advertising efficiency'. Grehan told them that, 'when he first entered on his late position in Dublin the advertising agency was looked upon as an evil, but now it represented an adjunct to the newspaper'.[47] One writer in Grehan's home county of Galway thought that:

---

42 Ibid., 26 Jan. 1933 & 17 Mar. 1933.   43 Ibid., 21 Nov. 1932 & 30 June 1933.   44 Ibid., 17 Apr. 1933.   45 *Irish Independent*, 14 Feb. 1933.   46 Ibid., 23 Dec. 1938.   47 *Irish Times* & *Irish Independent*, 23 Dec. 1938, including photograph; Oram, *Advertising book*: p. 376; for a photograph, p. 417.

It is difficult to imagine the Advertisement Department of 'The Irish Independent' without Tom Grehan. In his day he was one of the greatest of advertisement managers, and he richly deserves the handsome retiring allowance he is about to receive … he joined 'The Irish Independent' as its Advertisement Manager in days when few newspapers could afford the luxury. William Martin Murphy had been wise in his generation, for the success of 'The Independent' may be said to have marched in step with the success of Tom Grehan.[48]

After a lifetime working in print and having served on the state's broadcasting advisory committee, he himself briefly took to the airwaves. In July 1939 Grehan presented a short series on Radio Éireann about Irish towns, *Our Towns Talking,* including Drogheda and Kilkenny. Prior to his sudden death on 27 October 1943 he was preparing a book about Old Galway that was not completed.[49] The *Independent*'s competitor, the *Irish Times,* was warm in its praise of the man who had done so much to build the commercial success of Independent Newspapers. Grehan was, it noted, 'very popular in Dublin business and newspaper circles, where his big hearted and genial personality made him many friends'.[50]

---

48 *Connacht Tribune,* 8 Oct. 1938.  49 Ibid., 30 Oct. 1943.  50 *Irish Times,* 28 Oct. 1943.

# 6 / 'Irish-Ireland' and the *Irish Independent*, 1905–22

## AOIFE WHELAN

In its first editorial on 2 January 1905, the *Irish Independent* pledged: 'To the Irish Language and Industrial Revival Movements, as to every movement for the National and material regeneration of Ireland, we shall give our heartiest support'.[1] Thus began the use of the *Irish Independent* as a bilingual forum for the promotion of the 'Irish-Ireland' ideology throughout the early twentieth century. The 'Irish-Ireland' movement was rooted in the writings of D.P. Moran that were first published in the *New Ireland Review* from 1898 to 1900. At the crux of Moran's philosophy was the creation of a truly Irish nation that would have 'a native colour in arts, industries, literature, social habits, points of view, music, amusements and so on, throughout all phases of human activity'.[2] Moran's book, *The philosophy of Irish Ireland*, claimed to be a denunciation of the 'false standards of Nationality that have grown up everywhere' and offered the following advice to the Irish people:

> We must be original Irish, and not imitation English. Above all, we must re-learn our language, and become a bi-lingual people. For the great connecting link between us and the real Ireland, which few of us know anything about, is the Gaelic tongue.[3]

From the newspaper's inception the Irish language was considered an essential component of the 'Irish-Ireland' ideology and was pivotal in the formulation of Irish identity. Despite this emphasis on the revival of the Irish language, however, it must be noted that the 'Irish-Ireland' movement was often promoted through the medium of English. Moran's newspaper *The Leader*, launched in September 1900, became the movement's unofficial organ. Moran had previously argued that there was a need for a national newspaper in English to promote the 'Irish-Ireland' ideology among those who were not yet sympathetic to the revivalist cause: 'For many years to come we must have an active, vigilant, and merciless propaganda in the English language.'[4] Although Moran read Modern Irish quite well and joined the Keating branch of the Gaelic League, his weekly paper was published in English with just a small number of articles

I am grateful to Dr Regina Uí Chollatáin, Máire Daltúin and Dr Nollaig Mac Congáil for their advice regarding the material referred to in this chapter. 1 *Irish Independent*, 2 Jan. 1905. 2 D.P. Moran, *The philosophy of Irish Ireland* (Dublin, 1905), p. 1. 3 Ibid., pp 7 & 26. 4 Ibid., pp 81–2.

in Irish.[5] This use of a bilingual platform to promote the revival of the Irish language and all things Gaelic was mirrored in the *Irish Independent*. Analysis of this bilingual platform provides significant insights into the interpretation and promotion of the 'regeneration of Ireland'.

THE *IRISH INDEPENDENT* AND THE 'IRISH-IRELAND' MOVEMENT

A link between the 'Irish-Ireland' school of thought and the *Irish Independent* was, to some extent, contrary to the established policy of the 'Irish-Ireland' movement. The newspaper and its owner, William Martin Murphy, were often ridiculed in *The Leader*, the main 'Irish-Ireland' organ. According to Moran, Murphy symbolized the 'West Brit Catholic' and because Murphy's paper supported free trade, Moran had very little respect for what he called 'Murphy's ha'penny dreadful'.[6] In spite of these differences, it is clear from the outset that the 'Irish-Ireland' mentality influenced material published in the *Irish Independent* as its first Gaelic column used the very title of the movement: 'Irish Ireland – A Leaguer's Point of View – Éire na nGaedheal'. Through the use of this title, the columnist, Eoghan Ó Neachtain, was creating links with two distinct movements – 'Irish-Ireland' and the Gaelic League. This bilingual title is of particular relevance when considering the target readership of the *Irish Independent*'s Gaelic column. It is clear that Ó Neachtain sought to attract a wide readership, both Gaelic Leaguers and Irish-Irelanders alike.

The use of a bilingual, rather than wholly Gaelic title, is also worth considering. The *Irish Independent*'s pledge of support for the Irish language from its first edition onwards was made in English. The use of an English title and subtitle reflects the propagandist role of the Gaelic column in promoting the 'Irish-Ireland' ideal. Even though the *Independent*'s English-speaking readers were not all capable of understanding the content of the column (nor were they all sympathetic to the cause), they could not fail to notice that quite a sizeable portion of their daily newspaper was devoted to Irish language material printed in Gaelic font. In 1905, the *Independent* was a mere eight pages but the 'Irish Ireland' column was still afforded a prominent daily position alongside the editorial and 'Our London Letter'. In this respect, McLuhan's concept of the medium becoming the message is central to our interpretation of the column.[7] It was not merely the content, but also the context, of the 'Irish Ireland' column that attracted attention.[8]

5 P. Maume, *D.P. Moran* (Dundalk, 1995), pp 10 & 14.   6 Ibid., pp 14 & 45. It should be noted that Moran also referred to the *Irish Times* as 'The Bigots' Dust Bin' (See, Maume, *Moran*, p. 23).   7 See M. McLuhan, *Understanding media: the extensions of man* (New York, 1964), p. 13 for his famous dictum 'The medium is the message'.   8 This bilingual title is not as unusual as one may think. A journal entitled *Árd na hÉireann: An Irish-Ireland Magazine* was pub-

The inclusion of an Irish language column in the new *Irish Independent* may well have been a commercially motivated move, as William Martin Murphy sought to produce a commercially viable daily newspaper. The rise in cultural nationalism from the late nineteenth century onwards had resulted in the creation of an educated, cultural elite who were sympathetic to the 'Irish-Ireland' cause and to the revival of the Irish language and Gaelic customs. Had Murphy launched a new daily, nationalist newspaper without the inclusion of an Irish language column, he may have incurred the wrath of many Irish-Irelanders, especially given the fact that the Irish language and related material in English had appeared regularly in the preceding *Irish Daily Independent*.

## THE COLUMN IN CONTEXT

The 'Irish Ireland' column in the *Irish Independent* was penned by Eoghan Ó Neachtain from 1905 until the outbreak of the First World War in 1914. Ó Neachtain was a native speaker of Irish from Spiddal, Co. Galway, who had spent time in South Africa in the 1890s before the outbreak of the Boer War. Ó Neachtain was for a time editor of the Gaelic League newspaper, *An Claidheamh Soluis*.[9] Although he worked full time with Dublin Corporation, Ó Neachtain remained as Irish editor of the *Irish Independent* for almost 10 years, and recorded his occupation as *nuaidheachtóir* (journalist) in the 1911 Census.[10] In his first column, Ó Neachtain praised the work of the Gaelic League in promoting the Irish language and stated that his section of the *Independent* would discuss the events and activities of daily life as relevant to the Irish-speaking community, including international events:

> From day to day, this section of the paper will describe the events and happenings of life, from the Irish speaker's perspective. Not only will priority be given to Irish affairs – we should not abandon them on that account – the beginning and middle and end of our own affairs will be found here; but, on top of all that, we will not leave out the affairs of the human race, as they unfold in other countries.

> Beidh cur síos ar chúrsaibh 7 ar imeachtaibh an tsaoghail san roinn seo de'n pháipéar, ó lá go lá, do réir mar is léir d'on Ghaedhilgeóir an saoghal. Ní hé amháin go mbeidh tús 7 príomh-aire le fagháil ag

lished by the Gaelic League in Tullamore in 1903 and the title *Inis Fáil: A Magazine for the Irish in London* was founded in 1904. The use of bilingualism was quite common in Irish journalism during the early twentieth century, particularly in relation to the 'Irish-Ireland' movement.   9 For more on Eoghan Ó Neachtain (1867–1957) see Ainm.ie.  10 1911 Census return for Eoghan Ó Neachtain, National Archives of Ireland.

ghnothaibh na hÉireann – ní cóir iad a chur uainn taobh leis an méid
sin – beidh tús 7 lár 7 deireadh le faghail ag ár ngnothaibh féin; acht, ar
a shon sin 7 uile, ní díbreóchthar glan amach as ár n-amharc cúrsaí an
chineadh daonna, do réir mar a éirigheas siad i dtíorthaibh eile.[11]

In his debut article, Ó Neachtain also created links between contemporary
national and international issues while remaining loyal to the Irish tradition as
he saw it. This is evidenced in his proposal to occasionally include excerpts from
traditional Irish folktales, which he felt were beneficial to readers and worthy
of discussion, and his pledge to discuss the issue of higher education, which he
felt was imperative to the language movement:

> It doesn't occur to people that higher education has anything to do with
> the poor man who is, for example, cutting peat, mowing grass or carrying
> a load from a ship to the merchant's store on the quay. But higher
> education relates to every such thing to which man relates, and since it
> does and since merit and benefit and substance may be obtained from
> higher education it will be discussed in this section of the paper and an
> effort will be made to explain its benefits.

> Ní thuilleann sé sa gceann ag daoinibh go bhfuil aon bhaint ag árd-
> léigheann leis an bhfear bocht atá, cuir i gcás, ag baint móna, ag spealadh
> féir nó ag iomchar ualaighe ó luing go stór an cheannaidhe, ar an gcéibh.
> Acht tá baint ag árd-oideachas le gach uile nidh a bhfuil baint ag an duine
> leis, 7 ó thárla go bhfuil 7 ó thárla go dtagann brígh 7 tairbhe 7 substaint
> de bharr an árd-oideachais cuirfear síos air san roinn seo de'n pháipéar
> 7 déanfar iarracht a thairbhe a mhíniughadh.[12]

The growth of the nationalist movement and the ability of the Irish people to
overcome their foreign neighbour, *an fear thall*, were also worthy of comment and
Ó Neachtain's first column praised the new-found confidence of the Irish
people: 'A beautiful thing is growing among the people, that is, confidence in
themselves' ['Is áluinn an rud é sin atá ag fás imeasg na ndaoine .i. muinighin
asta féin.'][13] From the outset, it was apparent that Ó Neachtain's column would
champion the nationalist cause, and the 'Irish-Ireland' movement in particular.

## LANGUAGE PROMOTION AND DISCOURSE

The promotion of the Irish language was undoubtedly a visible thread in the
*Irish Independent*'s narrative in the years before the foundation of the Irish State.

11 *Irish Independent*, 2 Jan. 1905; translation by the author.  12 Ibid.  13 Ibid.

However, Ó Neachtain's column discussed such issues as education, national and international politics, economic and social problems, as well as examining the challenges facing the language movement. Foremost among these challenges was the status of the Irish language in the education system under the British administration. Ó Neachtain repeatedly advocated the inclusion of Irish in the primary school system, for matriculation purposes and on the curriculum of the National University.[14] This was a major debate of the time and one that was a focus of editorials in other Irish language journals.[15] Ó Neachtain was particularly concerned with issues surrounding education during the early days of his 'Irish Ireland' column. He believed that teachers should receive a higher salary and that schools should be comforting and welcoming:

> The school nowadays is not beside a hedge or in the woods as it was long ago, and, although many a good man received his early education in the hedge school, it is not natural not to send the younger generation to a healthy, warm place in search of education.

> Ní ar chúlaibh claidhe nó fá'n gcoill atá an sgoil indiu mar bhí sí fadó, 7, cé gur hiomdha fear maith a fuar a chéad-theagasg cois claidhe, ní luigheann sé le nádúr gan an t-aos óg a chur go háit fholláin teolaidhe ag iarraidh oideachais.[16]

The following day, Ó Neachtain's column considered the social implications of the warm schoolhouse mentioned above, considering that the tax payer was funding the education system: 'Fathers are paying for the best education and the children are getting third rate education ...' ['Tá na haithreacha ag íoc ar an oideachas is fearr agus tá na páisdí a fagháil an tríomhadh sgoth oideachais...'][17]

Ó Neachtain's column also discussed many news events, political issues and social problems that were not related to the Irish language. International events such as the fall of Port Arthur, the Irish roots of President Theodore Roosevelt and the outbreak of the First World War were discussed, as were general national news items.[18] Ó Neachtain was something of a social commentator, criticizing the behaviour and customs of the society of his day, and in one article in January 1905 he commented on the number of people brought before the courts on counts of drunkeness over the festive period. He praised a priest in Co. Wexford who had called on publicans not to serve alcohol to anyone

---

14 See *Irish Independent*, 6, 10 & 11 Jan. 1905. This was a particularly strong theme when the 'Irish-Ireland' column was first founded.   15 Examples include 'The University Crisis' in *An Claidheamh Soluis* in 1909. See R. Uí Chollatáin, *An Claidheamh Soluis agus Fáinne an Lae, 1899–1932* (Dublin, 2004), pp 95–102.   16 *Irish Independent*, 10 Jan. 1905.   17 Ibid., 11 Jan. 1905.   18 See *Irish Independent*, 4 Jan. 1905, 16 Feb. 1905 & 7 Aug. 1914.

already intoxicated.[19] This appeal for temperance was echoed in similar articles relating to the Irish language movement, particularly regarding proper observance of St Patrick's Day.[20]

Despite the inclusion in the 'Irish Ireland' column of material unconnected to the language movement, the main political question of the day, home rule, was tied to the Irish language cause in one particular column that welcomed the support of John Redmond and his followers:

> Redmond and his followers are now helping the Irish language and it's not long since they annoyed the Englishman, that is, the last time Redmond and the Irish speakers were on the platform of the meeting room in Parliament.

> Tá an Réamonnach agus a mhathshluagh ag cuidiughadh leis an nGaedhilg anois agus níl sé an-fhada ó shoin ó bhaineadar cor a thuaithbhil as an Sasanach .i. an uair dheireadh bhí An Réamonnach agus na Gaedhilgeoirí ar árdán an chruinn-tseomra sa gCruinn-Teach.[21]

Among the challenges facing the Irish language movement during the early years of Ó Neachtain's column was the refusal of the Post Office to handle letters and parcels addressed in Irish or in Gaelic script. This had a devasting impact on the Gaelic League's communication with its branch members and was discussed in many English language articles:

> This is apparently but the beginning of a tussle between the Gaelic League and the Post Office, and we believe the matter only requires to be resolutely followed up, when the victory will rest with the Gaelic League and Irish Ireland.[22]

While this dispute may appear trivial to non-Irish speakers, the post was essential for effective and speedy communication, particularly for the native Irish community who were very dependent on an efficient postal service. It was finally resolved after much agitation in the press. The fact that this was debated in the columns of the *Irish Independent* is significant in understanding the importance of this forum as one of further agitation for the language cause.[23]

Ó Neachtain's 'Irish Ireland' column came to an abrupt end in August 1914. This may have been a result of the war-induced paper shortage as the *Independent*

19 *Irish Independent*, 5 Jan. 1905. 20 For example, see 'Seachtmhain na Gaedhilge. An Appeal to the Nation'; 'St. Patrick's Day. Papal Dispensation. An Appeal to the Vitners', *Irish Independent*, 4 Mar. 1905. 21 *Irish Independent*, 28 Feb. 1905. 22 Ibid., 2 Mar. 1905. 23 See Uí Chollatáin, *An Claidheamh Soluis*, pp 80–2.

was reduced to four pages per edition.[24] After the war, Irish language articles were published regularly under the auspices of the 'Matters of Moment' editorial column from January 1919 onwards. Unfortunately, these articles are unsigned and the author's identity unknown. During the post-war period, occasional articles in Irish were provided by journalists such as the author and translator Liam Ó Rinn, and Aodh de Blácam, who is best remembered for his 'Roddy the Rover' column in the *Irish Press* from 1931 to 1947.[25] When the *Independent*'s Gaelic column was revived after the First World War, the articles published in Irish concentrated mainly on issues and events relating to the Irish language and the nationalist cause, in contrast to Ó Neachtain's column, which had discussed all facets of Irish and, occasionally, international life.

The 'Matters of Moment' column was a daily feature of the *Irish Independent* that appeared directly alongside the editorial. As this column was published predominantly in English, the Irish language appears to have been used mainly for matters relating to the language movement. That said, from 1919 onwards, the column regularly carried two to three articles in Irish each week. The status of the Irish language within the education system was a major feature of this column as the Gaelic League strove to ensure that the language was included on the compulsory primary school curriculum, rather than continuing as an extra subject outside of regular school hours:

> It's a long time since the Gaelic League undertook such important work as the new programme for education which they have devised. It is clear to all that there is an urgent need for the Gaelicization of the national schools, and although this has been talked about for some time, little has come of that all talking.

> Is fada anois ó thóg muinntir Chonnartha na Gaedhilge idir lámhaibh aon obair chómh tábhachtach leis an gClár nuadh oideachais seo atá ceapaithe aca. Is léir do chách go bhfuil dian-ghádh le Gaedhlú na mbun-scoileann, agus cidh go bhfuiltear ag trácht ar an sgéul le fada, is beag atá de thoradh aguinn de bhárr na cainnte go léir.[26]

The author of the Irish articles in the 'Matters of Moment' column may have changed over time. There is a shift in 1921 towards Roman font and a modernized spelling of words in Irish. The scope of these articles gradually

24 Nollaig Mac Congáil has suggested various reasons for the discontinuation of Ó Neachtain's column. See N. Mac Congáil, 'Saothrú na Gaeilge ar Nuachtáin Náisiúnta Bhéarla na hAoise Seo Caite: Sop nó Solamar?' in R. Ó Muireadhaigh (eag.), *Féilscríbhinn Anraí Mhic Giolla Chomhaill: tráchtais léannta in onóir don Athair Anraí Mac Giolla Chomhaill* (Dublin, 2011), pp 112–91. 25 P. Maume, 'Aodh de Blácam', *Dictionary of Irish biography* (online edition). 26 *Irish Independent*, 5 Apr. 1919.

widened to include more international topics although domestic politics and
the language movement continued to dominate. When the Anglo-Irish Treaty
was debated in late 1921, the 'Matters of Moment' column called for peace
and expressed optimism that the nationalist cause was on the cusp of achieving
freedom from British rule:

> We do not yet have all that we wish for but, with the help of God, we
> will. Ireland cannot go back. God has ordained that she shall progress.
> Her star is rising; England's star is continually falling.
>
> Níl againn fós gach rud ba mhaith linn a bheith againn ach, le cúnamh
> Dé, beidh. Ní féidir dEire dul siar. Dul ar aghaidh atá ceapaithe ag Dia
> dhi. Tá a réalt ag dul in áirde; tá réalt Shasana ag dul fé i gcomhnuí.[27]

Numerous articles signed by 'L.O.R.' also appeared in the *Irish Independent* on a
regular basis from 1919 onwards and can be attributed to the author, activist and
translator Liam Ó Rinn.[28] These occasional articles were, for the most part,
strongly worded and opinionated in tone. Ó Rinn's articles discussed a variey
of issues regarding the Irish language and its literature. He criticized the failure
of Irish writers to generate new literature in their native tongue: 'Novels must
be written based on the life we have in Ireland now and in times gone by.' ['Ni
miste tuirt fe urscealta cheapadh do reir an tsaoil ata againn in Eirinn fe lathir
agus le tamall.'][29] In another article, Ó Rinn proposed the establishment of a
standardized dialect for the *Galltacht*, or non-Gaelic speaking areas:

> Reference was made in this paper a while back to the standardizing of
> prayers in Irish, and that got me thinking that it would be worth
> considering what can be done to establish one single dialect for the
> *Galltacht*.
>
> Bhí tracht sa phápeur so tamal ó shin ar na húrnuithe Gaedhilge chur
> ar aon dhul amháin, agus do chuir san am cheann nár mhisde feuchaint
> cad dfeudfi a dheunamh chun aon chanúint amháin Ghaedhilge
> dheunamh don Ghalldacht.[30]

---

27 Ibid., 22 Dec. 1921. 28 For more on Liam Ó Rinn see Ainm.ie. 29 'I am afraid we won't have any proper,
natural literature in Irish until the people of the Gaeltacht awaken, not just as regards the Irish language but as
regards the world around them.' ['Is eagal liom na beidh aon litriocht cheart nadurtha againn sa Ghaedhilg go
mbeidh muintir na Gaeltachta ina nduiseacht, ní hamháin i dtaobh na Gaedhilge ach i dtaobh an tsaoil mhoir
bhraonaigh.'] *Irish Independent*, 13 Dec. 1921. 30 *Irish Independent*, 30 Dec. 1921. This sentiment was echoed in the article
'Schism fears for Gaeilgeoirí', *Irish Times*, 1 Jan. 2010.

## OUTSIDE THE COLUMN

Aside from the Gaelic column itself, much of the Irish language material in the *Irish Independent* took the form of letters, book reviews, advertisements and, most notably, reports of Gaelic League events and campaigns. Letters to the editor debated issues such as the Fáinne League (the Fáinne Association was founded by the journalist and political activist Piaras Béaslaí, a freelance contributor to the *Irish Independent*, prior to the 1916 Rising),[31] the salaries of Irish teachers, the work of the Gaelic League, the publication (or lack thereof) of Irish language literature, and home manufacture, again in both English and Irish.[32] The executive committee of the Gaelic League was criticized for its lack of action, particularly with regard to raising the status of Irish in the education system:

> Our patience is almost worn out, and if the Committee we have are unable to complete the work they are supposed to do, my advice to them is to retire altogether, and to give a chance to those who are ready for action rather than idle talk.

> Tá ár bhfoidhne nách mór caitte, agus muna féidir leis an gCoiste atá againn an obair atá ceapuighthe acu do chur i gcrich, isé mo chomhairle-se dhóibh eirighe as ar fad, agus seans do thabhairt dos na daoine atá ollamh chun obair do dhéanamh in'ionad cainnte.[33]

The proscription of the Gaelic League by the Dublin Castle administration in late 1918 resulted in a marked increase in birth, death, and marriage notices in Irish from early 1919 onwards. Many notices were published in Irish with an accompanying English translation, offering further proof of the importance attached to the Irish language during the struggle for Irish independence. The text of Dáil Éireann's message 'to the free nations of the world' was printed in full in both Irish and English in January 1919[34] and the use of Irish in the first meeting of Dáil Éireann was repeatedly praised in the *Independent*. It noted 'The predominence of Irish in the proceedings of Dáil Éireann is the most important thing which has been done in favour of the language for a long time'. ['An lámh in uachtair don Ghaedhilg i n-imeachtaí Dail Éireann, sin é an rud is tábhachtaighe dá ndearnadh ar son na teangan le fada fada an lá.'][35]

Advertisements for events organized by the Gaelic League and other language groups were occasionally published in Irish, but the use of bilingual

---

31 For further information on Piaras Béaslaí's contributions to the *Irish Independent* see Piaras Beaslaí papers, National Library of Ireland, MSS 33,911–33,987.  **32** See *Irish Independent*, 25 Oct. 1919, 18 Aug. 1919, 21 May 1919, 13 Feb. 1905, & 5 Nov. 1919.  **33** *Irish Independent*, 21 May 1919.  **34** Ibid., 22 Jan. 1919.  **35** Ibid., 17 Jan. 1919.

advertisements was more commonplace. Such advertisements included those for GAA fixtures, traditional Irish concerts and *céilithe* and schools where Irish was taught.[36] Bilingual advertisements for the Oireachtas competitions also featured regularly in the *Independent*, as did notices of the competition winners.[37] The use of a bilingual format was also common in reports of Gaelic League events and happenings. In the early years in particular, it was quite common to find an Irish language account of the latest Gaelic League news repeated in English directly below.[38]

Along with Irish language articles and bilingual material, the *Irish Independent* provided a forum for the promotion of the Irish language revival through the medium of English in the opening decades of the twentieth century. This was particularly evident in the 'Letters to the Editor' or 'Opinions of Our Readers' section. Many letters in English were signed in Irish as the use of the language in the public sphere of the media came to the fore during the war of independence. Letters in English relating to the language movement were frequently published, and stand-alone articles in English raised many controversial issues such as the use of Irish in the public service, the proclamation of the Gaelic League, the use of Roman rather than Gaelic font, and the phonetic teaching of Irish.[39] Reference was made to the fact that Professor Eoin MacNeill was elected president of the Gaelic League in August 1916, despite his active involvement with the Irish Volunteers.[40] Similarly, a report on the Oireachtas festival held in Cork in August 1919 indicated that the proclamation of the Gaelic League had only increased its popularity among the people of Ireland: 'The proclaiming of feiseanna by the English authorities was a great benefit to the Gaelic League, two or three feiseanna having been held where only one would have taken place.'[41] The *Independent* also made reference to the British prime minister, David Lloyd George, speaking in his native Welsh at public gatherings and thus acknowledging his own native language whilst the Gaelic League was suppressed.[42]

The content of the *Irish Independent*'s material relating to the Irish language was similar to that of Irish language publications of the time; therefore it is possible that there may have been a crossover in the articles that appeared in various publications. However, in addition to the impact of the English language on Irish language discourse, the incorporation of many Irish language words into the English narrative in the *Irish Independent* during this period is also significant. Terms such as 'Irish-speaking districts', 'ring', 'dance', 'assembly' and 'Parliament' gradu-

36 See *Irish Independent*, 27 Aug. 1919, 14 June 1919, 30 Aug. 1919 & 11 Sept. 1919.   37 *Irish Independent*, 2 Aug. 1920.   38 This journalistic format was also used by Pearse in *An Claidheamh Soluis* as he wrote over 300 editorials in both Irish and English. For further information see Uí Chollatáin, *An Claidheamh Soluis*, Bilingual Index of ACS.   39 See *Irish Independent*, 6 Mar. 1905, 4 Aug. 1919, 23 Sept. 1919 & 11 Aug. 1919.   40 *Irish Independent*, 9 Aug. 1916.   41 Ibid., 4 Aug. 1919.   42 Ibid., 29 Dec. 1919.

ally gave way to the accepted use of words such as *Gaeltacht, Fáinne, céilidh, aeridheacht, Dáil Éireann* and the like in English language articles. It is therefore possible to assert that the use of the bilingual media forum influenced the use of Irish terms in everyday speech regardless of the first language of the speaker.

In political reports, statements in Irish were often translated into English, leading to examples such as: 'Mr. De Valera, speaking in Irish, said it was fitting that the Dáil should make a solemn pronouncement on the League of Nations, thus demonstrating that Ireland was not selfish or self-absorbed, recognizing no obligation to anyone else.'[43] While the translation of these lines into English indicates the target readership of such news items, the fact that the reporter informs the readers that the speech was originally given in Irish is noteworthy. Translation such as this was a frequent feature of the political rhetoric of nationalism promoted in the *Independent*, perhaps implying that if our political leaders spoke in Irish so too should the people of Ireland. Clearly therefore, the linking of 'Irish-Ireland' with the Irish language acknowledged the need for the use of language in political debate and public discourse, promoting a sense of inclusion rather than exclusion. The translation of such passages indicated that the target audience, the Irish public, needed to fully understand what was being said in Irish on the political platform, creating an understanding, at least, of an equal platform for both languages.

## THE ECONOMIC IMPACT OF THE 'IRISH-IRELAND' IDEOLOGY

Another element of the 'Irish-Ireland' concept was the promotion of a truly Irish economic programme. Within the parameters of the *Irish Independent*, this economic aspect took the form of the ongoing promotion of Irish-made goods. Readers were urged to support home manufacture, or *déantús baile*, in line with the 'Irish-Ireland' mentality that 'Ireland, because she has lost her heart, imports today what on sound economic principles she could produce for herself'.[44] As the decades wore on, the terms of the debate on home manufacture widened to include the co-operative movement that was gaining popularity among certain sections of society. The *Independent* vowed to support the 'Industrial Revival Movement' from the outset and its promotion of home manufacture was most pronounced during Irish Week or *Seachtain na Gaeilge* each year. Advertisements promoted products such as 'Irish Goods at Clery's', Gaelic League publications and Bournville cocoa.[45]

---

43 Ibid., 12 Apr. 1919. Other examples include: 'Mr. R. Mulcahy, speaking in Irish …', 12 Apr. 1919, 'In an address, Mr. De Valera spoke first in Gaelic, reminding the audience that he did so at the beginning of every meeting, "for the language is one of the distinguishing marks of our nationhood".' 22 Aug. 1919.  44 Moran, *Philosophy of Irish Ireland*, p. 111.  45 *Irish Independent*, 18 Mar. 1919, 31 Jan. 1910, and 24 Nov. 1915.

From an economic perspective, many articles and letters were published in English regarding the wearing of Irish-made clothes, the establishment of co-operative movements, and the provision of employment in Irish-speaking districts.[46] One such letter advocated the establishment of a *Fáinne*-type badge for those who wore Irish-made clothing: 'No doubt many Irish Irelanders would not touch imported goods, but the wearing of a button would certainly remind others of their duty to their country.'[47] A report on the newly established Kerry Gaoltacht Association declared that 'The Irish language must be identified with the trade.'[48]

Notwithstanding the promotion of home manufacture and Irish economic endeavours, it must also be remembered that the *Irish Independent* was, during the opening decades of the twentieth century, functioning within the confines of the British Empire. Patrick Maume has analyzed the stance taken by the *Irish Daily Independent* and, later, the *Irish Independent*, under imperial influences.[49] This is particularly evident from a commercial standpoint as, while promoting Irish-made goods, the *Independent* also published advertisements for various British companies including Rowntrees, Cadburys and Beechams. Although the 'Irish-Ireland' mentality was evident from 1905 onwards, the *Independent* was very much a commercial entity within the British Empire, as indicated by its regular inclusion of rolls of honour or 'Military Intelligence' during the First World War and advertisements for subscriptions to an Irish National War Memorial.[50] References were regularly made to imperial appointments and fashionable marriages, particularly in the magazine page, and both 'Our London Letter' and the 'Social and Personal' column were daily fixtures during this period. A similar imperial stance was taken in the following notice that appeared regularly during the summer months: 'You cannot enjoy your holidays without "The Irish Independent". It will be sent to you by post to any part of the United Kingdom'.[51] While this notice appeared in 1919, it echoes the inferred dual mentality and interdependence previously referred to by D.P. Moran in 1905 as he spoke of how 'at one and the same time we are hating England and imitating her'.[52]

## SOCIAL AND POLITICAL IMPLICATIONS OF THE 'IRISH-IRELAND' DISCOURSE

The wider social and political implications of the bilingual forum provided by the *Irish Independent* for the 'Irish-Ireland' rhetoric have yet to be fully explored.

46 Ibid., 9 Aug. 1919, See also 13 & 31 Oct. 1919.   47 *Irish Independent*, 14 Mar. 1921.   48 Ibid., 13 Oct. 1919.   49 See P. Maume, 'The *Irish Independent* and empire, 1891–1919', in S. Potter (ed.), *Newspapers and empire in Ireland and Britain: reporting the British Empire, c.1857–1921* (Dublin, 2004), pp 124–42.   50 *Irish Independent*, 13 Jan. 1920.   51 Ibid., 9 June 1919.   52 Moran, *Philosophy of Irish Ireland*, p. 48.

Frequent references are made throughout the period in question to Irish danc-
ing, singing, music, recitation, literature and the Oireachtas competitions. Such
social and cultural events were widely publicized by the *Independent*, through
the medium of both English and Irish. On a more ideological plane, the
*Independent* presented a platform for other organizations such as the Catholic
Truth Society (the annual conference of which was given considerable coverage), the Catholic Total Abstinence Association, the Society against Evil
Literature, the Women's Franchise Association and others, not to mention more
politicized groups such as Cumann na mBan, the Ancient Order of Hibernia
and, of course, Sinn Féin. The politicization of the Gaelic League and, conse-
quently, the Irish language itself, is clearly visible on the pages of the *Irish
Independent* in the years before the foundation of the state. A prime example of
the use of the Irish language not only as a mark of distinction from other
nations but, more specifically, as a political tool, may be found in Eamon de
Valera's St Patrick's Day message that appeared on the front page of the
*Independent* on 17 March 1919. The text of the message reads:

> To save the national language is the special duty of this generation.
> The ultimate winning back of our statehood is not in doubt. Sooner
> or later Ireland will recover the sovereign independence she once enjoyed:
> should we fail a future generation will succeed – but the language, that
> must be saved by us or it is lost forever.[53]

At this particular time, de Valera was on the run, having escaped from Lincoln
Prison, and his efforts to encourage the Irish people to save their native language encapsulate a vigorous propaganda put forward by the Sinn Féin party
during this period. The position of this message on the front page of the
*Independent* is significant, as it demonstrates the use of the language movement
as a propagandist tool in political discourse.[54] Regular news articles appeared
in the *Independent* around this time centred on the arrest of individuals who
refused to speak English to members of the armed forces, including the incar-
ceration of a group of young girls who were charged with unlawful flag-sell-
ing on behalf of the Gaelic League.[55]

---

53 *Irish Independent*, 17 Mar. 1919.  54 This is also reflected in advertisements for the Gaelic League flag days, 'The
Gaelic League is resisting Conscription of the Soul as you resisted Conscription of the Body', 14 Mar. 1919, and
in a bilingual letter from Agnes O'Farrelly seeking re-election to the Senate as a National University candidate, 13
Sept. 1919.  55 See *Irish Independent*, 3 Nov. 1919. See also the arrest of Pádraig Fahy 'for refusing to speak English
to a policeman', 26 June 1919 and the case of James Sugrue, who was arrested for drilling, and 'spoke in Irish, refusing to recognize the Court', 12 Aug. 1919.

CONCLUSION

William Martin Murphy's revised *Irish Independent* promoted not only a nationalist ideology, but also the linguistic and cultural framework within which such an ideology could take hold. Paradoxically, to some extent, it may be considered a testament to the *Independent* that it continued to provide a platform for the Irish language even after the proscription of the Gaelic League, all the while functioning as both a supporter of 'Irish-Ireland' and a commercial entity within the British Empire. The *Irish Independent* certainly produced a valuable corpus of Irish-language material in the years prior to independence but it is important to consider this material in the wider context of the 'Irish-Ireland' doctrine under which the Irish language was often promoted through the use of English.

The *Irish Independent*'s interpretation and promotion of the 'regeneration of Ireland' certainly offers an insight into the varied political, sociological and linguistic facets of the newspaper in the early decades of the twentieth century. Clearly, therefore, the focus was not limited to the Irish language as a stand-alone value within Irish society, but acknowledged the forum provided for the promotion of the Irish language within a framework of fostering the Irish economy and Irish nationalist movements. This may actually have been a journalistic style that crossed, and even disregarded, both linguistic and political boundaries.

1 The first edition of the *Irish Independent*, 2 January 1905. Adverts remained on the front page until July 1961.

2 William Martin Murphy, founding proprietor of Independent Newspapers.

3 Advertising the *Irish Independent* ahead of the arrival of the papal delegation for the Eucharistic Congress in June 1932.

4 A newsstand poster to promote the 14 December 1934 edition of the *Irish Independent* coming off the printing press.

5 Night-time view of Independent House, 1935, home of Independent Newspapers from 1924 to 2004.

6 Editorial department, 1935. Note the metal pipes in the back-left corner used to transport copy around the building.

7 Etching department, 1935. Photographs were turned into half-tone plates that were etched with acid, mounted on a block and then inserted into the page.

8 The case room, 1935. For decades, headlines were assembled by hand. After printing, the individual letters had to be 'dissed' or dismantled – capital letters to the upper case and small letters to the lower case.

9 A Linotype operator, 1959. The Linotype machine allowed for the production of columns of text or 'slugs'. Prior to the Linotype, every column had to be assembled by hand.

10 The Linotype hall at Independent Newspapers. The Linotype machine remained at the centre of newspaper production until the 1980s.

11 Assembling the 'slugs' from the Linotype on the 'stone' to make up a page.

12 A completed page or 'forme' being moved from the 'stone' to the printing press.

13 The company's Crabtree rotary press. Installed in 1921, the three-deck machine was the most modern available.

14 Printers examining copies as they come off the press, 1935.

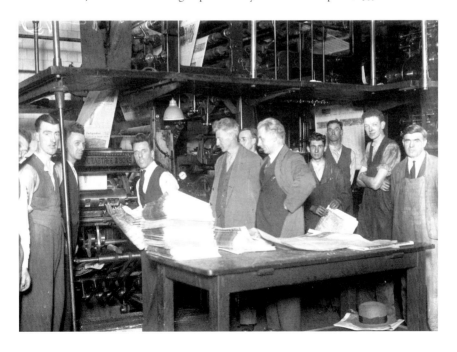

15 Distribution activity as the latest edition becomes available, 1935.

16 Cars and vans at the dispatch department on Prince's Street North (off O'Connell Street), 1935.

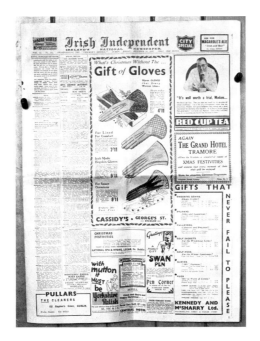

17, 18, 19 For half a century Independent Newspapers published four newspapers – the *Irish Independent*, the *Evening Herald*, the *Sunday Independent* and the *Irish Weekly Independent*. These front pages are from December 1934.

20 Presentation to chairman T.V. Murphy in the boardroom of Independent Newspapers in the early 1950s. Artist Leo Whelan (*left*), T.V. Murphy (*centre*) and Frank Geary, editor of the *Irish Independent* (*right*).

21 Independent House, the Middle Abbey Street home of
Independent Newspapers in 1955.

22 The broadsheet *Evening Herald*, 16 August 1957.

23 Printing press at Middle Abbey Street, 1959.

24 The *Irish Independent* newsroom in Middle Abbey Street during the count on the electoral system referendum in 1968. Pictured from left: journalist Isobel Geary, copytaker Anne Grogan, journalist Frank Byrne, journalist John Maddock, journalist Ned Murphy, religious affairs correspondent Joe Power, and on ladder journalist Jimmy Gallagher who compiled election results in the newsroom.

25 Frank Geary, editor of the *Irish Independent*, 1935–61.

26 Hector Legge, editor of the *Sunday Independent*, 1940–70.

27 Aengus Fanning on his appointment as editor of the *Sunday Independent* in January 1984. He edited the newspaper until his death in January 2012.

28 Vincent Doyle, editor of the *Irish Independent*, 1981–2005.

29 Veronica Guerin pictured reading the *Irish Independent* shortly before her murder on 26 June 1996.

30 Gavin O'Reilly and his father Sir Anthony (Tony) O'Reilly at the 2007 annual general meeting of Independent News and Media.

31, 32 Independent News and Media newsprint production centre at Citywest in Dublin.

## 7 / 'The best interests of the nation': Frank Geary, the *Irish Independent* and the Spanish civil war

### MARK O'BRIEN

In his 1937 review of Irish newspapers the Revd Stephen Brown noted that 'The *Independent* was first and foremost a commercial undertaking. Indeed its very essence was business. To this rather than to the popularity of its political opinions it owned its remarkable success'.[1] The newspaper was, Brown continued, 'the non-party organ of business interests in the country ... anxious to capture the support of independent readers and in particular of Irish Catholic sentiment'.[2] Both the *Independent*, and the *Irish Press*, he observed, 'vie with one other to capture the favour of the Catholic public'.[3] In terms of circulation the *Independent* was far ahead: Brown cites its circulation at being between 143,000 and 152,000 compared to 106,000 for the *Irish Press*. The *Irish Times*, still viewed as the organ of southern unionism, though slowly transforming itself, stood at 25,500.[4] As regards politics, Brown observed that the *Independent* 'had consistently supported the Anglo-Irish Treaty from the first, and ... had come more and more to be regarded as the semi-official organ of the Cosgrave party, though in fact it was independent of all party control'.[5]

Brown's review of the *Independent* was broadly accurate: it had been established as a commercial venture and it did support Cumann na nGaedheal and later Fine Gael, but only because it viewed both parties as being more business friendly than anti-Treaty Sinn Féin or Fianna Fáil. Also central to the *Independent*'s commercial sensibility was the devout catholicism of William Martin Murphy. Unlike its politics, the *Independent* wore its catholicism on its sleeve. This policy reached its zenith during the Spanish civil war, when the *Independent*, then edited by Frank Geary, raged against de Valera's policy of non-intervention in what the *Irish Press* dismissed as a cynical circulation building exercise. But while Geary may have amplified this editorial philosophy of uncritical support for the Catholic church, he had, in fact, inherited it from his predecessors. Both Timothy R. Harrington (1905–31) and Tim Quilty (1931–5) had, to varying degrees, established the *Independent*'s position in relation to Fianna Fáil and the Catholic church during the late 1920s and early 1930s.

---

1 S. Brown, *The press in Ireland: a survey and a guide* (Dublin, 1937), p. 40. 2 Ibid., p. 49. 3 Ibid., p. 168. 4 M. O'Brien, *The Irish Times: a history* (Dublin, 2008), p. 82. 5 Brown, *The press in Ireland*, p. 49.

SETTING THE TONE

Under the editorship of T.R. Harrington the *Independent* consistently supported
Cumann na nGaedheal. As Fianna Fáil prepared to contest its first general election in 1927, the newspaper was forced to take stock of its politics. It acknowledged that, in relation to the Cumann na nGaedheal government, it had 'dealt
with the imperfections of some of its proposals and drawn attention to omis-
sions on its part' but had 'always given it credit for the many splendid services
it had rendered'. Such service, it concluded, 'so far outweigh its mistakes that
in appraising its record as a whole it must be admitted that it deserves a renewal
of confidence'.[6] Mindful of commercial realities though, the *Independent* published half-page adverts for Fianna Fáil that criticized the government's record.[7]
On election day it declared that a Fianna Fáil victory would see the party 'repudiate the nation's financial obligations, tax almost every article coming into our
ports, and strike a mortal blow at the whole system of finance by setting up a
state bank'. In contrast, it praised the government's 'stupendous achievements
in achieving peace at home and credit abroad' and concluded that 'patriotism
and commonsense urge the people to rally to the side of the Government'.[8]

In terms of its coverage of ecclesiastical matters throughout the 1920s, the
*Independent* devoted two full-page length columns every year to the bishops'
Lenten pastorals. Such reportage was often accompanied by an editorial, such
as that of 1924, which noted that the pastorals reminded Catholics 'of the
fundamental truths of their religion and of their obligatory Christian duties'.[9]
Throughout the 1920s the *Independent* sent a 'special representative' to report on
the Catholic Truth Society's annual pilgrimage to Lourdes.[10] It welcomed the
government's decision in February 1926 to establish a committee on evil literature and warned that those appearing before the committee should not 'confine
themselves to vague generalities about the objectionable tone of some publications'; advocates should 'come with their proofs in black and white, giving
the name of each publication, and the extracts that show its objectionable character'.[11] The committee's report, which framed the 1929 Censorship of
Publications Act, was described by the *Independent* as 'very modest recommen-
dations [to which] no objection can be raised',[12] while the censorship bill itself
was described as 'a fair and reasonable scheme for checking a grave menace to
public and private morality without unduly interfering either with the liberty
of the Press or the liberty of the subject'.[13]

Harrington's successor, Tim Quilty, maintained this editorial policy of supporting Cumann na nGaedheal and the teachings of the Catholic church. Quilty

6 *Irish Independent*, 21 May 1927. (Hereinafter, the *Irish Independent* is abbreviated to II.)  7 II, 2 June 1927.  8 II, 9
June 1927.  9 II, 3 Mar. 1924.  10 II, 7 Sept. 1927.  11 II, 19 Feb. 1926.  12 II, 1 Feb. 1927.  13 II, 13 Aug. 1928.

was appointed editor in September 1931, some five months before the 1932 general election. As in previous campaigns the *Independent* published advertisements for Fianna Fáil but gave editorial support to Cumann na nGaedheal.[14] It noted that it was 'tied neither to party nor to politician', but concluded that 'in this election we unhesitatingly give our support to Cumann na nGaedheal'.[15] With this caveat the *Independent* then attacked Fianna Fáil's programme for government as communism Irish-style. Its editorials raised the spectre of a land tax and 'State control and State interference' in industry.[16] These declarations put Fianna Fáil on the back-foot and it was forced to deny there was anything communist in its plans. This only further fuelled the *Independent*'s attack:

> Mr de Valera speaking at Carrick-on-Shannon, declared that there was nothing Communistic or Socialistic in the policy of Fianna Fáil and nothing to interfere with the rights of private property. Has he forgotten what he said at the Ard-Fheis when he announced that 'wherever private enterprises fail to take advantage of the opportunities provided by the State, the Government will provide capital for a Board that will establish and conduct the industry in the public interest'? What does this mean if not the introduction of Russian methods?[17]

Nonetheless, when Fianna Fáil took office in March 1932, the *Independent* asserted that 'the new Ministers have every right, moral, legal and political, to the allegiance of the community'.[18] In fairness, the *Independent* had no time for the antics of Eoin O'Duffy and his National Guard (Blueshirts). When the organization was proclaimed an unlawful association, the newspaper politely devoted its editorial to matters closer to its heart – 'Tariffs, Tea and Trade'.[19] It did, however, welcome the establishment of Fine Gael as a demonstration of 'sanity and wisdom in statesmanship'.[20]

Quilty also maintained the *Independent*'s commitment to reporting ecclesiastical matters. Extensive space continued to be allocated to the reportage of the bishops' Lenten pastorals. In March 1930 the newspaper devoted three full-page columns on the hierarchy's pronouncements on topics as diverse as the dangers awaiting females who emigrated, poteen making, mixed marriages, birth control, blasphemy, modern dress and foreign fashions.[21] It also reported on the first national pilgrimage to the Holy Land, which was accompanied by one of its reporters.[22] It was, however, the Eucharistic Congress of 1932 that allowed Quilty and the *Independent* to demonstrate their commitment to the church. The

14 See II, 30 Jan. 1932 & 5 & 13 Feb. 1932. For Cumann na nGaedheal adverts see 10–13 & 15–16 Feb. 1932.  15 II, 30 Jan. 1932.  16 Ibid.  17 II, 1 Feb. 1932.  18 II, 10 Mar. 1932.  19 II, 28 Aug. 1933.  20 II, 9 Sept. 1933.  21 II, 4 Mar. 1930.  22 II, 10 Mar. 1930.

arrival of the Papal Legate, Cardinal Lorenzo Lauri, was described as 'one of the proudest days in one of the greatest weeks in our history',[23] while the Congress itself was described as 'one of the greatest events in the long and not inglorious history of our Catholic nation'.[24]

## A NEW EDITOR

When Quilty retired as editor in September 1935 his successor was his assistant editor, Frank Geary. Born in Kilkenny in 1891 Geary began his journalistic career on the *Kilkenny People* under E.T. Keane, whose influence he later acknowledged.[25] He joined the *Independent* in early 1922 and on his first day covered seven coroners inquests, which was, as he put it, 'a bit of a shock for a reporter just up from the country'.[26] Shortly afterwards, he was dispatched to Belfast to cover the conflict that had erupted there. Geary spent three months in Belfast – 'spending many, many days of fear and nights of terror' – before being recalled to Dublin to report on the shelling of the Four Courts.[27] As the civil war began Geary was assigned to cover the Free State army's advance on Limerick. Having caught the train to Nenagh, Co. Tipperary, Geary had to borrow a bicycle to complete the journey to Limerick. Every alternate day he cycled between the two locations as Nenagh's post office was the only telegraph facility he could use to send his reports to Dublin.[28]

Geary's first scoop came in August 1922. While in Kilmallock, Co. Limerick, covering the Free State army's advance on Cork he received a message that T.R. Harrington wished to see him in Dublin. When they met, Harrington ordered Geary to go to Cork, then still in the hands of anti-Treaty forces. When Geary protested that cars and trains had ceased entering the city due to blockades, Harrington told him to go by sea.[29] Thus began a 48-hour sea journey from Dublin to Liverpool and from there to Cork. He arrived in Cork on 3 August, five days before the city fell. His first report, 'Days of Waiting and Fearing', which outlined his journey to the city, was published on 10 August. Two days later, his full-page story, 'Capture of the City of Cork: Exclusive Account of the Operations', gave a graphic day-by-day countdown to the arrival of Free State troops. As the city's telecommunications infrastructure had been destroyed Geary had to hire a driver to take him to Waterford so that he could telegraph his story to Dublin. After a torturous 12-hour drive that involved several encounters with retreating anti-Treaty forces Geary reached Waterford and telegraphed his 5,000 word story for inclusion in the next day's *Independent*.

23 II, 21 June 1932. 24 II, 22 June 1932. 25 II, 22 Dec. 1961. 26 II, 3 Jan. 1955. 27 Ibid. 28 Ibid. 29 II, 25 Sept. 1937. I am grateful to Felix Larkin for alerting me to this episode.

The exclusive seven-column story caused quite a stir: it was, in Geary's own words, 'the greatest "scoop" of a generation'.[30] The *Independent* called it 'one of the best achievements in the annals of Irish journalism'.[31]

In 1925 Geary was one of four reporters who accompanied a group from Cork's Farmers' Union that visited Denmark to study Danish agricultural methods.[32] Praise for the series and Geary's writing came from all quarters: the *Enniscorthy Echo* noted that 'the value in this country of the visit to Denmark is increased a hundred-fold by means of his readable and well-instructed narrative'.[33] The *Independent* declared that the articles had 'aroused such great interest' that it had decided to publish them in pamphlet form.[34] Geary's writing skills also resulted in him being sent to some tragic scenes to report on what he found. In September 1926 he was dispatched to Drumcollogher, Co. Limerick, the scene of a horrific fire that had occurred in a makeshift cinema when the reels of film had combusted. Under the subheading 'Coffins, Coffins, Coffins', Geary described the scene he encountered: 'Messages', he wrote, 'had been sent out for coffins, coffins, coffins – what a message'.[35] Similarly, in October 1927, he was dispatched to counties Mayo and Galway after forty-five fishermen died in a freak storm.[36] He also accompanied W.T. Cosgrave on his state visit to the USA and Canada in early 1928 and was on the train carrying Cosgrave to Ottawa that derailed due to ice on the tracks.[37] Geary was promoted to assistant editor when T.R. Harrington retired in 1931, and finally editor when Tim Quilty retired in September 1935.[38] In most respects, while the editorship had changed hands, the editorial philosophy of the newspaper remained the same – not tied to any party, but pro-Fine Gael and unswerving loyal to the Catholic church. This loyalty reached its highpoint during the Spanish civil war.

## 'A FIGHT TO THE DEATH'

In the wake of the Wall Street Crash and the resultant global depression the Spanish republic had been declared in April 1931. The republic's new constitution established freedom of speech and association, granted voting rights to women, allowed for divorce, stripped the nobility of its special legal status, allowed for the nationalization of essential public services and effectively disestablished the Catholic church. Articles 26 and 27 of the new constitution curtailed the right of the church to own property and its involvement in education. These developments were denounced by Pope Pius XI[39] and the conservative

30 Ibid.  31 II, 14 Aug. 1922.  32 The series ran on 26 & 28 Sept. and 2, 3, 5, 6, 7, 8, 9, 10, 12, 13, and 17 Oct. 1925.  33 II, 10 Oct. 1925.  34 Ibid.  35 II, 7 Sept. 1926.  36 II, 31 Oct. & 1 Nov. 1927.  37 II, 3 Jan. 1953. See also II, 1 Feb. 1928. Many US newspapers described the incident as a plot to kill Cosgrave.  38 II, 1 Sept. 1961.  39 The encycli-

party in Spain, the supporters of which were determined to protect the power and privilege they had previously enjoyed. From there, the fate of Spain was, in broad terms, a bloody civil war between a left-leaning republican government, and a right-wing military revolt led by General Franciso Franco and supported by the Catholic church. The conflict was, as the historian J. Bowyer Bell noted, whatever anyone wanted it to be; it was a war where 'Fascism fought Democracy or God met the anti-Christ or Tradition wrestled with Revolution'.[40]

For the *Independent*, the war was solely a battle between communism and catholicism. In his 1937 review of newspapers, Brown declared that, in relation to the war, the *Independent*, 'alone among the metropolitan dailies, took definitely the side of the Spanish national army against the Socialist-Communist-Anarchist combination. Alone it gave the Irish public the full facts about the persecution of the Church and the atrocities committed against priests and nuns'.[41] Browne did not refer to the coverage of the *Irish Press*, which supported de Valera's policy of non-intervention,[42] nor to that of the *Irish Times*, which viewed the conflict as a battle between 'a Fascist junta which seeks to impose a military despotism upon the country and a population which has tasted, for the first time, some of the sweets of democracy, and does not want to forego them'.[43]

For the *Independent*, however, it was not the fate of democracy or the rise of fascism but rather the fate of the Catholic church that informed its reportage and editorial policy. It carried its first report of the conflict on 20 July 1936, accompanied by a photograph of members of the Sisters of Mercy order leaving a Madrid convent.[44] Two days later, it declared where it stood on the conflict:

> It is, in fact, a fight to the death between Communism and the combined forces of the Right for control of Spain ... Either the Right will triumph and a military dictatorship will emerge and strive to bar the advance of the Bolshevistic movement which has already gained such a considerable hold upon the people of the Peninsula, or, the Left will come out victorious and open up the way for a Spanish Soviet State upon the Russian model ... All who stand for the ancient Faith and the tradition of Spain are behind the present revolt against the Marxist regime in Madrid.[45]

In the early stages of the war, the *Independent* was dependent on the services of press agencies and unverified second-hand accounts of events that were lifted from other publications. For example, under the headline 'Priests Shot, Cathedral Burned', it reproduced a story from *Petite Parisien* that described a raid by

cal 'Dilectissima Nobis' (1933) condemned the Spanish government's actions.   **40** J. Bower-Bell, 'Ireland and the Spanish civil war, 1936–39', *Studia Hibernica*, 9 (1969), 137–63 at 141.   **41** Brown, *The press in Ireland*, p. 49.   **42** *Irish Press*, 29 Aug. 1936.   **43** *Irish Times*, 19 Aug. 1926.   **44** II, 20 July 1936.   **45** II, 22 July 1936.

republican forces on the cathedral in Figueras, Catalonia. According to the report, the cathedral was defended by priests, two of whom were shot before the cathedral was burned down.[46] Similarly, under the headline 'Priests Massacred', it reproduced an interview with a French citizen who had fled Barcelona. According to the interviewee, 'during the sacking of the convents and churches, which followed the Communists' victory, several Jesuits were massacred and their heads cut off and paraded through the streets on a huge silver salver. Nuns were also mistreated, many of them being stripped by the Reds and then turned into the streets'.[47] Whatever about the veracity of these reports, the *Independent* felt compelled to outline where it stood. It criticized the 'armchair democrats' who viewed the conflict as 'nothing more than an attempted military coup by disgruntled army men against a duly elected Government of the people'. The Spanish government had, it declared, abdicated power to 'the Red Militia – the forerunners of social revolution and the would-be fulfillers of Lenin's prophecy that Europe would one day witness the birth, in blood and terror, of the Spanish Soviet Republic'. The battle lines had, it contended, been clearly drawn:

> The issue at stake in the present struggle in Spain is of infinitely more importance than a mere contest for power between two political factions. It is, in fact, a struggle to the death between Christianity and Communism. On the side of the insurgents are ranged all who stand for the Catholic and national ideals which animated the life of Spain when she was one of the greatest of European states … On the side of Senor Giral's Government there is ranged an unholy alliance of Communists, Anarchists, and anti-Christian revolutionaries of every sort and description in Spain. The Red assassination squads who slaughter defenceless nuns and priests, who loot and burn the convents and churches, who desecrate the tombs of the dead, and who destroy the property of the living – these and the mob are the upholders of the junta which we are sometimes invited to regard as the sacrosanct democratic Government of Spain.[48]

Having set out where it stood in relation to the conflict's protagonists, the *Independent* then clearly set its sights on the non-interventionist policy of the Irish government.

### 'MORE CATHOLIC THAN THE POPE'

As the month of August 1936 progressed, the newspaper became sharper in its demand that the Irish government do something. In an editorial entitled 'Red

46 II, 23 July 1936.  47 II, 24 July 1936.  48 II, 6 Aug. 1936.

Savagery in Spain' it began to use the 'Catholic card' in its call for government action:

> Thousands of defenceless priests, nuns, and Catholic citizens have been massacred all over Spain by the Red legions; churches, monasteries, and convents without number have been looted, desecrated, and burned, and fiendish indignities have been perpetrated at the very Alter steps upon those whose only crime against 'democracy' was that they were ordained priests, professed nuns, or practising members of the Catholic Church. Even the very crypts of the churches and the cemeteries attached to Religious Houses have not been safe from the barbaric attentions of the Red champions of 'Liberal democratic thought'. The bodies alike of long dead and recently interred priests, nuns, and Catholic lay folk have been torn from their tombs and exposed in the public streets of Red controlled cities, to make a Communist holiday for jeering and degenerate savages, whom we are sometimes invited to regard with sympathetic approval as the defenders of democratic rights and liberties in Spain!

It queried why the Free State had maintained diplomatic relations with the Spanish government and called on de Valera and his government to introduce a ban on Spanish and Russian goods.[49] When one Fianna Fáil TD, Hugo Flinn, declared that the Spanish conflict was 'between Fascism and Democracy' and that 'Fianna Fáil has no use for Fascism', the *Independent* expressed concern that this position reflected the government's position. It also asked why the government did not 'raise its voice to speak out the Irish people's horror and condemnation of the fiendish Red campaign'.[50] In mid-August it returned to the fray in explicit terms:

> And what an agony Catholic Spain has endured these last few terrible weeks in those areas where those sacrilegious savages of the Red Militia hold sway ... Not content with the wholesale destruction of the Houses of God throughout Spain, the Red barbarians have in many instances sacrilegiously rifled the Tabernacle on the Alters, hurled the Blessed Sacrament on the ground, and trampled upon it. They have profaned the sacred vestments of the Alter by wearing them in derision before jeering Red mobs in the public places of those cities and towns of Spain where Red Terror reigned. Could Red Barbarism masquerading as the championship of 'liberty' and 'democratic rights' against reactionary 'Fascism' go

49 II, 11 Aug. 1936.  50 II, 14 Aug. 1936.

further? Yes, there were defenceless priests and nuns to be 'hunted like
wild beasts' and butchered wherever found by the Red Legions of Madrid
... Certainly the Red levies of Madrid are carrying out with a ruthless
ferocity the dictates of Lenin, the apostle of Bolshevism, 'to fight without mercy religion and all allies of religion' ... Surely even the most
purblind 'democrat' in Western Europe must be convinced by this of
the fact that this struggle in Spain is nothing else but a battle between
Christianity and Communism in which there can be only one victor.[51]

The broad European policy of non-intervention in Spain was denounced as a
tactic 'to deny any material or moral assistance to those who are fighting
Catholic Europe's battle against Red Savagery in Spain' and it expressed the
hope 'that the Catholic Government of our Catholic land has not completely
tied its hands in face of the Spanish situation'. An acceptance of non-intervention would, the *Independent* asserted, 'not be in accord with our national traditions, or the will and desires of the Irish people, the overwhelming majority
of whom look with horror and detestation upon the criminal and anti-Christian
campaign which the Red militia is so relentlessly pursuing in Spain against
our fellow Catholics there ...'[52] Within the hierarchy, the *Independent* found an
ally in the bishop of Killaloe, Michael Fogarty, who expressed his 'warm appreciation' of the newspaper's 'uncompromising denunciation of the brutal outrages which have been going on in Spain under the aegis of the so-call legitimate
Government'. He also expressed regret that the Irish government had not
declared 'its abhorrence of the savagery of the Spanish "Reds"' and called on
the government to sever diplomatic relations with 'the communists of Madrid'.[53]

Having secured the public support of the hierarchy, the *Independent* stepped
up its campaign. 'Time and again' it noted, it had 'called on our Government to
speak out the Irish people's horror and condemnation of the Red war on Catholicism in Spain'. But the response had been 'not a word, apparently, of condemnation from Dublin of Red savagery'. The 'Catholic Government of the
Catholic Saorstat' was, it concluded, 'in a better position than any government,
perhaps, to give a lead to the world by expressing condemnation of the barbarous
Red campaign against the Catholics of Spain' but it had neglected its 'obvious
duty to do so'.[54] A few days later, it again called on de Valera's government to
'sever diplomatic relations with Madrid, and express its abhorrence of the hor-
rible deeds committed by the forces waging war on Christianity'.[55]

When the government confirmed it was adopting a policy of non-
intervention the *Independent* responded with unbridled hostility. 'In the govern-

---

51 II, 17 Aug. 1936.  52 Ibid.  53 II, 18 Aug. 1936.  54 II, 19 Aug. 1936.  55 II, 22 Aug. 1936.

ment communication', it thundered, 'the defenders of Christianity in Spain are put on the same plane as the mobs of Anarchists and Communists who are murdering Bishops, priests and nuns, who are burning churches and convents, and who do not conceal that their devilish aim is to exterminate religion from Spain'. The failure of the government 'to utter disapproval or condemnation of these ferocious destroyers of Christian civilization' would be, it asserted, 'a disappointment to the Irish people'.[56] But, determined not to let the *Independent* play the 'Catholic card' and portray de Valera as some sort of communist fellow-traveller, the *Irish Press* criticized the *Independent* for what it called its 'ill-considered and insincere criticism of the Government'. The policy of non-intervention, it asserted, was devised to prevent 'a general conflagration in Europe'. The *Independent's* call for the severance of diplomatic relations arose, the *Press* countered, 'from no nobler motive than its customary one of attempting to embarrass Mr de Valera's Ministry'. It noted that the Vatican had not gone as far as the *Independent* was urging de Valera to go and concluded that the newspaper 'when it suits its own purpose, does not hesitate to be more Catholic than the Pope'.[57]

In response, the *Independent* noted that 'the tied organ of the Government … must, as on other topics, respond to the whip of its controlling director – who is also head of the Government – and swear that the Government must be right'. It also noted that while the *Press* had finally broken its silence on the war to support government policy, it had not printed 'a single word of protest against the blasphemous and fiendish onslaught by the Reds on Christianity'. Neither, it observed, had the government 'condemned the atrocities committed by the Reds'. Why, it wondered, did de Valera's government 'have such tender regard for the Red murders and despoilers in Spain?' Describing the government's silence as 'an expression of cowardice' it noted that, apparently, 'the correct thing for the Catholics of this nation is not to say even boo to the murderers of bishops, priests and nuns, the destroyers of churches, and the exterminators of religion'. As for being 'more Catholic than the Pope', it had no problem with such a characterization: 'What the Pope has said', it declared, 'epitomizes the attitude of the *Irish Independent* and what we have written in exposure and denunciation of the detestable godless orgy by the Reds'. For expounding this position, the *Independent* would offer 'no apology to the "Irish Press" or to the other newly-found defenders of "democracy," or to the apologists and excuse-finders for the barbarities of the Red rabble of Spain, the destroyers of Christian civilization'.[58] When the *Press* accused the *Independent* of attempting 'to brand all those who refuse to share in its hysteria as enemies of the Church in

56 II, 26 Aug. 1936.   57 *Irish Press*, 28 Aug. 1936.   58 II, 29 Aug. 1936.

Spain',[59] the latter replied that it would 'leave it to the people to judge whether it is hysteria to support Catholicity and Christianity against Communism and Paganism'.[60]

In September 1936 the *Independent* began to publish accounts of the war written by seasoned war correspondent, Francis McCullagh. In an advert the newspaper declared that in his first article McCullagh would 'prove conclusively that a Communist plot engineered from Moscow aimed at the overthrow of the Constitution and the establishment of a Soviet'.[61] The article, of course, did no such thing: it simply speculated that a contact of McCullagh's may have seen reports sent to Moscow from agents in Spain.[62] In October the newspaper devoted a full page to one of McCullagh's articles, in which he criticized de Valera for not engaging in 'armed intervention' in Spain.[63] The *Irish Press* responded by pointing out that it had turned down McCullagh's offer to write for the paper because of his use of hyperbole. It also accused the *Independent* of cynically using the war as a circulation boosting exercise:

> when the *Independent* was servilely [sic] publishing the reports of English news agencies in which those whom it now describes as 'patriots' were daily held up as 'rebels' we published independent accounts showing the real origin of the rising, setting forth the outrages and excesses which compelled the Catholic population to resort to arms … It was after we had been doing this for some time, that the *Independent,* whose knowledge of foreign politics generally approaches zero, suddenly woke up to the fact that there were great Catholic interests involved … and that it was a situation which could be usefully exploited for circulation purposes.[64]

The following year the *Independent* sent it own reporter, Gertrude Gaffney, to Spain. Her first series of articles, 'In War-Torn Spain', was described by the newspaper as 'a first-hand, authentic account of conditions behind the war-fronts in Spain'.[65] A second series of articles was published in October and November 1937.[66]

When, in November 1936, Fianna Fáil's majority defeated a proposal by W.T. Cosgrave that the government recognize General Franco as leader of Spain, the *Independent* described de Valera's position as 'peculiar and deplorable'. 'Not a word', it asserted 'by the President or Government of this Christian nation

---

59 *Irish Press*, 31 Aug. 1936.   60 II, 5 Sept. 1936.   61 II, 22 Sept. 1936.   62 II, 23 Sept. 1936. Other articles by McCullagh appeared on 1, 3, 9 & 12 Dec. 1936 and 8 & 13 Jan. and 7 Apr. 1938. For more on McCullagh, see J. Horgan, 'The Irishness of Francis McCullagh' in K. Rafter (ed.), *Irish journalism before independence* (Manchester, 2011), pp 106–19. 63 II, 16 Oct. 1936.   64 *Irish Press*, 17 Oct. 1936.   65 II, 19 Feb. 1937. The series began on 22 Feb. 1937 and continued throughout Feb. and March.   66 The second series of articles was published between 25–30 Oct. and 1, 2, and 4 Nov. 1937. Gaffney's death was reported in II, 12 Dec. 1959, but no obituary was published.

has been uttered in condemnation of these Red brutalities, barbarities and blasphemies'.[67] In February 1937 the Dáil passed a Non-Intervention Act, and the *Independent* noted that while an Irishman was free to join the British army or the French foreign legion 'he will be a criminal if he attempts to join the Army that is fighting for Christ against anti-Christ in Spain'.[68] After that, interest in the Spanish war declined as wider war clouds gathered. On 11 February 1939 the Irish government finally recognized Franco as the leader of Spain. It was a case of the most fortunate, or perhaps, opportunistic, timing: Pope Pius XI had died the day before and the *Independent* was too consumed with coverage of this event to even notice de Valera's action. For two days the newspaper's editorial page was outlined in bold black borders to indicate its grief.[69] Similarly, by the time the Spanish war ended on 1 April 1939 the newspaper's attention had long switched to the looming conflict between Britain and Germany.

### TOO LONG AT THE HELM

The Spanish civil war marked the *Independent*'s highpoint of Catholic conservatism. And, while there is no definitive proof that Geary wrote the quoted editorials, according to his son, he would not have disapproved of them as they rang true of his attitude.[70] Many years later, amid the Mother and Child Crisis of 1951, Geary would maintain an unusual editorial silence when, given the newspaper's policy of supporting the church, it would have been expected to come out with all guns blazing.[71] Nonetheless, four years later, when the *Independent* celebrated its fiftieth anniversary, its editorial page was festooned with messages of goodwill from leading church figures. The cardinal archbishop of Armagh, John D'Alton, told the newspaper it could 'justly claim that during the fifty years of its existence it has maintained a high standard of journalism ... [and] ... has always endeavoured to promote the best interests of the nation'. The archbishop of Dublin, John Charles McQuaid, noted that the newspaper had been marked by its 'policy of distinctive loyalty towards the Church'. In his editorial, Geary declared the newspaper's intention 'to live up to our title, to be both Irish and independent, allied to no party, free to criticize or to help any or all as the interests of the nation may demand'.[72] One may wonder, however, how free it was to critique the power of the Catholic church in Irish society. But for all that, Geary was, no more or less than any of his contemporaries, a product of the Ireland of the times. There existed a seemingly unbreakable symbiotic relationship between church and state, and catholicism was part and

67 II, 28 Nov. 1936.  68 II, 25 Feb. 1937.  69 II, 10 & 11 Feb. 1939.  70 Interview with Paddy Geary, 8 Dec. 2011.  71 See chapter 9.  72 II, 3 Jan. 1955.

parcel of national identity, and reflected as such by the press, until the 1960s.

Geary was also cognisant of the commercial realities of producing a daily newspaper. He was reluctant to remove advertising from the front page, but when, in July 1961, the board insisted, the compromise reached was that the adverts and death notices be moved to the back page.[73] When Geary celebrated his silver jubilee as editor, he received a telegram from Cardinal Tardini, papal secretary of state, conveying the pope's 'fraternal felicitations'. He also received an autographed colour photograph of Pope John XXIII.[74] Against his own wishes, Geary retired in September 1961 and assumed the position of editorial advisor to the board of directors.[75] The following November it was announced that the pope had conferred the distinction of Knight of St Sylvester on Geary.[76] This rare distinction is awarded to lay people who are either actively involved in the life of the church or exemplify the teaching of the church in the exercise of their professional duties. He died three weeks later on 21 December 1961, his plans for a memoir unfulfilled.[77]

Frank Geary undoubtedly left an indelible mark on the *Independent*, but arguably stayed at the helm for too long. During his editorship the newspaper accepted the status quo of post-independence Catholic Ireland and the safe commercial environment that an insular society provided. It never, unlike, the *Irish Press* or the *Irish Times,* advocated social or economic change or challenged any power-bloc in Irish society, with the exception of Fianna Fáil, and only then when it could make a play for demonstrating that it was more loyal to the church than de Valera. In 1960s Ireland, as economic growth and social change accelerated, Independent Newspapers was forced to make a choice about the future of the *Irish Independent*: whether to allow it to become a socially aware and critically informed journal under the editorship of Louis McRedmond or have it continue on its commercially successful middle-of-the road conservative path. The board ultimately chose the latter option.

73 Interview with Paddy Geary, 8 Dec. 2011. See II, 3 July 1961 for Geary's explanation for the change.  74 II, 22 Dec. 1961.  75 II, 1 Sept. 1961.  76 II, 30 Nov. 1961.  77 For obituaries see II, 22 Dec. 1961, & *Irish Times*, 22 Dec. 1961.

## 8 / 'May we safely refer to the Land League?': Independent Newspapers and Emergency censorship, 1939–45

### DONAL Ó DRISCEOIL

Censorship in Ireland during the Second World War — one of the harshest regimes of its kind — had the objective of contributing to the preservation of the state and its neutrality. 'By and large', according to the minister in charge, Frank Aiken, 'we operate this censorship to keep the temperature down internally and to prevent it from rising between ourselves and other countries.'[1] As well as the neutralization of war news, coverage of Irish social, economic and political issues was severely restricted and the expression of opinions on the war, neutrality and much else of importance, contemporary and historical, was ruthlessly curtailed.[2] The Emergency, as the Second World War was known in Ireland, was a torrid time for the newspaper industry even without censorship, with newsprint shortages reducing issues to four pages and transport difficulties playing havoc with distribution. This chapter examines the relations of the three Independent titles — the *Irish Independent*, *Sunday Independent* and *Evening Herald* — with the press censor, exploring how the restrictions impacted on the papers' production and content, while highlighting some key clashes and controversies. This episode is a fascinating part of the history of the relationship between Independent Newspapers and Irish society and offers a glimpse behind the censorship curtain at the curious, secret world of Irish neutrality.

### A 'FRANK-AIKENSTEIN MONSTER': EMERGENCY CENSORSHIP IS BORN

Ireland declared its neutrality on the outbreak of war in September 1939 and the Dáil passed the Emergency Powers Act, which provided the period with its peculiar Irish moniker — the Emergency.[3] It also provided the Fianna Fáil government

---

1 Seanad Éireann Debates, vol. 24, cols. 2614–15 (4 Dec. 1940). 2 For a detailed account and analysis of wartime censorship, see D. Ó Drisceoil, *Censorship in Ireland, 1939-1945* (Cork, 1996). 3 'Is it smugness or insurgency, That makes them say "Emergency"?, I feel it lacks the urgency, Of World War Two', sings a British intelligence officer in Arthur Riordan's musical comedy *Improbable frequency*, set in wartime Dublin (A. Riordan and Bell Helicopter (2005), *Improbable frequency*, p. 11).

with a range of extraordinary and arbitrary powers, including censorship. Frank Aiken was appointed wartime minister for the co-ordination of defensive measures, and the censorship organization was created under this ad-hoc ministry – prompting one parliamentary critic to dub it a 'Frank-aikenstein monster'.[4] While all media and communications were controlled and censored, the Emergency censorship organization was directly responsible for the press and posts and telegraphs. The cinema was controlled by the existing film censor, whose remit was extended to include war-related productions, while army intelligence monitored telephones and the state broadcaster Raidió Éireann censored itself. The censorship regime was initially headed up by Joseph Connolly, a Fianna Fáil stalwart, former senator and minister, and long-time de Valera confidante, who was chair of the Office of Public Works (OPW). Connolly remained as controller of censorship until September 1941, when he returned to the OPW and was replaced by civil servant Thomas J. Coyne, who had been assistant controller. The post of chief press censor went to 1916 veteran and former *Irish Independent* journalist Michael Knightly, who had been editor of the Oireachtas debates, a post he returned to following the end of the war.

On 17 September 1939 the press received a list of censorable matters in the form of 'Directions to the Press'. These were listed under headings such as defence forces, supplies, financial, foreign military forces and 'safeguarding neutrality', the latter including anything that cast doubt on the 'the reality' of Irish neutrality or the 'wisdom or practicability of maintaining' it.[5] This created a double political protection: first, the censor would ensure that the image of Irish neutrality the government wanted to portray was maintained, and second the policy of the government in this regard was beyond question. The 'reality' of Irish neutrality was that it was, of necessity, highly compromised and Irish policy was secretly partial towards the Allies from the outset. In the absence of a military deterrent, the survival of the state and its policy was disproportionately dependant on the maintenance of internal political and socio-economic stability – to prevent hostile forces from being tempted to fish in troubled waters – together with diplomatic manoeuvring and secret co-operation with the Allies. Once the lines of censorship policy had been drawn and the organization was in place, the editors of the Independent titles joined their colleagues from the *Irish Press*, *Irish Times*, *Cork Examiner* and the *Evening Mail* at Dublin Castle on 19 September 1939, where they had a 'frank exchange of views' with Connolly, Coyne and Knightly. The newspapermen, while accepting the need for censorship, were anxious to preserve as much freedom as they could,

4 T.C. Kingsmill-Moore, Seanad Éireann Debates, vol. 28, col. 754 (27 Jan. 1944).　5 National Archives (NA)/DJ, WC, 'Directions to the Press', 17 Sept. 1939.

but were met with a stern determination from their hosts that boded ill for the future. A particular issue of concern was the censors' insistence on minimizing expression of opinion on the belligerents. 'Am I to say that there is nothing to choose between the sides?' asked Bertie Smyllie, editor of the *Irish Times*. Connolly's reply was unequivocal: 'Yes'.[6]

The task of keeping the papers in line fell to Knightly and his staff of nine press censors, based in Dublin Castle, as was the office of the controller. Coyne, Connolly and Aiken made judgement calls as issues arose and were referred to them, and effectively made policy on the hoof. Coyne was a subtle and nuanced justifier of often absurd decisions; Connolly was less concerned with the niceties of explanation and justification, telling the censors bluntly – 'in case of any doubt, cut it out.'[7] Newspapers were expected to submit before publication any matter listed in the 17 September 1939 order. The proofs were pored over by the censors and the pieces were passed, passed subject to deletions or alterations being carried out, or stopped. When newspapers published matter that came under the purview of the 'Directions to the Press' but had not been submitted, explanations were sought and reprimands and warnings given. Repeat or serious offenders were subjected to the temporary inconvenience of having to submit galley proofs of each issue in full before publication, a penalty that only the *Irish Times* had to endure for an extended period. The only one of the Independent titles to suffer this penalty was the *Irish Independent*, which had to submit in full for over three weeks in August 1940.

PRESS CENSORSHIP IN ACTION

The extent to which the censorship interfered with the daily content of newspapers is illustrated by the ban on weather reports and forecasts, which extended even to mentions of the weather in sports reports. The reason for this prohibition was the military value of meteorological information. However, while the Irish public and the Axis powers had to do without this information, the Irish Meteorological Service was supplying the British with full data for the duration of the war. The Irish, then, were being publicly impartial while simultaneously aiding the Allied war effort. This perfectly symbolized the 'double game' the government felt it necessary to play to ensure the state's survival.[8]

With regard to war coverage, the aim was to make it as objective and balanced as possible, removing as much of the propaganda slant as possible and excising any colour or embellishment, such as human interest stories, that might

6 NA/DJ, WC, 'Press Conferences', 1939.   7 Ibid.   8 The term 'double game' is used in this context by J.J. Lee, *Ireland, 1912–85: politics and society* (Cambridge, 1989), p. 244.

elicit 'unneutral' sympathy. This left war coverage in the Irish press anodyne and flat, which was exactly the objective. A major obstacle to achieving what Smyllie dubbed 'newspaper neutrality'[9] was the fact that most war news in the Irish press came from British and American news agencies such as Reuters and Associated Press. There was no Irish agency, and no Irish newspaper had its own reporters covering the war. These agencies supplied news that was censored at source and slanted in favour of the Allies. For reasons of bias or convenience, Irish papers often used the headings, introductions and captions provided, thus reproducing the propagandist slant. Neutralizing them was a major task of the censor, though, unusually, the *Irish Independent* mainly did this job itself. All three Independent titles carried war news mainly in the form of columns summarizing 'yesterday's communiqués' from all sides.

The desire to minimize what Coyne called 'war appeal' amongst the population – part of a process I have elsewhere called 'the neutralization of Irish public opinion'[10] – extended even to advertisements that referred to the war, such as 'Blitz that Cough with CHEKS' or 'Longine – The Watch that Fought in Two World Wars.' The perceived need to create a clear distance between Ireland and the war, and especially to downplay Ireland's close relationship with its belligerent nearest neighbour and the direct and indirect involvement of Irish citizens in the conflict, led to a ban on references to Irish people in the British forces, including social announcements, death notices and obituaries. Otherwise, according to the censors, it was certain that 'our papers would be plastered day in day out with pictures and announcements about the British forces'. This, it was argued, would 'mislead' opinion abroad about Irish neutrality and provoke a response at home that might lead to internal disorder.[11] (It was this fear of provoking internal conflict that was a major reason for neutrality – allying with Britain, the only realistic alternative policy, was fraught with danger, especially with renewed IRA activity.) The highlighting of the Irishness of prominent figures such as Brendan Bracken, British minister for information, and Field Marshal Montgomery was stopped. When the *Sunday Independent* submitted an article by Irish playwright Denis Johnson, a BBC war correspondent, entitled 'An Irishman Sees Desert Battle', it was stopped in full.[12] Following the onset of the 'blitz', the *Irish Independent* wanted to run a series about the air raid experiences of Irish citizens in Britain. Connolly informed its editor Frank Geary in December 1940 that 'it is not considered desirable nor in the interests of our neutrality to lay emphasis on any Irish connection with the war. The grouping

9 R.M. Smyllie, 'Unneutral neutral Éire', *Foreign Affairs*, 24 (1946), 317–26 at 324. 10 See D. Ó Drisceoil, 'Censorship as propaganda: the neutralization of Irish public opinion during the Second World War' in B. Girvin & G. Roberts (eds), *Ireland and the Second World War* (Dublin, 2000). 11 NA/DT, S12381, 'Note for Minister', Mar. 1941. 12 NA/DJ WC, 'Press Censorship Reviews: Sunday Independent'.

of isolated incidents in which Irish people are involved is liable to give a wrong impression of the extent to which Irish people are involved.'[13]

Both sides in the war controlled reports of air raids carefully, for security and propaganda purposes, attempting a balance between playing up the impact where anger at home and sympathy abroad was required, and playing it down to discourage the enemy and not create panic at home. Damage to church property was something the *Irish Independent* – with its strong Roman Catholic sensitivities – would have highlighted, as it did often in its pro-Franco coverage of the recent Spanish civil war, but was now prohibited from doing. 'Matter of this kind', Coyne informed Geary, 'can hardly fail to be propagandist in fact if not in intention.'[14] Following the stopping of a report reproduced from a Swiss newspaper about the effects of air raids on Hamburg in August 1943, *Sunday Independent* editor Hector Legge protested vociferously. Coyne, in response, accused Legge of suggesting that:

> Irish people are so deficient in imagination that unless the 't's are crossed and the 'i's dotted they may fail to realize the havoc wrought in a built up area by the dropping of several hundred tons of high explosives and remain in ignorance of the natural and probable reactions of the population of a heavily bombed city whether it be England or Germany.[15]

When the *Irish Independent* used the agency headline 'German Arms City Bombed' when reporting on a raid on Frankfurt in 1944, it was altered to read 'German City Bombed.' Coyne correctly pointed out to Geary that this was an example of how both sides tried to give the impression that they were concerned with military targets, while the enemy targeted civilians.[16] While the approach of the censor in the propaganda war zone was often reasonable, the propensity for absurdity was ever-present. For example, in March 1943, Aiken changed 'Battle of Britain' to 'the air battle over Southern England and the Channel in 1940' in a *Sunday Independent* article. When the same paper submitted a photograph the previous August with the caption 'Malta subjected to grim ordeal – A view from the air above Malta', it was altered to: 'Malta subjected to bombs – A view from the air over Malta'.[17]

The Soviet news agency used well-known literary figures like Vassily Grossman and Konstantin Siminov as war correspondents. The latter was one of the few reporters present during the siege and battle of Stalingrad, and in

---

13 Ibid., 'Irish Independent'.   14 NA/DJ, WC, No. 2, 'Irish Independent', Coyne to Geary, 16 Oct. 1943.   15 NA/DJ, WC, 'Press Censorship Reviews: Sunday Independent', Coyne to Legge, Aug. 1943.   16 NA/DJ, WC, No. 2, 'Irish Independent', Coyne to Geary, 17 Feb. 1944.   17 NA/DJ, WC, R25, 'Sunday Independent': stopped and deleted proofs, 16 Mar. 1943 & 8 Aug. 1942.

October 1942 the *Sunday Independent* submitted his report, 'The Human Picture of Stalingrad.' Aiken made extensive cuts and deletions: he changed the title to 'A Russian Picture of Stalingrad' and deleted the final two paragraphs dealing with the suffering and courage of the civilian population; 'women and children' became 'non-combatants' and the wrecked 'German bombers' became 'aeroplanes'.[18] The suffering of many others across war-torn Europe, Asia and Africa was likewise kept from the pages of the Irish press for fear of eliciting unneutral sympathy. This included the litany of German atrocities, as news gradually emerged from 1941 onwards of the murderous Holocaust. 'The publication of atrocity stories', wrote Coyne, 'whether true or false, can do this country no good and may do it much harm.'[19] The policy remained rigid as the horrors of the Nazi death camps were revealed. Even in retrospect, Aiken believed his policy was justified and that each side was 'as bad' as the other: in a 1979 interview, he stated: 'What was going on in the camps was pretty well known to us early on. But the Russians were as bad – you only have to look at what happened in Katyn forest.'[20] When the censors altered the story of the deliberate burning to death of four Irish missionary priests in Manila by the Japanese in March 1945 so that they died simply 'in the fighting at Manila', the US Minister, David Gray, wrote to the *Irish Independent* quoting an American account of the incident. The account was prohibited and replaced by: 'The telegram quoted by Mr Gray places sole responsibility for the deaths ... on the Japanese forces.' When Geary informed Gray of the change, he refused to approve publication. On 14 May 1945, three days after the lifting of censorship, the *Irish Independent* published Gray's letter in full.[21]

The zeal of the censors to fulfil their duties to the letter meant that even the pronouncements of Catholic bishops were censored, giving rise to much controversy. Being the most pious of Irish national newspapers, the Independent titles were often at the forefront of this issue. In January 1941, for example, selections from the Lenten pastoral of Bishop Patrick Morrisroe of Achonry submitted by the *Irish Independent* made reference to Germany's 'godless plans' and the persecution of the church in Poland and Germany. The article was stopped, raising a storm of protest in the Dáil. The censor argued that the *Independent* had deliberately selected only those portions of the pastoral that gave offence to Germany.[22] The following January, Bishop Daniel Coholan of Cork was censored in the *Sunday Independent* when he wrote that the 'evil' done by 'Totalitarian leaders' was inconsiderable when compared with 'the evil caused and transmitted by

---

18 Ibid., 2 Oct. 1942 and *Sunday Independent*, 4 Oct. 1942.   19 NA/DJ, WC, 'Press Censorship Monthly Reports', May 1945.   20 Quoted in R. Fisk, *In time of war* (London, 1985), p. 419.   21 Military Archives (MA)/OCC 2/150, 'Irish missionaries in the Far East' and *Irish Independent*, 14 May 1945.   22 NA/DJ, WC, 'Press Censorship Monthly Reports', Jan. 1941.

two other leaders, Martin Luther and John Calvin.' It was the reference to totalitarian leaders, not the sectarian slur, needless to say, that led to its suppression.[23]

Censorship was applied to home news also, and to matters that on first
glance could hardly be said to fall within the purview of wartime security censorship. In 1943 publicity for the memoirs of a former RIC inspector Vere
Gregory, titled *The house of Gregory*, was prohibited on the basis that reviews
would 'inevitably lead to controversy harmful of national security [by] stirring
up memories of the Black and Tan atrocities.' An outraged Frank Geary noted
that on a previous occasion he had been forbidden to publish something related
to the civil war; 'May we', he sarcastically enquired of the censor, 'safely refer
to the Land League, the Fenian period or the Insurrection of 1798, without
imperilling our neutrality in 1943 or 1944?'[24] The occasion in which the civil war
arose related to a review the *Irish Independent* had submitted in 1941 of Daniel
Binchy's *Church and state in Fascist Italy*. The censors had mutilated it, deleting
references to Binchy's dislike of fascism, the reviewer's defence of the Blueshirts
and attacks on Fianna Fáil and de Valera's civil war stance. Geary was told that
it was 'contrary to public interest' to allow a controversy along such lines to
develop 'at a time when the unity of our people was more than ever called for.'[25]
For Geary, the censor was here revealing a party-political bias towards Fianna
Fáil.

It is true that on many occasions the lines between state and government,
between the national interest and Fianna Fáil's interests, were blurred. For example, the censor stopped a letter to the *Irish Independent* from former Cumann na
nGaedheal TD Seán Milroy on the subject of the apparent contradiction
between a speech Aiken made in the Dáil in January 1941 – when he stated
that 'even if every damn ship were at the bottom of the sea, we could have twice
as high a standard of living in a few years' – and a speech in Drogheda days
later in which he bemoaned the unemployment brought about by the lack of
imported raw materials. Milroy asked whether the minister for the co-ordination of defensive measures could co-ordinate with Frank Aiken to 'find out
whether he means what he says in Dáil Éireann or what he says in Drogheda'.
The prohibition was raised in the Dáil, where James Dillon asked 'Is it treason
in this country to pull Frank Aiken's leg?'[26] Likewise, criticisms of de Valera
were censored as contrary to the national interest, and a range of Fianna Fáil
policies, neutrality first and foremost, became synonymous with the security of
the state, which made their censorship defensible.[27]

23 NA/DJ, WC, R14, 'Censorship of Irish Church Dignitaries', 11 Jan. 1942.  24 MA/OCC 2/143, Purcell (censor)
to Geary, 17 Nov. 1943 and Geary to Censorship, 18 Nov. 1943.  25 NA/DJ, WC, 'Press Censorship Reviews: Irish
Independent'.  26 Dáil Éireann Debates, vol. 82, col. 1456 (3 Apr. 1941).  27 See Ó Drisceoil, *Censorship in Ireland*,
pp 258–74.

The *Independent* submitted far less material to the censor than its competitors, Geary having decided early on that he would conform to the guidelines and directions closely. This was in line with his self-censorship policy in relation to cultural matters, and his instruction to staff not to review books that contained objectionable matter.[28] Geary was broadly supportive of the existing cultural censorship, but his policy of self-censorship during the Emergency was a pragmatic decision, based on a wish to have as little to do with the censorship authorities as possible. The censor noted at the war's end that the paper effectively did its 'own censorship … [and] did it reasonably well.'[29] The German Minister, Eduard Hempel, agreed, regarding the *Independent* as the most objective of the daily Irish newspapers with regard to war coverage, though he did express amazement at how even 'strongly Catholic papers' like it appeared to 'take the side of Russia against Germany' through its reproduction of the tone and structure, if not the exact content, of British propagandist coverage of the war in the East.[30] There was a certain amount of conflict between the censor and Geary, but less than there was with Bertie Smyllie of the *Irish Times* and, more surprisingly, William Sweetman of the *Irish Press*. The former was a constant thorn in the side of the censors, breaking the rules and pushing the limits until in December 1942 the *Irish Times* was ordered to submit each issue in full before publication, a huge inconvenience that it had to endure until the cessation of censorship in 1945. Just before the order was made, Coyne told Knightly: 'I don't want to break with him altogether. It has always been our great strength that Smyllie and Geary cannot stand each other and I don't want to force them into an unholy alliance.'[31]

Sweetman believed that chief press censor Michael Knightly's former association with the *Independent* led him to discriminate in its favour. Knightly strongly resented the accusation that he was 'activated by any motive other than the discharge of my duty to the Government' and requested that Coyne ask Aiken to raise the issue with the *Irish Press* management. The *Press*, of course, was de Valera's newspaper, and the censorship had to be careful not to show it any favouritism, especially as the Germans regarded it as the 'organ of the Government party' and expected it to be 'pledged to particular care' in its war coverage. Sweetman believed that this expectation led to reverse discrimination against his paper, and he constantly complained about anomalies that arose in the treatment of similar stories in the *Press* and *Independent*.[32] One reason for these anomalies was

28 P. Travers and B. Hourican, 'Geary, Francis (Frank) Joseph', *Dictionary of Irish biography*, http://dib.cambridge.org (accessed 24 Oct. 2011).  29 NA/DJ, WC, 'Press Censorship Reviews: Irish Independent'.  30 NA/DFA (Sec.), P 51, Memorandum, 12 Aug. 1941.  31 NA/DJ, WC, 'Press Censorship Reviews: Irish Times'.  32 Ibid., 'Irish Press',

the fact that Sweetman's paper submitted far more material than the *Independent*. There may also have been a tendency, in an effort to stave off any accusation of bias, to make doubly sure nothing objectionable appeared in the *Press*.

The *Independent*'s first serious clash with the censors occurred in August 1940 when it carried a report on the bombing of the SS *Kerry Head* by the Germans off the Cork coast, prior to the official release of the story. As Geary had just recently transgressed the censorship regulations by publishing a photograph of an Irishman in British uniform, an order to submit in full before publication was issued on 6 August. In the course of correspondence with Geary, Knightly admitted that the paper 'was generally doing the censorship quite well – quite possibly better than we would do it', and recommended that the order be lifted, which it was on 30 August.[33] There was a general improvement in relations with the paper thereafter, according to the censors, coinciding with the departure of Hector Legge as chief sub-editor. Legge felt that the censorship regime was operated in a petty and party-political manner, and, as we shall see, continued his hostility towards it when he was appointed editor of the *Sunday Independent* in August 1940.

In advance of a Seanad debate on censorship in January 1941, Geary wrote a leader headed 'Our Charges Against the Censorship', which claimed that the censors were biased against the *Irish Independent* and were exceeding their powers by demanding control over how news was presented, including headline size.[34] The leader was stopped, and Senator Frank MacDermot used parliamentary privilege to read out extracts from it during the debate. Aiken, in response, raised the notorious call by the *Irish Independent* for the execution of James Connolly: 'If the Senator had been here at a certain stage of Irish history, he would remember another leading article which the Irish people would have been glad to see stopped in 1916.' In his notes for the minister, Knightly had written that 'As long as Irishmen live, two newspaper articles will live in their memories, one the notorious article in the *London Times* gloating over the disappearance of the Celt from Ireland and the other, the article of the *Independent* calling for the blood of the 1916 leaders.'[35]

There were five separate occasions from February 1942 when the *Irish Independent* appeared without a leader due to censorship interference. The final occasion was on 14 February 1945, following the deletion of comments 'calculated to cause offence to the US and Great Britain as well as to Russia' in a piece on the Crimea Conference at Yalta and headed 'New Partition of Poland'. Coyne told Geary that 'much mischief' could be created if the *Independent*

Knightly to Coyne, 6 Mar. 1940 and Sweetman to Censorship, 9 Nov. 1943. 33 NA/DJ, WC, No. 2 'Irish Independent'. 34 Ibid., Geary to Coyne, 20 Jan. 1941. 35 Seanad Éireann Debates, vol. 25, cols. 216–17 and 241–3 (29 Jan. 1941) and MA/OCC 7/58, 'Notes for Minister', Jan. 1941.

revealed that the censor had stopped such an editorial; Geary refused to give assurances that he would not repeat the offence of revealing the actions of the censor by implication. Coyne and Aiken discussed taking the paper to court, but did not proceed.[36] Within months the war was over and the censorship disappeared as quickly as it had arrived.

### SUNDAY INDEPENDENT

Until the emergence of the *Sunday Press* in 1949, the *Sunday Independent* was Ireland's only Sunday newspaper, and was in direct competition with the many British titles that continued to circulate during the war. Though the British newspapers were compelled to tone down their war coverage and produce special Irish editions to conform to the demands of neutrality,[37] they still had far more leeway than the Irish press, which put the *Sunday Independent* in particular at an unfair disadvantage. Further cause for regular complaint from the paper arose when stories broke at the weekends and publication was delayed, often until an official statement was released. 'If we think it right to stop a story on a Saturday night', an unsympathetic Knightly informed the editor, 'and release it on a Sunday we have no alternative but to do so even if the result is to deprive the *Sunday Independent* of a story.'[38]

The *Sunday Independent*'s relations with the censor were relatively friendly under the editorship of Thomas O'Donnell, but took a turn for the worse, as mentioned earlier, when Hector Legge replaced O'Donnell in August 1940. Legge wanted the censors to extend their working hours to facilitate him on Saturday nights and began publishing censorable matter without submission in increasing quantities, while his general attitude, according to the censor, was 'hostile'. Coyne described it as 'a case of his judgement against ours and he preferred his own judgement.'[39] In general, a little more latitude was accorded to the *Sunday Independent* because of its unique position, but Legge's persistent minor transgressions led to a warning in June 1943 that the paper would be forced to submit in full if the situation continued.[40] The threat was never carried out (one reason may have been that it would have meant extending the Saturday night shift, as Legge had wanted), and the editor continued to prefer his own judgement. He accused the censorship organization of being 'very squeamish about "hurting the feelings" of the people of certain countries' (i.e., Axis states). 'Does it ever think', he asked Coyne, 'that it hurts the intelligence of its own people?'[41]

36 NA/DJ, WC, 'Press Censorship Reviews: Irish Independent'.   37 See Ó Drisceoil, *Censorship in Ireland*, pp 188–99.   38 NA/DJ, WC, 'Press Censorship Reviews: Sunday Independent', Knightly to Legge, 6 Aug. 1940.   39 Ibid., general.   40 Ibid., Knightly to Legge, 7 June 1943.   41 Ibid., Legge to Coyne, 11 Aug. 1943.

In general, the censors were relatively even-handed in their treatment of matter viewed to be critical of belligerent countries, their governments, people and political systems. The two exceptions were the latitude given to anti-partition-ist opinion, which was technically propaganda against a belligerent, and criti-cisms of the Soviet Union in the Catholic press, because of the Irish people's supposed 'natural ... antipathy towards Communism'.

Once the Soviets joined the Allied war effort in December 1941, a more benign attitude was taken towards them in unexpected quarters. A bland arti-cle in the 10 October 1943 edition of the *Sunday Independent* headed 'Dubliners Are Acquiring A Knowledge of Russian' caught the eye of Thomas Coyne. The piece referred to a visit to Ireland of a delegation of foreign press men, who had suggested that 'in a post-war world Russia was bound to play a big part politically and economically' and that a knowledge of Russian would be a huge advantage. Trinity College in Dublin began its first Russian courses in 1942, and the paper reported that many Dubliners were receiving private lessons also. 'Soviet Russia – who would believe it – is all the rage today', wrote Coyne to Legge, 'and I notice that the *Sunday Independent* is in the fashion.' He admitted that the article was largely unobjectionable, 'but I think it as well to tell you that we expect you to submit this sort of thing for censorship beforehand in future and that you will find us wholly unsympathetic to the idea of a "build-up" for any particular belligerent no matter what form it may take.'[42]

When deletions were made to a report of a speech by Northern Ireland pre-mier Basil Brooke in March 1945, Legge argued that though 'the authorities here may disagree with what Sir Basil Brooke says, censorship of his speeches raised the big question of freedom of speech and freedom of the press.' Coyne, who liked nothing better than jousting on such issues, replied that it was the very existence of censorship that raised the 'big question' of press freedom and not any specific act, and indeed settled it so long as the censorship continued, 'for, as everyone knows, the two things are wholly incompatible'.[43]

### EVENING HERALD

In contrast to its troublesome and defiant stable mates, the *Evening Herald*, for the first couple of months under long-time editor Michael Brunicardi and from late 1939 under John J. Murphy, was extremely compliant. According to the censor, the *Evening Herald* was 'the most satisfactory of the daily newspapers with which we had to deal. Except in one instance, a ready willingness to co-oper-ate was shown and relations with the staff throughout the censorship were quite

42 *Sunday Independent*, 10 Oct. 1943 and ibid., Coyne to Legge, Oct. 1943.   43 Ibid., Coyne to Legge, 12 Mar. 1945.

friendly.'[44] The 'one instance' occurred in September 1942, and related to the highly problematic IRA campaign north and south of the border. The IRA was targeted with particular ferocity by the state in this period. Its dalliance with Nazi Germany, declaration of 'war' on Britain and raid on the Irish army's magazine fort in the Phoenix Park in December 1939 provided pretext enough to repress it, but it also posed a threat through its continuing ability to mobilize republican support at times of crisis and threaten de Valera politically. Internment, military courts and executions were supplemented by a censorship clampdown aimed at denying the organization the life-blood of publicity and any suggestion of legitimacy. A complicating factor was that the Northern state was acting against armed republicans in the same manner, but for many in Fianna Fáil's support base, the IRA's activities there were legitimate because of the continuation of what was regarded as British occupation.

In August 1942 six young IRA men were sentenced to death in Northern Ireland for the killing of a policeman. De Valera supported the reprieve campaign and full publicity was allowed for it, with the exception of 'unhelpful matter' that pointed out the hypocrisy of the Irish government's position. The censor insisted that 'killing' rather than 'murder' be used in reports of the RUC man's death.[45] Five of the sentences were reprieved, and only one of the men, Tommy McWilliams, was executed, on 2 September 1942. A week later one of the most hated of the IRA's Special Branch foes, detective sergeant Dinny O'Brien, was shot dead in Dublin. The press censors were instructed to stop the word 'gunmen' and replace it with 'murderers'. The *Irish Independent* omitted the passages where this change had been made from its published reports.[46] 'Apparently', noted US Minister in Ireland David Gray, 'murder by the IRA is murder only in Éire and not when committed north of the border.'[47] The *Herald* headed its report 'Rathfarnham Shooting – Detective Killed', deliberately following the policy as applied in the McWilliams case. The censor refused to pass the report unless the newspaper described 'the crime by its proper name', i.e., 'murder'. Murphy, the editor, held firm, and preferred to go to press with no report of the shooting.[48]

## CONCLUSION

The lifting of censorship on 11 May 1945 was greeted with joy and relief in Irish press circles. While the public was aware of the existence of the censorship, little was known of how extensive and pervasive it had been. At the *Irish Times* Smyllie gorged on his new freedom, publishing a series of photographs – 'They

44 NA/DJ, WC, 'Press Censorship Reviews: Evening Herald and Evening Mail'.   45 NA/DJ, WC, No. 5, 'Evening Herald'.   46 NA/DJ, WC, 'Instructions to Press Censors', 10 and 12 Sept. 1942   47 David Gray papers, FDR Library, 'Censorship in Eire', 1942.   48 NA/DJ, WC, No. 5, 'Evening Herald'.

Can be Published Now: Pictures that were Stopped by the Censor during the War' – over the following weeks, and wrote of the many absurdities and injustices he had had to endure. Sweetman in the *Irish Press* loyally toed the party line, presumably with gritted teeth, praising the censors' 'good sense' and 'impartiality', and admitting only having to endure 'minor errors or irritations'.[49] The most honest assessment probably came from the Clonmel-based *Nationalist*, which asked readers to appreciate the 'prolonged mental torture' editors and journalists had endured and how they now felt 'at this moment of release from bondage'.[50] 'Let us rejoice!', declared Legge in the *Sunday Independent*.[51] He condemned the system's 'petty tyranny' and listed some examples of its absurdity, such as the 'daft extremes' of pretending that no Irishmen were fighting in belligerent armies, but, in general, was rather subdued. Geary raged against the 'stupid, clumsy, and unjust manner' in which censorship had been operated and claimed it had been 'frequently inspired not by national but by party political motives'.[52] And that, really, was that. There were no follow-up pieces over the coming days and weeks in any of the Independent titles, as one might have expected, demonstrating how the censorship had been 'unreasonably and unfairly exercised' and exposing the 'tyranny' that had been endured, with the exception of the David Gray letter regarding the death of Irish missionaries referred to earlier. Some of the excesses of the system were brought to light in various fora, but, for the most part, the true extent of the censorship remained hidden, and what was revealed provoked little discussion or debate.

Relief that the war and the Emergency were over at last, and a sense of pride in the survival of the state and its neutrality, enhanced by de Valera's famous reply to Churchill's attack on the policy, probably contributed to a public feeling that the end had justified the means. What Brian Farrell has called 'the thickened cobwebs of accumulated habitual suppression'[53] were doubtless a factor in blunting the critical edge of the Irish press, but the lack of attention to the recently departed censorship was primarily a result of the relieving return to 'business-as-usual' – a gradual increase in supplies of newsprint, more advertising, improved distribution, and the restoration of relative editorial freedom – that acted like a fast-acting balm on propreitorial, editorial and journalistic wounds. Besides which, the nature of the newspaper business – its competitive pressures, deadlines, and primarily present-centred dynamic – compelled editors and journalists to 'move on', which they did, leaving Emergency censorship behind like a bad dream they were loath to recall.

---

49 *Irish Press*, 12 May 1945.   50 NA/DJ, WC, No. 51, 'The Nationalist (Clonmel)'.   51 *Sunday Independent*, 13 May 1945.   52 *Irish Independent*, 12 May 1945.   53 *Irish Times*, 8 Jan. 1994.

# 9 / The politics of despair: Independent Newspapers and post-war Irish society

## GARY MURPHY

This chapter examines the reaction of Independent Newspapers to political and economic events from the end of the Second World War to the brake that was placed on Ireland's application for entry to the European Economic Community (EEC) in 1963 following the French veto of British membership. It posits the view that the orthodox historical interpretation that the *Irish Independent* was a proxy voice for Fine Gael, 'essentially a Fine Gael paper'[1] along similar lines to the *Irish Press* and Fianna Fáil, is overstated. The dismal economic conditions of post-war Ireland brought with it significant political uncertainty. The fluidity of politics during this period saw successive changes of government in the four elections between 1948 and 1957 where the voters, tired of economic privation, simply took out their frustrations on the parties in government. Momentous shifts in political thinking at both governmental and non-governmental level in the mid-1950s led eventually to the adoption of an interdependent approach to economic policy making symbolized by T.K. Whitaker's famous plan to literally rescue Ireland, *Economic Development*. Prior to this landmark approach to planning, Irish governments for the most part pursued economic policy through the dictum of keep taxation low, public spending low, and sell agricultural produce to the British market. This policy for the most part found favour in Middle Abbey Street, but no party, not even Fine Gael, could count on the *Irish Independent* to support it unconditionally in an era where buyers of the newspaper were fickle in their political choices.

### A DARK AND DISMAL LAND

Post-war Ireland was different to rest of western Europe. While the Continent was ravaged by war, Ireland, apart from the odd German bombing and an occasional explosion caused by drifting mines, suffered not a jot and, unlike the continental neutrals, the Irish were, for the most part, shielded from any sight or sound of the catastrophe that had befallen most of Europe.[2] Moreover, the Irish state did not have to face the seemingly never-ending streams of importunate

1 T. Garvin, *News from a new republic: Ireland in the 1950s* (Dublin, 2010), p. 20.   2 E. O'Halpin, *Defending Ireland: the Irish state and its enemies since 1922* (Oxford, 1999), pp 254–5.

refugees at border crossings or seaports pleading for their lives, as was the case with mainland European states. The extraordinary trading conditions engendered by the war meant that Ireland exported more than it imported, so that by the time the conflict had ended, the country had built up large reserves of sterling.[3] Judged by its external assets, Ireland was one of the wealthiest countries in the world on a population basis; judged by less theoretical measures, Ireland's wealth was a chimera. At a very basic level, judging wealth per head of population in a country with mass emigration was a poor gauge of national wealth. The emigration figure, for instance, for a neutral state was colossal, with at least 100,000 leaving Ireland for civilian employment in Britain during the war. While emigration was regarded in some quarters – including at the highest level in the department of finance – as 'a safety-valve against revolution' given that would-be malcontents (i.e., the unemployed) would be kept busy in another country, it was only towards the end of the war that these same bureaucrats began to wonder what fate would befall the country when these men and women returned from their sojourn in godless England, having imbibed the teachings of welfarism while domiciled there.[4]

In the end, however, most of these emigrants did not come home. In fact, the rate of emigration to Britain actually increased after the war. Between road and house building and the Attlee government's new national health service Britain had become a magnet for Irish men and women, many of whom had low paid, low status and irregular employment at home. In the post-war world it was accepted that the solution to emigration lay in improving the wider economic and social environment. In Ireland though, things were different. While the principle might have been accepted, what was not was the view that the government could do anything about it. In fact it seemed that no Irish post-war government could do anything about anything in macro economic terms. Even more unique, and practically alone among small European countries, Ireland seemed incapable of benefiting from the post-war reconstruction boom, in spite of having received almost $50 million in loans from the Marshall Plan.[5]

This, then, was the Ireland that Independent Newspapers operated in; a country in which a vast amount of people had either left or wanted to leave, feeling that it was a state that offered no future. The *Irish Independent* looked at this Ireland with a quizzical eye. The newspaper is often seen as nothing but the political voice of Fine Gael in this period. Tom Garvin in his 2010 study on newspapers and Ireland in the 1950s notes that while 'the *Irish Press* was obviously and explicitly the mouthpiece of Fianna Fáil and echo of Seán Lemass, theo-

3 G. Murphy, *In search of the promised land: the politics of post war Ireland* (Cork, 2009), p. 27.   4 E. Delaney, *Demography, state and society: Irish migration to Britain, 1921–1971* (Liverpool, 2000), p. 113.   5 B. Whelan, *Ireland and the Marshall Plan, 1947–57* (Dublin, 2000).

retically the *Irish Times* and *Irish Independent* were non-partisan. In reality the *Independent* was Fine Gael'.[6] The true picture is, however, slightly more complex. While the paper editorialized about the evils of Fianna Fáil and particularly of Eamon de Valera, it did not exactly spare the whip when it came to Fine Gael and proved quite critical at times of Fine Gael's first Taoiseach, John A. Costello.

### THE FIRST INTER-PARTY GOVERNMENT

At the end of the Second World War the *Irish Independent*'s circulation, at 143,000, was only 5,000 above its 1933 level. By 1949, however, this had risen to 193,000 and by 1952 to 203,000, an extraordinary rise of more than a third in only six years. This, then, was a newspaper with a significant political reach. Moreover, the *Sunday Independent* by this time had a circulation of close to 400,000.[6a] And it was to be the Sunday title that would deliver the most significant scoop in Irish political journalism to that time on 5 September 1948, under the headline: 'External Relations Act to go' (see chapter 10). The first inter-party government would eventually collapse under the weight of its own inherent contradictions and while it would formally be the price of milk that would cause its ultimate downfall this was preceded by the famous controversy over the Mother and Child scheme from which there was no way back for the government. The Mother and Child health scheme was promoted by the Clann na Poblachta minister for health, Dr Noel Browne, and devoutly opposed by both the medical profession and the Catholic hierarchy. The scheme was first broken to the public by the *Sunday Independent* on 3 September 1950. It was Browne, however, who forced the bishops into public disagreement with the government by issuing his correspondence with them.[7] Despite the fact that the hierarchy had some years earlier meekly accepted a national health service in Northern Ireland that had many of the same characteristics, they regarded the system in the new Republic of Ireland as a matter of principle. In this, like in so many other things, Ireland was different.

Given the extremely public nature of the debate it might have been expected that the *Irish Independent* would have come out unambiguously on the side of the bishops given both its robust support for Catholic causes and the fact that its editor Frank Geary was himself a devout Catholic. However, while the *Irish Independent* did give significantly more space to attacks on Browne by both politicians and clerics, it maintained a remarkable reticence about getting involved in

6 Garvin, *News from a new republic*, p. 61.   6a I am grateful to Prof. John Horgan for his assistance in locating this information.   7 The most comprehensive and balanced account of the Mother and Child scheme and its various machinations is to be found in J. Horgan, *Noel Browne: passionate outsider* (Dublin, 2002).

the conflict editorially. While this might well have betrayed its Fine Gael lean-
ings, and its unwillingness to further destabilize a government that was already
falling apart at the seams, there was another factor of which neither its readers
in general nor the Catholic hierarchy would have been aware. This was that, as
Browne's biographer John Horgan points out, the embattled minister, had as a
child, through an extraordinary combination of circumstances, been informally
adopted by the wealthy Chance medical family, who were not only allied to
the Murphys of the Independent Group by marriage but were now substantial
shareholders in, and represented on the board of, Independent Newspapers.[8]
We can only speculate as to the editorial silence emanating from Middle Abbey
Street over an issue that was convulsing the nation in 1951, but there clearly were
different agendas at play throughout the whole episode; one of which was
that the Chance family could see to it that, if nothing else, Browne would not
be publicly traduced in the pages of the *Irish Independent*.[9]

## A NATIONAL GOVERNMENT FOR IRELAND

The election that followed the inevitable fall of the government in May 1951
saw the *Irish Independent* enter the fray with a call for a national government. In
the run-up to the election, it advocated an all-party government that would
include Fianna Fáil. This is certainly not a typical Blueshirt political organ. 'The
best brains for governing the country and guiding it through the difficult years
ahead are not to be found in any one party'[10] the paper noted, while two days
later it advocated 'a government representing all parties because in our opinion Fianna Fáil should have agreed to participate with the other parties in 1948
and should agree to do so now.'[11] In the immediate aftermath of the election, at
which Fianna Fáil failed to secure an overall majority, it interpreted the result
as a 'mandate for an all-party government'.[12] The *Irish Independent*'s electoral viewpoint can if anything be seen as anti-Fianna Fáil as distinct from simply pro-
Fine Gael. And even this stance was somewhat nuanced. For Geary, the role of
public watchdog was one the *Independent* had no option but to fill considering
that as early as 1938 the *Irish Times* was beginning to befriend de Valera and
Fianna Fáil.

But the *Irish Independent*'s habitual pre-poll hostility to Fianna Fáil and de
Valera was only infrequently one of outright opposition. One editorial, on the
eve of the 1944 election, suggests a patent desire on the part of Geary, who
would have known many of the civil war protagonists personally, not for the

8 Horgan, *Noel Browne*, p. 153. 9 Ibid. 10 *Irish Independent*, 24 May 1951. 11 Ibid., 26 May 1951. 12 Ibid., 6 June 1951.

defeat of Fianna Fáil as such, but for a healing of the deep divide in Irish society that the civil war had engineered. Although the greater part of the editorial was taken up with a trenchant response to a speech by de Valera in which he had accused the *Irish Independent* of carrying on a 'vendetta' against him, it concluded in what were, given the temper of the times, unusually placatory tones. De Valera, Geary wrote, had travelled far since he evoked a spirit of national unity in response to the conscription crisis of 1918:

> Now he seems determined to perpetuate party divisions at a time when every call of good sense and patriotism urges the wisdom of a united national front to meet the future. We still believe that this nation is greater than any leader or any party. We still believe that the unity which defeated conscription in 1918, and which gave the people such confidence when this war began, is the unity upon which the people should insist on Tuesday next.[13]

A decade later at the 1954 election the newspaper was harping on the same theme noting that 'one-party rule has not solved the nation's problems; it has kept alive old feuds and personal spleens.'[14] It is certainly noteworthy, however, that the *Irish Independent*'s calls for Fianna Fáil participation in an all-party government tended to be loudest when the outgoing inter-party government appeared to be on the ropes.[15] This could be seen as a tactic designed to ensure the continuance in government of Fine Gael, or even as an outgrowth of a certain type of corporatism, involving not only interest groups but political parties as well, but it is certainly not the voice of the civil war victors. Indeed, in his verdict on the 1957 election, at which Fianna Fáil defeated the Fine Gael-led inter-party administration, Geary noted severely that in some respects the verdict on Costello was a fitting one:

> In our view it was a negative but very effective way of showing their dissatisfaction with the conduct of national affairs in the last three years. On numerous occasions this newspaper has warned the ministers that their administration was extravagant, that public expenditure was excessive, and that the people were being asked to maintain a welfare state that we cannot afford. The ministers did not heed our warnings and they have paid the price.[16]

Although Geary retired in September 1961, the editorial line in the general election of the following month was almost a replica of the one he had adopted

---

13 Ibid., 24 May 1944. 14 Ibid., 17 May 1954. 15 Ibid., and 27 Feb. & 4 Mar. 1957. 16 Ibid., 8 Mar. 1957.

in earlier years: if anything, it was even more middle-of-the-road. All party leaders were invited to contribute articles to the newspaper, and did so: a similar
facility, for instance, would not be accorded by the *Irish Press*.[17] On the day before
the poll, it expressed the hope that the result, 'whatever it may be, will be such
as to dispose of any suggestion that it is inconclusive or incomplete'.[18] As the
result of the election became clear – Fianna Fáil was four seats short of an overall majority – it argued strongly that the politicians should accept the intelligence and wisdom they professed to discern in the electorate, and 'get together
in the united fashion that the public has so manifestly demanded.'[19]

Five days later, as Lemass formed his first post-election government with
the support of a number of independents, the new *Irish Independent* editor, Michael
Rooney, while lamenting the missed opportunity to respond to the electorate's
wish for a national government 'with representatives of at least the three major
parties in the Dáil', advocated that the decision, now made, should be 'loyally
accepted on all sides'.[20] The *Irish Independent* never went as far as the *Irish Times* in
calling for a merger of Fianna Fáil and Fine Gael as that paper did during the
election of 1957[21] but what can be observed for the *Irish Independent* over the post-
war period, is a move away from simply criticizing Fianna Fáil on the grounds
that it was going to repudiate the Treaty or introduce forced agricultural collec-
tivization, and a concentration on issues that traditionally exercised the minds of
the newspaper's directors, shareholders and readers: high levels of taxation, government extravagance in both social and capital spending and the burden of hard
pressed rate-payers. Indeed, it was as critical of the first inter-party government's
social welfare legislation on the familiar grounds that the country could not
afford it as it was of any of Fianna Fail's policies.[22] In that context the *Irish
Independent* was a steadfast defender of the emergent professional middle class and
a bitter foe of what it saw as the redistribution of income from that middle class
to the working class and farming community.[23]

## TAXATION AND EXTRAVAGANCE:
## IRISH ECONOMIC DEVELOPMENT

The publication of T.K. Whitaker's *Economic Development* accompanied by a government white paper on economic expansion would eventually lead the way to
Ireland engaging with the twin precepts of opening up its economy to foreign
trade and applying to join a European trading bloc. Its most critical feature was

---

17 Murphy, *Promised land*, p. 162.  18 *Irish Independent*, 3 Oct. 1961.  19 Ibid., 7 Oct. 1961.  20 Ibid., 12 Oct. 1961.  21
*Irish Times*, 8 Mar. 1957.  22 *Irish Independent*, 26 Oct. 1949 & 11 Dec. 1950.  23 Garvin, *News from a new republic*, p. 20.

its premise to shift from protection towards free trade and from discouragement to encouragement of foreign investment in Ireland. This involved a dramatic reversal of the rhetoric, and to a large extent of the practice of all policy, but especially Fianna Fáil policy, since 1932. Whitaker argued that the government should encourage industries that would be competitive in world markets and provide a continuing source of employment at home:

> we can no longer rely for industrial development on extensive tariff and quota protection. Foreign industrialists will bring skills and techniques we need, and continuous and widespread publicity abroad is essential to attract them. If foreign industrial investment does not rapidly increase, a more radical removal of statutory restrictions on such investments should take place.[24]

The main theme of both documents was that an increase in investment and an expansion in demand, coming from agriculture, would set in motion a general expansion in the national product. In conjunction with this was the aim of attracting foreign industry. Whitaker outlined two ways to attract foreign corporations: removing restrictions and giving incentives for foreign firms to establish bases in Ireland. The Control of Manufactures Act was amended and a series of proposals intended to attract outside investors to Ireland was recommended. He proposed that the IDA should expand its staff, particularly in North America, in an intensification of its efforts to attract foreign capital.

All this, however, left the *Irish Independent*, and the rest of the newspaper media, rather underwhelmed: when *Economic Development* was published in November 1958 it was to the less than stunning plaudits that it would subsequently enjoy. The *Irish Independent* pretty much ignored the issue of foreign direct investment and found much to criticize in the document, not least its apparent ignorance of the principle at the core of the newspaper's economic philosophy – that of reducing taxation:

> The best incentive that could be given to economic expansion would be to reduce taxation so that everybody could again have a prospect of saving. The White Paper has some merits: its insistence on exports and efficiency is not the least of them. But it stultifies itself by covering too wide a field. Greater progress would be made and a smaller strain placed on the taxpayer if priority were given to those forms of production, such as agriculture, from which the prospects of an early return are most promising.[25]

24 T.K. Whitaker, *Economic development* (Dublin, 1958), p. 218.   25 *Irish Independent*, 15 Nov. 1958.

This seemed to miss the rather important point that the Irish state itself was teetering on the brink of existence, unable to keep its people at home, while those who lived at home did so in living standards markedly inferior to that of the rest of western Europe.

But excessive levels of taxation had long been a bugbear of the *Irish Independent*. After Seán MacEntee's famous hairshirt budget in April 1952, an editorial entitled 'Everybody in the casualty list' had argued that it was as if the government had 'looked around to see how it could strike the hardest blow at every section of the community', and that MacEntee's stated policy of 'redistributing the national income' appeared to take the form of 'having the citizens earn the money and the Government spend it'. Geary then launched into an attack on Fianna Fáil that has resonance for those who believe that Fianna Fáil has long mastered the art of saying one thing in opposition and doing the complete opposite in power:

> However, Fianna Fáil has been consistent in one thing. Once again the party has shown with what agility it can betray those who put it in power. Less than a year ago the present ministers denounced at every crossroads a scale of taxation that was mild in comparison with that now imposed. What the consequences of this budget will be on employment and industrial enterprise it is disturbing to imagine.[26]

While this editorial response was certainly milder than some other media attacks on MacEntee's budget (most notably the editorial in the *Irish Times* entitled *Dies Irae* or 'days of wrath', which suggested that the budget would quickly spawn a general election),[27] it is instructive in showing the *Irish Independent's* obsession with taxation as the cause of all evils in the Irish economy. It would return to this theme regularly throughout the dismal 1950s. An editorial entitled 'Taxation and Extravagance' in January 1954 sums up the newspaper's view that taxation was a penal crime against the Irish people that only benefitted those who were out of work:

> The industrious citizen, be he shopkeeper, farmer, professional man or manufacturer is sadly aware that the income tax is part of a penal code under which his punishment grows the heavier with every effort that brings him a greater return. Only the ne'er-do-wells and the never-works are unconcerned; under the welfare state they will be provided for by those who work and who are therefore taxed and punished for their industry.[28]

26 Ibid., 3 Apr. 1952. 27 *Irish Times*, 3 Apr. 1952. See also T. Feeney, *Seán MacEntee: a political life* (Dublin, 2009), p. 188. 28 *Irish Independent*, 21 Jan. 1954.

The unemployed and social welfare recipients could expect no support from the *Irish Independent*. This had always been its approach. The commitment to economic planning that was the hallmark of *Economic Development* would not be welcomed by the *Irish Independent* when the principal cause of Ireland's woes, its extreme levels of taxation, were not addressed.

## STANDING UP FOR THE PEOPLE

The late 1950s saw the Irish state adopt a proto-corporatist western European-style democracy where the main interest groups, farmers, employers and unions, were effectively co-opted into the economic governance of the state and planning, at least in terms of reaching targets, was introduced.[29] The *Irish Independent* was somewhat sceptical of this approach but it did finally accept by the turn of the decade that Ireland's industrial development would have to be given priority over agriculture in both government policy and economic leadership; it finally went to Canossa as Tom Garvin most eloquently puts it.[30] There were, however, still many political targets for the *Irish Independent* to cast its beady eye at. Eamon de Valera, long the bugbear of those in charge of the newspaper, resigned as Taoiseach to take up the position as president in 1959 following his election in June of that year. The presidential election that saw de Valera comfortably defeat the Fine Gael candidate General Seán MacEoin was held on the same day as a proposal to effect a change in the voting system by ditching proportional representation via the single transferrable vote for the much simpler first past the post system.

The *Irish Independent* was having none of it, however, and saw the proposal as nothing but the worst kind of political opportunism by Fianna Fáil. In a coruscating editorial two days before the referendum the newspaper turned its guns squarely on the new Taoiseach to be, Seán Lemass, wryly noting that when Lemass announced:

> that when Proportional Representation is abolished Labour should hope to be much more strongly represented, one passes over for the moment the ludicrous implication that Mr Lemass, of all people, is concerned about Labour. But one is entitled surely to ask under which thimble is the Fianna Fáil pea.

This was in reference to the view voiced by pretty much all Fianna Fáil supporters that the change to the electoral system would be much fairer to all polit-

29 See Murphy, *Promised land*, for a further elucidation of this theme.   30 Garvin, *News from a new republic*, p. 68.

ical parties and to the electorate itself who would now be able to understand the system of voting:

> That is what the Fianna Fáil spokesmen call 'simple, fair, democratic'. It is clearly neither fair, nor democratic; it is simple only in the sense that it is simple downright dishonest politics. The people should stand firmly by the method that gives fair play to minorities. They do not want to prepare a way for the totalitarian one party state.[31]

The people, in their wisdom, accepted this view and narrowly rejected the proposed change by just over 30,000 votes with 51.8 per cent voting to keep the status quo. Notwithstanding its dire warnings of perpetual Fianna Fáil government the *Irish Independent* waved de Valera off to the park with a delicate warning that his new role was in effect ceremonial and that he should let Lemass get on with the job of governing. It then offered an olive branch to Lemass: 'We wish him and his colleagues well: may their efforts to promote the prosperity and the well-being of the country be rewarded with success.'[32] A public rather weary of politicians, given the dire state of the country at the end of the decade, was then rather amazingly urged by the newspaper to show an appreciation of the hard work that cabinet responsibility entailed. With a broader appreciation of the magnitude of their task the newspaper asserted, 'the burden of ministers can be lightened and public life can be sweetened. They are entitled to this consideration.'[33] A new political era had clearly dawned.

It was to be an era where Irish membership of a trading bloc, more specifically the EEC, began to take centre stage in political life. The prospect of Irish involvement in European economic integration was not an explicit feature of either *Economic Development* or of the government's *First Programme for Economic Expansion*. Yet both documents did recognize that the country would have to engage substantially more with western Europe at least in trade terms if it was to prosper economically. Most policy makers, though somewhat committed to change, continued to believe that for the immediate future the country's economic prospects rested on access to British markets. Nor did the accession of Lemass to Taoiseach mark a completely radical departure in this respect. A distinction was drawn between the movement to free trade and a decision to join any multilateral organization. The former policy was adopted towards the end of the 1950s, but the latter was avoided until July 1961. Throughout 1960 and into 1961 Lemass reiterated the view that it was not to Ireland's advantage to join either the EEC or the European Free Trade Association. While examining

---

31 *Irish Independent*, 15 June 1959.   32 Ibid., 26 June 1959.   33 Ibid.

the options, the conclusion drawn was that Ireland's economic development would not be significantly improved by membership of any multilateral group. This all changed dramatically once the Irish government became aware in July 1961 that the British were ready to apply. It quickly prepared its application and forwarded it to Brussels to anticipate the British application. This was for public consumption in order to claim that the Irish decision was not a consequence of British pressure or example.[34] While such behaviour might be considered somewhat bizarre, the application itself made sense because Ireland could not afford to be outside the community if Britain was a member. Lemass admitted that the application was inevitable once Britain had decided to apply. He told *The Economist* in February 1962:

> It was Britain's decision to apply for membership that opened the way for our own application. The predominant position of British trade on our economy, as a market for our exports, and the special character of the trading arrangements between the two countries, made it difficult to contemplate membership unless Britain were also to become a member.[35]

While Lemass was primarily concerned about the economic implications of membership, he did realize that there were political ramifications as well. He told the secretary of his department that he considered it 'essential to the success of Ireland's application to include in the draft statement a declaration of Ireland's attitude to the political aims of the Community'.[36] He outlined this publically in a speech in Brussels on 18 March 1962 where he stated baldly: 'I desire to emphasize that the political aims of the Community are aims to which the Irish Government and people are ready to subscribe and in the realization of which they wish to play an active part'. The *Irish Independent* was not so sure:

> As far as the people are concerned this is hardly the truth. How many people in the country have any inkling what the political aims of the EEC are? How much has the Government done to enlighten us in any detail? From the economic point of view it is fair to say that the sentiment of the country is in favour of the Common Market. That will obviously have political effects in the sense that many economic decisions will be taken out of the hands of the legislature. But that is only accepting legally what is to a large extent already happening in fact. Defence treaties and a common policy towards the Afro Asian world are other

34 D. Keogh, *Ireland and Europe, 1919–1989: a diplomatic and political history* (Cork, 1990), pp 232–3.  35 *The Economist*, 9 Feb. 1962.  36 National Archives; NA/T: S.16877X/62, Lemass to N.G. O'Nuaillain, secretary, department of the Taoiseach, 1 Jan. 1962.

matters however. Perhaps the people will come around to Mr Lemass'
line but it is essential that the full implications of that line are put before
them. The foreign and defence policies which the people have supported
deserve better than to be dumped without ceremony. Europe will respect
us more if we enter with a point of view than if, to quote a celebrated
phrase, we go in with our hands up.[37]

The newspaper's point about the public's awareness of the political aims of the
EEC was very well made. Only the previous week the *Sunday Independent* had
claimed that the cabinet itself was split on that very same issue.[38] More problematic was that the EEC itself, not to mention its political aims, had made
very little imprint on the public consciousness. When, in July 1961, just before
the government applied for membership, the *Irish Press* asked 943 people if they
had *heard* of the Common Market, 36 percent of those polled said they had a
'vague idea' of it while the same percentage said they had 'never heard of it'.[39]
Even if the survey was not conducted under rigorous scientific methods, the
fact that a clear majority expressed either a complete or general lack of knowledge of the nature of the EEC, let alone what membership of the communities would mean for Ireland, hardly gave succour to Lemass' belief that the Irish
people were fully in support of the EEC's political aims.[40]

CONCLUSION

Frank Geary's retirement as editor of the *Irish Independent* in September 1961
marked the end of an era. He had been editor since 1935 and was in a prime
position to comment on the calamitous decade that was the 1950s. But under
his editorship the paper would, if anything, become even more conservative than
in its formative years as it enunciated strict conservative values and offered only
low taxation and low public spending as the way out of the quagmire in which
the Irish people found themselves in the dismal decade that was Ireland in the
1950s. The newspaper was no Fine Gael lackey in this period and did live up to
its premise of being 'allied to no party, free to criticize'.[41] It did not, however,
use its significant voice to serve the Irish people by offering realistic solutions
to the problems that threatened to sink the Irish state. In that it missed a sin-
gular opportunity to make a difference to a state that looked like it had nowhere
to go.

37 *Irish Independent*, 19 Jan. 1962.   38 *Sunday Independent*, 11 Feb. 1962.   39 *Irish Press*, 12 July 1961.   40 G. Murphy, & N.
Puirséil, 'Is it a new allowance? Irish entry to the EEC and popular opinion', *Irish Political Studies*, 23:4 (2008) 533–53
at 536.   41 *Irish Independent*, 3 Jan. 1955.

# 10 / A tale of 'womanly intuition': Hector Legge at the *Sunday Independent*, 1940–70

KEVIN RAFTER

The *Sunday Independent* has with some justification acquired the reputation as Ireland's most controversial newspaper although equally it remains the most successful publication in the national newspaper market. In more recent times the newspaper has had to withstand criticism over its editorial stances ranging from coverage of John Hume's role in the Northern Ireland peace process, to support for Bertie Ahern during his tenure as leader of Fianna Fáil. Even the fall-out from the murder of crime correspondent Veronica Guerin in June 1996 – and claims of a 'cult of personality and cynical controversialism'[1] – did not prevent the newspaper maintaining its dominant position. Weekly sales in 2011 reached over 250,000 copies – almost 25 per cent of the Sunday newspaper market. The foundations of this editorial and commercial success were laid in an earlier period during the editorship of Hector Legge. During his thirty-year tenure Legge defined the broad parameters of the weekly publication from Independent House. Yet, remarkably, given Legge's pivotal role in establishing the *Sunday Independent* as a modern mid-market national newspaper, little attention has been paid to this period in the history of the newspaper. This chapter sets out to present a fuller biographical profile of this longstanding editor. In doing so, the chapter presents new evidence not just on Legge's editorial style and approach to journalism but also offers new evidence on what was one of the greatest exclusives in twentieth century Irish journalism.

## WHO WAS HECTOR LEGGE?

Hector Legge was born on 9 January 1901 in the Curragh, Co. Kildare. He was one of four children – their father was a bombardier in the Royal Horse Artillery at the Curragh; their mother was a teacher who encouraged reading and study. In his teenage years alongside day studies Legge also took night

I would like to acknowledge the assistance of Independent News and Media in researching this chapter and, in particular, the generous help of Peter Legge in providing access to his late father's papers and to David McCullagh for sharing research material on the first inter-party government.   1 See E. O'Reilly, *Veronica Guerin: the life and death of a crime reporter* (London, 1998).

classes at the vocational school in Naas including introductory courses in book-
keeping and shorthand. The college principal A.J. Smyth recorded that Legge
had made 'very good' progress and had shorthand at a rate of sixty words per
minute along with the ability to transcribe the same accurately into longhand.
In late 1919 Legge secured a teaching position at the Christian Brothers sec-
ondary school in Monasterevan, Co. Kildare, but after six months decided
that his future lay beyond the classroom. He subsequently worked as a clerk
with D.E. Williams, a wholesale and retail company, in Tullamore, Co. Offaly.
It was in Tullamore – by a curious route – that Legge's knowledge of shorthand
brought him into the world of newspapers. The national mood at that time was
defined by insurrection. British rule in Ireland was being challenged – politically by Sinn Féin and militarily by the Irish Republican Army – and Legge was
drawn to the nationalist cause:

> At that time [1920] the War of Independence was quickening. Members
> of the R.I.C. were looked upon as enemies, as agents of the British
> oppressors. Some of them were shot. It was obvious that the men of the
> D.E. Williams staff were changing from their normal after-hours relax-
> ation and leisure habits.[2]

Legge joined a local republican brigade and with his work colleagues would cycle
to isolated rural areas for training: 'There we would go through some drilling –
all good soldiers have drilling! – and get practice in the use of firearms – rifles
and revolvers. I was now a member of the I.R.A.! However, I was never to fire a
shot in anger.'[3] Two local journalists, whom Legge befriend in the town's commercial club where billiards was played to pass the time, asked if he would do
some reports for them on evening time meetings and functions. 'Probably they
had engagements to meet their girl friends on those occasions,' Legge surmised.[4]
The journalists subsequently brought a job notice to his attention. The *Catholic
Herald* newspaper in Manchester had a vacancy for a junior reporter. The editor,
Michael J. O'Neill was a native of Monasterevan – a point of discussion when
Legge attended for interview in November 1920. O'Neill, who was coming close
to retirement, had learned his journalistic trade during the Parnell era working
with the *Leinster Leader* and the *Carlow Nationalist*. Now in Manchester the veteran
editor helped Legge find his own way as a reporter:

> I used to spend part of the week visiting Catholic priests in the many
> town throughout Lancashire – Bolton, Preston, Rochdale, St. Helens,

2 Notes for draft memoir (unpublished), p. 4, Hector Legge (HL) papers.   3 Notes for draft memoir (unpublished), p. 5, HL papers.   4 Ibid., p. 3, HL papers.

Salford, Pendelbury, Wigan – picking up news on parish activities. The back-end of the week would find me in the office doing sub-editing, or subbing as journalists call it. It was very good training for a beginner.[5]

Legge was obviously well regarded. Not long after his appointment he secured a pay increase. He also supplemented his income by filing stories for the *Manchester Guardian*, 'I had become a kind of Catholic Affairs correspondent'.[6] When the opportunity came to return to Ireland O'Neill sought to persuade his young reporter to remain by offering his own job as editor. Legge declined and instead joined the staff of the *Irish Independent* as a junior sub-editor in 1922 – the start of a forty-eight year relationship with Independent Newspapers.

T.R. Harrington, who had edited the newspaper since 1905, interviewed Legge for the vacant position. Legge later recalled of Harrington: 'He had no outside interests. The *Irish Independent* was given all his time. He rarely laughed or even smiled.'[7] During the war of independence the IRA raided the newspaper offices and smashed up machinery; during the civil war Harrington's life was threatened and he lived in Independent House for a period. The energetic editor did not, however, appear too distracted from his role as Legge observed:

> Land mine explosions were common. [One] night we all heard a very heavy explosion. Unless you were deaf you would have heard it. Shortly afterwards, Harrington took a phone call in the sub-editors room. We heard him say: 'Yes, they tell me there was a big explosion but I was very busy and I did not hear it.' We all laughed when he left the room.[8]

By the time Harrington retired as editor in August 1931 Legge had been promoted to deputy chief sub-editor at the *Irish Independent*. Harrington retained a seat on the board of Independent Newspapers and although no longer editing the national morning title he sent regular notes to Legge pointing out spelling and grammatical errors that had slipped through the subbing process. In an appropriate piece of journalistic symmetry half a century later Legge would himself send similar missives to his own successors in the editorial chair at the *Sunday Independent*.

Legge was a commanding figure and, with an outgoing and opinionated personality, he demanded – and secured – attention. He was a keen sportsman – playing a variety of sports including rugby and Gaelic games but he had a particular interest in hockey and golf. During the 1920s and 1930s success on the hockey field with Monkstown brought four Leinster Cup medals and a

5 Ibid., p. 7, HL papers.   6 Ibid., p. 7, HL papers.   7 Ibid., p. 10, HL papers.   8 Ibid., p. 10, HL papers.

Leinster league title. Between balancing these sporting interests and family life[9] Legge was promoted to chief sub-editor. He was a demanding boss. His personal papers contain a number of notes sent to his colleagues enquiring why stories had been missed or had appeared in rival newspapers before the pages of the *Irish Independent*. This toughness with colleagues was a hallmark of his tenure as editor. For example, in May 1948 a sub-editor who was found asleep at his desk was told to 'clear out his desk' and when he turned up for work as normal the following week the unfortunate fellow was met by hostility from his editor: 'I bawl[ed] him out' and [told him to] 'go away and stay away'.

Throughout the 1930s Legge was also writing news reports and had secured a regular by-lined column that treated subjects with a brashness that would have found a comfortable home in later manifestations of the *Sunday Independent*. For example, on 27 July 1939, Legge's column – a recollection of a conversation with friends over dinner – was headlined: 'How to recognize the perfect wife'.[10] Legge's career progression was steady and upwards. In August 1940, eighteen years after he first arrived in Independent House, he was appointed editor of the *Sunday Independent*. He also edited the *Irish Weekly Independent* – a Thursday publication that was aimed at famers attending weekly marts and emigrants seeking a summary of news from home. Legge continued in this dual role until the weekly met its demise in 1960.

The first issue of the *Sunday Independent* had appeared on 10 December 1905. The newly formed Independent Newspapers was now publishing four newspapers – the *Irish Independent*, the *Evening Herald*, the *Irish Weekly Independent* and the *Sunday Independent*. The latest addition to the Murphy stable was the only Irish-published Sunday newspaper. The development of this new market met some initial public and commercial scepticism. Attachment to the idea of Sunday as a day of worship and rest was declining but had still not totally disappeared. William Martin Murphy, the proprietor, sought to win over advertisers with the offer of placing adverts in both weekly newspapers at a single charge.[11] There was also a clever marketing campaign setting readers the challenge of locating the 'Missing Man' with a £20 prize for the reader who identified and approached the man described as 'Mr Baffler'. The competition ran for three weeks before the 'Missing Man' was eventually identified in Co. Donegal. The new venture had solid circulation growth. Certified weekly sales for the *Sunday Independent* in 1909 were 21,391 but within a year had climbed to 56,727 copies. While without a direct domestic rival until the arrival of the *Sunday Press* in 1949, the Murphy Sunday newspaper still faced competition from titles imported

---

9 Hector Legge and his wife Thelma had two sons, Peter and Simon.   10 *Irish Independent*, 27 July 1939.   11 I am grateful to Professor John Horgan for drawing my attention to this information.

from the United Kingdom – the *News of the World* and the *Sporting Times* report-
edly had a combined Irish circulation of 250,000 in 1926.[12]

By the time Legge was appointed editor in August 1940 wartime rationing
of newsprint meant he was overseeing a publication that consisted of a double
sheet of paper. The lack of space did not stop the new editor battling strongly
with the wartime censor (as recounted in chapter 8). In the post-war period
Legge built a hugely successful newspaper subsequently defined as 'a lively and
serious broadsheet with the biggest circulation in Ireland of any national newspaper.'[13] In many respects Legge's longevity as editor – in contrast to the more
frequent changes at the Press Group – can be explained by his outlook coinciding with those of the proprietors at Independent House. Legge was a devout
Catholic – a regular mass-goer and a frequent confession goer – who had been
educated by the Christian Brothers and who held the order in high esteem. He
was also distinctly Fine Gael-leaning in his politics, and was personally close to
a number of leading party figures, in particular, James Dillon, a fact which, as
discussed below, was significant in the publication of the controversial exclusive story about Ireland's declaration as a republic in 1948.

The Legge-Dillon friendship went beyond politics and was long lasting and
lifelong.[14] Legge's wife Thelma had introduced Dillon to his future wife Maura
while on holidays in the west of Ireland in 1942.[15] The two couples had almost
daily contact, enjoyed overlapping social diaries in Dublin and holidayed
together. For example, in October 1945 Legge wrote a diary entry: 'at our place,
James and his future in politics', while in April 1947 he recorded 'had long
chat on the political situation' with Dillon, who was throughout this period
an independent TD having parted with Fine Gael in 1942 over Ireland's wartime
neutrality.[16] Discussion of political events continued after Dillon was appointed
minister for agriculture in February 1948. For example, on 27 September 1949
Legge wrote: 'I met J.D. in the Shelbourne + had a chat – men, women, world
affairs.' News that Dillon was rejoining Fine Gael was exclusively reported by
Legge in the *Sunday Independent* on 11 May 1952 while Dillon's decision to resign
as party president (a position he attained in 1960) was noted as a 'Bombshell'
in a diary entry on 21 April 1965. Indeed, such was the closeness of the relationship that Legge recorded calling to the Dillon house at 11.15pm on the
evening of the resignation: 'sat on their bed till 120'c. Maura all worked up.
Spent nearly an hour in front of the mirror trying to put in hair clips. James
sat on a stool at the end of the bed. He had collar + tie off. He put [his] coat
back on when I called.'

12 Committee on Evil Literature, Minutes of Evidence, p. 8. National Archives of Ireland.   13 *Irish Times*, 11 Nov.
1994.   14 Information supplied by Peter Legge, 17 Sept. 2011.   15 M. Manning, *James Dillon* (Dublin, 1999), pp 178–
82.   16 All diary entries are from Hector Legge's diaries; 1946, 1948, 1949, 1952 & 1965.

The Murphys would have been content for Legge to produce a commercially successful newspaper that was Fine Gael-leaning and also sympathetic to the Catholic church. The *Sunday Independent* was not, however, a partisan party-organ like its equivalent at Burgh Quay and Legge cultivated sources well beyond these two constituencies including in Fianna Fáil where Seán Lemass has been credited as a source for leaked stories.[17] In the late 1950s and 1960s he enjoyed the company of many of the new generation of ministers who emerged in Fianna Fáil and who were obviously good sources of information.

During the 1940s and 1950s under Legge's editorship the *Sunday Independent* was socially conservative – like Irish society at large – and there was serious regard for the position of the Catholic Church in Irish life. The bishops held great sway and they were quick to write to the newspapers with their complaints – sometimes directly to the editor but more often than not to the chairman of the board. The outcome was, however, not always to their liking. For example, in May 1955 the *Sunday Independent* published a photograph of seven female members of the Cork Ballet Group who were in rehearsal for a forthcoming production, 'Coppelia', at the local Opera House. The bishop of Ossory, Patrick Collier, took offence at the photograph and wrote, along with several other clergy, in protest:

> We, the undersigned, consider it a very unbecoming picture for a Sunday Catholic paper, a bad picture, dangerous for young and old. We take objection to a female figure almost nude in the group [...] We like decent pictures: the indecent we abhor, as our religion demands.[18]

Interestingly, the correspondence was not received with automatic acceptance of the bishop's authority. In fact, Legge considered the protest 'ridiculous' and ultimately no reply was sent. But he was sufficiently concerned that he sent the correspondence for guidance to Fr J.G. McGarry – editor of the *The Furrow* magazine – in St Patrick's College, Maynooth. McGarry was dismissive of the bishop's protest:

> The life of the Editor of a Sunday newspaper is no easy one. He is between the Devil and the Holy See, as the late Jimmy Montgomery [film censor] said jokingly of his job. You know well that there is an unenlightened element in clerical – and lay – opinion, purely negative, focussing its spectacles to find something that will shock it [...] in the print I see the girl is actually wearing net stockings! The roll of signatures does not impress me. A bishop might call up a hundred such.[19]

17 J. Horgan, *Seán Lemass: The enigmatic patriot* (Dublin, 1997), p. 180.  18 Notes for draft memoir (unpublished), p. 45, HL papers.  19 Correspondence between McGarry and Legge, HL papers.

Despite his political and social outlook Legge, personally and professionally, was no mouthpiece for any specific constituency. He had an independent streak and enjoyed the company of those whose views were not his own. In the latter regard the Legge home in Ranelagh was the venue for social occasions involving writers, Sean O'Faoláin and Frank O'Connor, and was 'frequently the scene of vigorous and heated arguments.'[20] Indeed, Legge took a risk in commissioning articles from O'Connor in the 1940s when the author's work was banned: 'We had a managing-director who was more Catholic than the Pope. If O'Connor had walked in the hall of Independent House he would probably have had it disinfected. For him to write for one of the 'Independent' papers would have been impossible.'[21]

A clandestine arrangement saw O'Connor writing under the pen-name 'Ben Mayo'. Legge met with the writer on Tuesdays to discuss possible column topics and they would regroup on Fridays when O'Connor would hand over his copy. Cheques were passed from the accounts department at Independent House to Legge who ensured the writer received his fee. 'The articles created great interest. He was bringing a fresh and scholarly approach to many subjects. I remember Sean O'Faoláin asking me, 'Who is this Ben Mayo?' I expressed surprise that he didn't know and got away with it.'[22] The arrangement lasted for almost two years and in subsequent decades O'Connor again wrote for the *Sunday Independent* but under his own name. When O'Connor – a non-believer – died from a sudden heart attack in March 1966 there was some surprise that his funeral arrangements included mass at St Andrew's Church on Westland Row in Dublin. Legge was in the church with James Dillon and Sean O'Faoláin when former government minister Ernest Blythe approached them. Blythe expressed surprise at the religious arrangements. Legge responded: 'Did you not know? Frank has been at mass every day for over a year.' Blythe replied, as he moved on, 'I never knew that'. As Legge turned again to Dillon and O'Faoláin, the latter said, 'That's the best short story I ever heard.'[23]

## SCOOPS, LEAKS AND INTUITION

The arrival of the *Sunday Press* saw Legge facing new pressures, although on viewing the first edition – 4 September 1949 – he noted: 'My reaction was – a pleasant surprise. Not as good as I thought it wd be.' The threat of the new competitor, however, remained a significant issue. Legge judged the weekly contest in terms of which newspaper was published first – allowing

20 Manning, *James Dillon*, pp 152–3. 21 Notes for draft memoir (unpublished), p. 54, HL papers. 22 Ibid., p. 58, HL papers. 23 Ibid., p. 61, HL papers.

for early distribution around the country – and also the quality of the stories on the respective front pages. Typical examples of entries in Legge's diaries include: 'Got flying start on Press' (6 September 1952); 'Paper off in good time. To us it appeared better than the Press. Are we fair judges?' (24 December 1955); 'Two scoops over the Press ...' (15 February 1959); 'Press agn 28 to our 24 – 3rd week in succession' (10 March 1962); 'Missed 2 stories (1st ed) both splashed on Page 1 of the Press ... such frustration and annoyance' (18 January 1964). Legge was also vigilant in responding to any apparent threat from his competitor. When Vivion de Valera, the managing director of the Press Group, attempted to recruit one of Legge's staff – Ita Hynes – to edit a new woman's page Legge responded by getting her to edit a similar page in the *Sunday Independent* that would commence within two weeks.[24] De Valera had a measure of revenge twelve months later when he scuppered an attempt by Legge to recruit photographer Coleman Doyle to work on the *Sunday Independent*'s new colour magazine.[25]

Despite the launch of the *Sunday Press* in 1949, by the end of the 1950s weekly circulation of the *Sunday Independent* was almost 400,000. The arrival of the competitor newspaper had not damaged the Murphy publication. On 18 October 1959 Legge oversaw production of a twenty-eight page edition, the largest in the history of the *Sunday Independent*, and two weeks later he bettered that achievement with a thirty-two page edition. He noted in his diary: 'Considering the way it was got together it looked alright.' The Murphys invested in a costly colour magazine in 1963 for six months – and an equally short lived English edition that allowed Legge to write in his diary on 27 October 1963: 'Historic Day: We invade England with Sunday Inds. All went well.'

These innovations were, however, poorly considered while planning was insufficient. There was an apparent absence of any serious consultation by the board or communication with senior editorial staff. The investments proved costly while Legge's ongoing requests for more editorial staff including a designated photographer were unsuccessful. Two separate entries in Legge's diaries provide a sense of his frustration at not being able to expand the newspaper: 'Mind very agitated abt office, late printing, bad reporting staff etc etc + awake a lot' (24 November 1962); 'We are working on the proverbial shoe string' (23 August 1963); 'Still an Angry Young Man!!! But feeling far from YOUNG these days' (4 August 1964). Yet, whatever the editorial limitations experienced by Legge his newspaper was commercially successful – circulation was holding up against the *Sunday Press* while advertising was strong. There were presentations from the board – and social functions with staff – to mark Legge's 21st

24 Diary, 20 Mar. 1962, HL papers.   25 Diary, 14 Sept. 1963, HL papers.

(in 1961) and 25th (in 1965) years as editor. There was some talk of succession in the early 1960s but the Murphys were happy for their editor to continue on.

Legge was not just delivering for his proprietor, he was also good value for money – he continued as a working reporter throughout his entire period as editor. He wrote weekly editorials, regularly delivered front page stories (under the pen name 'Fergus Wright') and oversaw the 'Panorama' column. He was driven by a need for front-page exclusives. When the *Evening Press* reported that Edward Kennedy was expected to visit Ireland in 1962 Legge's diary response was typical of his journalistic outlook: 'I had hoped to have it Excl. in Sunday'.[26] Indeed, even as late as his twenty-ninth year as editor Legge was out and about gathering stories. In February 1969 Legge interviewed Terence O'Neill, the prime minister of Northern Ireland, at Ahoghill near Ballymena. The two men sat in armchairs on either side of a fireplace as they spoke for half an hour. Legge's first question asked about the political situation to which O'Neill replied, 'You are like Lemass. You people in the South have no idea of how we work in Northern Ireland.' The interview – and the internal difficulties within union- ism – was the front page story in the subsequent edition of the *Sunday Independent*.[27]

Legge made short entries in small pocket diaries throughout his career as editor. The references range from brief mentions of work meetings and office related activities to social functions and family engagements. There is no par- ticular consistency to the entries although they offer tantalizing glimpses into his professional life. Subjects and people come and go across days, weeks, months and years. Words that feature regularly in Saturday diary entries include 'scoop' and 'exclusive'. Legge placed great store in what he described as 'wom- anly intuition' in seeking out exclusive stories.[28] He was also a risk taker – and prepared to push stories as far as possible. His brash approach was evident one evening in 1938 when Neville Chamberlain sought to prevent war in Europe. As chief sub-editor at the *Irish Independent*, Legge arranged the lead story on the basis that a peace pact would emerge. But with the print deadline approach- ing in Independent House urgent messages over the private wires to Reuters and the Press Association brought only negative replies.

> So were we to start a complete new make-up of the page and thus be late and lose our transport connections? Hell! A steadying watchword to have is – always be calm in a crisis. Behold, at that very critical moment Chamberlain landed in London and produced what has become a famous – or infamous – piece of paper ... The relief![29]

26 Diary, 21 Feb. 1962, HL papers.   27 *Sunday Independent*, 23 Feb. 1969.   28 Notes for draft memoir (unpublished), p. 14, HL papers.   29 Ibid., p. 15, HL papers.

There was a message of congratulations the following day from the newspaper's editor Frank Geary who was on holidays in Tramore, Co. Waterford. As Legge observed, 'we were the only one in Tramore that had the story of the peace pact. Womanly intuition.'[30] Eleven years later, on 18 September 1949, Legge wrote what he considered the 'scoop of the year' when predicting that the British pound was about to be devalued. 'I see you scooped the world,' one of his colleagues remarked some days later when the story was proven to be true.[31] In the article Legge placed his source as the *Irish Independent*'s London correspondent – a deliberate misstatement – and subsequently claimed journalistic intuition rather than a leak from a political source. He failed, however, to explain how he came to know that the Dublin government was, that same Saturday evening, meeting to discuss the implications for the Irish currency. Interestingly, Legge was to fall back on the same 'nose for a story' rationale in also explaining what was probably one of the biggest exclusives of twentieth-century journalism in Ireland.

## DECLARATION OF A REPUBLIC

On 5 September 1948 the *Sunday Independent* published an exclusive story – under the by-line 'by our political correspondent' – that Ireland was to leave the Commonwealth. Under the front page headline – 'External Relations Act to go' – Legge, the author of the story, wrote with some authority that with repeal of the legislation in question Ireland would be formally declared a republic. It was a journalistic scoop that not only embarrassed Taoiseach John A. Costello – then on his first trip abroad since the formation of his inter-party government seven months previously – but also ultimately caused the formal announcement to be mired in controversy.

Legge insisted there was no leak for the story but that it had arisen from journalistic intuition arising from a close monitoring of political events. In notes prepared for an unpublished memoir Legge recalled 'having let some week-ends pass ... intuition' urged him to move on the story. His attitude was framed as, 'Write it now. The daily papers may stick you for it. So the story was written after lunch on a Saturday afternoon.'[32] There is some support for Legge's explanation – not only in terms of his record for pushing stories to the limit but also disparate information already in the public domain. Moves to take Ireland out of the Commonwealth had in fact predated Costello's government.[33] The previous Fianna Fáil administration had systematically dis-

---

30 Ibid., p. 15, HL papers.   31 Diary, 18 Sept. 1949, HL papers.   32 Notes for draft memoir (unpublished), p. 16, HL papers.   33 For a detailed examination of this period see E. Keane, *Seán MacBride: a life* (Dublin, 2007).

mantled links. De Valera had, however, stopped short of declaring Ireland a republic for a variety of reasons including a fear of copper-fastening partition and a wish to prevent a standoff with the British authorities. But the formation of a new republican party, Clann na Poblachta – and its declared policy of delivering beyond de Valera's 'dictionary republic' – renewed attention on Ireland's ambiguous official status. The outgoing Fianna Fáil government had, in fact, prepared draft legislation to give effect to Commonwealth withdrawal.

There were certainly differing views on membership within the new government. Clann na Poblachta's desire for change contrasted sharply with Fine Gael's public policy of wanting to maintain Commonwealth links. In a Dáil debate on the day the new government was formed in February 1948, Sean MacBride referred to the election results as not delivering a mandate to repeal the External Relations Act.[34] There were, however, reassuring words from within the wider Fine Gael family where alternative perspectives prevailed. In the same Dáil debate, James Dillon – then an independent TD but one with influential Fine Gael connections – clearly anticipated an early announcement when he observed that MacBride, 'contemplates a long postponement of some objective near his heart, but I am more optimistic than he.'[35] Significantly, the new Taoiseach, John A. Costello – also from Fine Gael stock – considered the imprecise nature of Ireland's status 'untidy and inadequate'.[36]

There is sufficient evidence from the early months in the life of the new government to strongly suggest that an unofficial decision had been taken – what was not decided was the moment for making a public announcement. In a Dáil debate on 21 July 1948, one Clann na Poblachta TD spoke positively about taking 'steps' to establish a republic while a little over two weeks later on 6 August 1948, the Labour Party Tanaiste William Norton observed that it would do 'our national self respect good both at home and abroad if we were to proceed without delay to abolish the External Relations Act'.[37] Moreover, at a cabinet meeting some days later, MacBride recommended that Ireland not be represented at a forthcoming Commonwealth gathering. While no record exists to show that an official decision had been made, the evidence suggests that there was consensus within government and that an early declaration was expected. So Legge may have been very clever in reading the tealeaves. But such intuition would not explain the curious timing of his story on the weekend when Costello was in Canada, which effectively bounced him into confirming the change.

Legge long protested innocence about the source for the story – insisting that he had no official or political assistance – and argued that there was no

34 Sean MacBride, Dáil Éireann Debates, vol. 110, col. 25 (18 Feb. 1948).   35 James Dillon, Dáil Éireann Debates, vol. 110, col. 28 (18 Feb. 1948).   36 Keane, *Sean MacBride*, p.110.   37 Ibid., p. 109.

significance in the article's timing, even claiming that he could have written the story earlier.[38] 'We did not talk to one member of his [Costello's] Government, or any of his officials, on the Government's intentions on this matter.'[39] The emphatic and consistent nature of Legge's denials of any governmental assistance remains admirable in terms of journalistic integrity in protecting sources. But the credibility of his stance has long been questioned, especially given the authority of the written article, the timing of its publication, and the fact that Legge was on good terms with several members of Costello's cabinet.

While Liam Cosgrave accepted the source as 'More likely "journalistic inspiration"'[40] others refused to accept Legge's explanation. Patrick Lynch, Costello's private secretary at the time, observed that, 'Hector believes that it was editorial inspiration that led him to produce that headline … I am certain he was informed from some source … My personal view is that it was Dillon.'[41] Costello apparently believed that MacBride was behind the leak.[42] Louie O'Brien – personal secretary to MacBride – ultimately came to believe that the Clann na Poblachta leader was the source and that 'MacBride had gone to Legge and cooked up this …'[43] MacBride was apparently aware of the *Sunday Independent* story prior to publication. As Louie O'Brien recalled in a 1996 interview: 'Sean got onto Costello on the phone and told him this thing was coming out on Sunday, and Sean gave him three alternatives [most likely to confirm, to deny or issue no comment].'[44]

There are no significant entries in Legge's diary for August and September 1948 except for a single mention of Dillon, on 29 August 1948: 'James Dillon in tonight but I did not see him.' There is no entry on the date that the External Relations exclusive was published. Indeed, if Legge's diaries are to be accepted, his contacts with MacBride appear to be confined to a period in 1949 when he had regular engagement with the minister for external affairs. There are several references in the early months of 1949 to Saturday evening contact when Legge had left Independent House with work complete on that week's *Sunday Independent*. For example, on Saturday 22 January 1949: 'Saw Sean MacB on way home. Discussed partition etc'; on Saturday 29 January 'Saw Sean MacB on way home'; on Saturday 12 February 1949 'Called into J.D on way home. Before lunch saw Sean MacB'.

MacBride apparently cultivated these links. On 12 March 1949 Legge wrote: 'Sean MacB phoned – Per. Sec. – he wd like to see me, so called in on way

38 *Irish Times*, 11 Nov. 1994.   39 *Sunday Independent*, 1 Nov. 1970.   40 Liam Cosgrave. Correspondence with David McCullagh, 12 Aug. 1996.   41 RTÉ Archive Tape A 4184: The Republic of Ireland Act, 1948. Tx 26/3/89.   42 N. Mansergh, *Nationalism and independence* (Cork, 1997), p. 187.   43 Louie O'Brien. Interview with David McCullagh, 24 July 1996.   44 Ibid.

home. Had interesting gossip re world affairs. F.H. Boland there.' There is an intriguing entry on 1 May 1949 that points to the minister providing material to the newspaper editor: 'Talked with Sean MacBride at 6.45–7.15pm re. current political situation. Interesting documents and letters. James Dillon was on the phone later in evg.' MacBride's involvement with Legge was apparently not sustained. There are no meetings or conversations between the two men recorded in Legge's diaries, outside the references in 1949. If taken at face value these entries leave open the strong possibility that MacBride established links with Legge in the aftermath of the External Relations Act story as he saw the *Sunday Independent* editor as a good media contact.

In assessing the origins of the External Relations Act story, significance must be placed on the fact that James Dillon was a regular source of political news for the *Sunday Independent* editor. For example, at 4.30p.m. on Saturday 2 February 1957 Legge called to Dillon's house. The future of the second Inter-party government was threatened after Sean MacBride – and Fianna Fáil – had tabled motions of no confidence. Legge wrote of his conversation with Dillon: 'Talked things general + political situation. Sean MacB never consulted any member of Govt re his censure motion.' Legge arrived at Independent House at 6.40p.m., and by 7.30p.m. he had finished writing the paper's lead story based on information provided by Dillon. The regularity of Dillon as a source was such that in January 1965 when Fianna Fáil minister Donagh O'Malley met Legge in the Shelbourne Hotel he chided him about the Dillon association: 'Talked abt J. Dillon writing editorials for us!!! Said the paper showed bitterness. I pointed to cases of opposite.'

While Legge always insisted that there had been no 'leak' from any cabinet member the balance of probabilities – and evidence of ongoing provision by the politician to his journalistic friend – would suggest that Dillon was the source for the External Relations Act exclusive. Dillon had advised MacBride in the Dáil in February 1948 that movement would be sooner than he contemplated. Discussions had been ongoing in government and political circles without a formal decision being reached. Legge's exclusive forced Costello into action and secured the required outcome for MacBride – delivering a pre-election pledge and confirming his party's republican credentials *vis-à-vis* Fianna Fáil. Dillon got to see Fine Gael shake-off its negative image as a pro-British party. In this regard Legge's repeated denial of assistance with the story may be explained not just by a desire to protect his source but also to protect the name and reputation of his great friend. If 'womanly intuition' was involved in publishing this great scoop, it was most likely very well informed intuition.

CONCLUSION

Hector Legge's final night as editor on 31 October 1970 was marked by a thunderous metallic salute from printing staff that rattled throughout Independent House in tandem with a chorus of shouts of 'bravo' from colleagues on duty as the edition of 1 November 1970 was put to bed. The retirement of a man who had spent thirty years in the editorial chair was recorded in a short inside piece accompanied by a photograph of Legge addressing the staff: 'It was a unique farewell for a unique journalist … a colossus of the Irish newspaper world if there ever was one.'[45] Drama remained with Legge even in this final period as editor. Controversially, he had declined to publish an exclusive story revealling that a unnamed government minister was involved in gun-running. Apparently 'womanly intuition' was set aside over libel fears arising from 'the scoop I could not publish'.[46]

In typical Legge style he wrote the front-page story in his final edition under his pen name, 'Fergus Wright'. He was followed in the editorial chair by Conor O'Brien (1970–6) and Michael Hand (1976–84). When Aengus Fanning (1984–2012) succeeded Hand another long, and equally controversial and successful, editorship commenced. The world of newspapers was transformed in these years not only in terms of size, layout and design but also editorial priorities. The Sunday market – marked by a single local newspaper from 1905 to 1949 and an effective duopoly over subsequent decades – became an intense battleground between numerous broadsheet and tabloid titles. Legge maintained a watchful eye on his former publication – there was frequent correspondence with the new proprietor. In early 1985 he sent a memo to Tony O'Reilly and several other management executives at Independent Newspapers. He bemoaned a recent decision by the *Sunday Independent*'s new editor, Aengus Fanning, to drop the regular cookery column, questioned the absence of an obituary page and lamented the neglect of the letters to the editor page. 'A page – plus some advertisements – devoted to letters in the Sunday Independent would be one of the most widely read and, in terms of cost, one of the cheapest.'[47] While the Sunday market had moved on from Legge's era, even in retirement he still had a sense of the priorities underpinning success at Independent House – high circulation and low costs.[48]

---

45 *Sunday Independent*, 1 Nov. 1970  46 *Sunday Independent*, 15 June 1975.  47 Untitled memo sent by Hector Legge to A.J.F. O'Reilly, Bartle Pitcher, John Meagher, Liam Healy, Joe Hayes and Gerry McGuinness. Undated, but most likely early 1985. HL papers.  48 Hector Legge passed away on 3 Nov. 1994.

# 11 / The changing of the guard at Middle Abbey Street, 1961–73

## JOHN HORGAN

In 1961 the *Irish Independent* underwent a number of significant changes that marked, in a way, the end of an era. Frank Geary resigned as editor (he was to die very shortly afterwards), and the newspaper put news on its front page for the first time. At the same time, a readership survey, possibly the first of its kind, was published in 1961, giving a picture of an Ireland that was still in many ways static, but on the cusp of change.[1] The survey was commissioned for the Association of Irish Newspapers, an organization that, despite its name, largely represented regional and local weekly newspapers. For this reason it excluded Dublin and Cork from its purview. Nonetheless, given that urbanization had still not got into its swing, the survey presents a fair picture of the 1,265,000 inhabitants over 16 years of age living outside these two areas.[2]

Television sets were owned by only 8 per cent of respondents; 72 per cent cooked with solid fuel, and 61 per cent owned a vehicle of some kind (often, one imagines, a tractor). Some 60 per cent of respondents never went to a dance or céilí: the cinema was the choice of 57 per cent. Fewer than 10 per cent of respondents 'never' listened to Raidió Éireann: the overwhelming majority listened to the station 'regularly' or 'occasionally' and in an unmistakeable sign of the times almost as many listened regularly or occasionally to Radio Luxembourg. It was, nonetheless, a public in love with newspapers. Almost three-quarters of the respondents (73 per cent) read both their local weekly newspaper and a Sunday newspaper while 83 per cent read 'one or more' Sunday newspapers. Only 6 per cent read no newspaper at all. The prevalence of multiple purchasing is clearly shown by the overlap in the percentages for Sunday newspaper purchasers: some 61 per cent read the *Sunday Press* against 59 per cent for the *Sunday Independent* and 33 per cent for the *Sunday Review*. The relative weakness of the morning and evening newspapers outside the major conurbations, certainly compared to the Sunday papers, is graphically illustrated in Table 1, as is the strength of the *Irish Independent*.

---

1 *Readership in Ireland: June 1961*, S.H. Benson Ltd, and Social Surveys (Gallop Poll), Ltd, for the Association of Irish Newspapers. NLI ILB 070 a 1.   2 The sample size was 971.

Table 1: Newspaper Purchasing Habits, 1961

| Title | % |
|---|---|
| *Irish Independent* | 34% |
| *Irish Press* | 27% |
| *Cork Examiner* | 10% |
| *Irish Times* | 4% |
| *Evening Press* | 16% |
| *Evening Herald* | 12% |
| *Evening Echo* | 5% |
| *Evening Mail* | 2% |

Source: *Gallop*

Change was, however, taking place, even if it was at first subterranean in character. Socially and politically, as well as economically, the tide was turning. In 1959 Eamon de Valera, who had led his political party, Fianna Fáil, for more than three decades – most of them as Taoiseach – had finally given way to his successor, Seán Lemass. James Dillon bowed out in Fine Gael, William Norton in Labour. Lemass' economic approach was to abandon the policies of protectionism and high tariffs as export-led growth and foreign investment became the twin mantras of economic progress.

The creation of the national television service on the last day of 1961 marked another epochal change. It opened up the electronic media to a new wave of journalists who had, in many cases, not come up through the ranks from the provincial and national newspapers, but straight from university. It did so, moreover, in a new structural framework, one in which national public service broadcasting was, for the first time, removed from direct political control. The whole news agenda was also changing. Ireland's new domestic policies were reinforced by a new foreign policy, as Irish troops went to the Congo at the beginning of the decade to fight for the United Nations. In 1963 the Second Vatican Council opened: for three years, it was to challenge many of the well-worn patterns of traditional Irish Catholic piety and practice. In 1965 Lemass visited the Northern Ireland prime minister, Terence O'Neill, in Stormont, and a year later he gave way to Jack Lynch, the first Taoiseach from the post-revolutionary generation of Irish political leaders. In the summer of 1968, in a controversial rejection of post-Conciliar expectations, Pope Paul VI issued his encyclical on birth control, *Humanae Vitae*. Earlier in the same year, students and workers in a whole range of European countries threw off the shackles of conformity, almost toppling General de Gaulle in France as they did so; Irish university students followed suit, if more decorously. Later, in Prague, the first cracks began to appear in the Iron Curtain. For those Irishmen and women who had been schooled in the old certainties, it was all puzzling at best, threatening and deeply disturbing at worst. To journalism, it was meat and drink.

Frank Geary's successor as editor of the daily newspaper, Michael Rooney, had joined the *Irish Independent* as a sub-editor in 1931 and was appointed assistant editor in 1935.[3] He had, in effect, served as deputy editor for so long that he had acquired almost coadjutor status. Like many coadjutors whose accession to power is long delayed, however, Rooney was no new broom and was to retire some seven years later without having made any dramatic changes in the paper. His generally relaxed attitude to newspapering was exemplified by the occasion on which he opted for a prior engagement with a foursome on the golf links at Portmarnock rather than meet a visiting United States senator by the name of John Fitzgerald Kennedy. He did, however, reassure readers that the change of editorship did not mean that there would be any change of heart, at least insofar as foreign policy was concerned. As communist China applied for membership of the United Nations in November 1961, Rooney warned his readers: 'If the Charter [of the UN] has any meaning, it must reject Red China, or go the way of the spineless League of Nations.'[4]

Unusually, given the actual or presumed politics of the newspaper, Rooney had a republican background, and had actually been interned on a prison ship in Belfast Lough by the British authorities during the war of independence. He did, however, encourage a younger, literate group of journalists, many of them coming from the Law Library and from the universities rather than from the stuffy confines of small-town provincial newspapers, to spread their wings to some degree in the editorial and feature columns, and also in the book review section. Louis McRedmond, a young barrister who initially combined Law Library work with writing editorials, and who was eventually to succeed Rooney as editor, made a name for himself in writing about the Second Vatican Council, particularly the final session in the autumn of 1965, on which he reported personally. Frank D'Arcy was another import, from the university rather than from the Law Library, with a wide knowledge of Europe. Gerry Quinn, a young economics lecturer in UCD, took over the task of writing editorials on economic matters in succession to James Meenan, for many years professor of national economy at University College Dublin.

It is doubtful whether Geary would have agreed to print an editorial, as Rooney unexpectedly did, objecting to the banning of John McGahern's second novel, *The Dark*, in 1965.[5] His residual, anti-authoritarian republicanism was no

3 *Irish Independent*, 1 Sept. 1961.   4 Editorial, *Irish Independent*, 4 Nov. 1961.   5 *Irish Independent*, 31 July 1965.

doubt responsible for this decision, and indeed the *Irish Independent* was the only Dublin morning newspaper to protest on this occasion. That said, the Abbey Street newspapers were generally slower to react editorially to the social and other changes ushered in by the Sixties – in particular the introduction of television – than the *Irish Times*, which, although not yet a serious rival (that role was still, and properly, reserved for the titles in the Irish Press Group), was beginning to make stealthy gains on the colossi of Abbey Street and Burgh Quay. There was no features department, properly speaking; that function was exercised by a team of editorial writers, who would also attend press conferences to familiarize themselves directly with the news of the day before commenting in leaders.

The general election in May 1965 was marked by an identifiable shift in the newspaper's editorial attitude. The idea of a national government was no longer being canvassed, and there is more than a hint of impatience with Fianna Fáil, which had been in power for some eight years. Two days before the election, the editorial came down emphatically on the side of Fine Gael in relation to the health issue; Fine Gael, it averred, was the party best equipped and motivated to reform the health services.[6] The following day, the *Independent* emphasized that it had tried to maintain impartiality, but the mask slipped slightly even as it did so:

> A newspaper exists to reflect public opinion, to inform and guide it. It has neither duty nor right to hector; if, therefore, on the eve of polling, you look to this corner for a specific recommendation on how to vote, you can stop reading now. We shall not usurp the citizen's privilege of deciding for himself.[7]

This did not prevent the paper from observing, in the same editorial, that Fine Gael offered 'constructive and workable alternatives to the present defective systems' in the areas of pensions and health. Constructive or not, Fine Gael was defeated: there would be no change of government for another two elections, by which time the *Irish Independent* was itself beginning to change.

Part of the reason for this change came with the appointment of Louis McRedmond as editor on Rooney's retirement in 1968. McRedmond had a fondness for the eternal verities of journalism: good writing, solid research, getting it right. He was unshowy and unspectacular.[8] These attributes, it turned out, were in danger of becoming increasingly devalued as the brashness of television, in particular, began to make inroads into other branches of journalism. This was more evident initially in the evening market, where the *Evening Herald*

6 *Irish Independent*, 5 Apr. 1965.  7 Ibid., 6 Apr. 1965.  8 Louis McRedmond died on 16 Jan. 2011.

was engaged in a dog-eat-dog contest with the *Evening Press*. The latter paper had, since its foundation in 1954, been making huge inroads into the *Evening Herald*'s original quasi-monopoly (there had also been the *Evening Mail*, but that had been in terminal decline for years and posed no serious threat to either of the other two titles). Frank Kilfeather, whose father had worked for the Abbey Street titles and who joined the group from the *Wicklow People* in 1965, was rather bruised by the experience, and eventually left to join the *Irish Times*:

> I enjoyed working on the [*Irish*] *Independent* and the *Sunday Independent*, but hated being rostered for the [*Evening*] *Herald*. Two years after I arrived a major decision was taken at the top to 'liven up' the [*Evening*] *Herald*, jazz it up and dramatize stories. A wildly enthusiastic news editor was put in charge of the operation and he terrorized the staff from early morning until 4 p.m. in the afternoon. [...] This was quite traumatic for the staff and it pressurized us all into hyping up and exaggerating even the most trivial of stories. If you were not prepared to carry out orders without question you were categorized as driftwood ... The atmosphere was, to say the least, very sour.[9]

Journalists working for the *Evening Herald* held a number of meetings to protest about these practices, but were effectively powerless to challenge them. This in itself underlines two aspects of mid-twentieth-century national journalism. The first was the practice of rotating journalists across titles: each title might have its designated editorial executives, but the journalistic foot-soldiers were expected to learn and practise different styles, depending on the title they were working for on any given day. This was also true for the *Irish Times* (which at one point also ran a Sunday and an evening paper) and for the Irish Press Group. More significant, however, was the degree to which power resides, in any newspaper, with the editor and the news editor. Editors, in turn, create editorial cultures, and the quotation above exemplifies the degree to which these cultures could differ, even under the same proprietorial roof.

This reality, of course, had been the case for many years, but it was, if anything, accentuated by the growing ferocity of the competition for circulation. In 1960 the *Evening Herald* was out-selling the *Evening Press* by the bare margin of 1,000 copies. The following year, that had been reversed, and the *Evening Herald* circulation had slipped by almost 8,000 to 108,845, while its rival was selling 116,077.[10] This was the last year in which there were three evening newspapers in

---

9 F. Kilfeather, *Changing times: a life in journalism* (Dublin, 1997), p. 21.   10 All figures in this section are from the Audit Bureau of Circulation, courtesy of McConnell's Advertising Ltd.

Dublin. When it closed in 1961, the *Evening Mail* was selling an average of 44,577 copies an issue, and on its demise, although these went disproportionately to the *Evening Herald*, the *Evening Press* was still almost 4,000 copies ahead of its Abbey Street competitor, which was losing money. By 1969, although the *Evening Press* was 5,500 ahead, the combination of economic growth, an enhanced news agenda, more aggressive journalism, and the introduction of television, had created a situation in which the two remaining evening papers were selling more copies than the three papers combined had in 1960, and approximately three times as many evening papers as the lone survivor, the *Evening Herald*, would sell at the end of the century thirty years later.

The *Sunday Independent* was doing rather worse, relatively speaking. At the beginning of the decade, in 1960, it was selling an average of 330,919 weekly copies, compared with 364,397 for the *Sunday Press* and 164,749 for the *Sunday Review*. The *Sunday Review* closed in 1962, when it was still selling an average of 154,551 copies an issue, but those of its readers who transferred to the surviving papers did so by a ratio of almost 4:3 in favour of the *Sunday Press*. The *Sunday Independent* counter-attacked by launching the first colour supplement ever produced for an Irish Sunday paper, in 1963, and this narrowed the circulation gap with the *Sunday Press* to a little over 40,000 copies a week. The magazine, however, folded after nine months and a loss of about £750,000, and even though the *Sunday Independent* circulation kept on increasing, the gap between it and the *Sunday Press* continued to widen. By 1968 the latter title was selling an astonishing 422,000 copies weekly, almost 90,000 more than its Abbey Street rival. Noel Browne, who still maintained distant connections with the Chance family, was to allege at around this time that the advantage won by the *Sunday Press* was in part related to the way in which it capitalized on growing political unrest in Northern Ireland by publishing series of articles about Ireland's republican past that were designed to blur the distinctions between the IRA of the war of independence and its modern successor in title. There is no doubt that the *Sunday Press*, under its energetic editor Matt Feehan, represented the wilder shores of irredentism within Fianna Fáil. All of this, and the by now declining powers of Hector Legge, prompted the Independent board to finally persuade their veteran editor to retire in 1970, at the age of almost 70. Legge's successor was Conor O'Brien, editor of the *Evening Press*, where he had been consistently keeping the *Evening Herald* in second place.[11]

The situation in the morning market was more complex. The *Irish Independent*'s circulation rose for two years after Geary's departure, reaching a high

---

11 The present author owes his introduction to journalism to Conor O'Brien, who gave him his first job, as a trainee sub-editor on the *Evening Press* in November 1960.

of 180,801 in 1963. Thereafter, however, progress was very uneven, and by 1968 average daily circulation fluctuated at around 178,000 copies. At this point Rooney retired, and was succeeded by McRedmond, whom he had appointed as deputy editor the previous year and whose right of succession had been implied for at least that period of time. The *Irish Press*, on the other hand, reached its circulation high point of the decade the following year, when it sold an average of 122,844 copies. The slow burner, however, was the *Irish Times*, which by 1970 had increased its circulation by almost two-thirds, from 35,024 in 1960 to its new average of 57,443. Over a period since 1964 this increase, which dated essentially from 1965, was noteworthy, particularly as the total circulation of the Irish morning papers had remained more or less unchanged over the decade (328,000 in 1970 as against 325,000 in 1960).

In the boardroom at Abbey Street, the figures were being noted with some concern. This was all the more so because the company had begun a process of expansion and re-design that would, in the short term, increase the company's overheads. A pivotal figure in this period was Bartle Pitcher, an accountant who joined the company in December 1958 after a period with the *Irish Times*. Pitcher was appointed a member of the board in 1960, secretary of the company in 1962 and a year later became manager following the untimely death of his predecessor, John O'Riordan.[12]

At the time Pitcher joined the company, the modus operandi of the business side of the house was characterized by values and practices that at times seemed to hark back to the Edwardian era. Clerical staff used pencils; when a pencil was finished, they had to go and see the company secretary personally to acquire a replacement. The company secretary, in those pre-Pitcher days, would produce a pencil – and then a razor blade, with which he would cut the pencil in half, before giving one half to the supplicant.[13] The same was true for erasers. Pitcher, who was appointed group general manager in late 1968, was to play a role of extraordinary significance in the development of the Independent Group, both before and after its change of ownership in 1973. With the encouragement of the chairman of the board, T.V. Murphy, he oversaw the first acquisition of a new title in 1967–8, when the Independent group acquired the *Drogheda Independent* for some £40,000.

In the autumn of 1969 there were two other factors that created ripples in the otherwise smooth running of the Abbey Street machine. One was an attempt, the first of its kind in Independent House, and a rarity in Irish industry at this time, to strike a productivity agreement with the pre-press employees, in particular the printers. The second was a re-design of the daily title itself,

12 *Irish Independent*, 28 June 1962 & 2 May 1963.   13 Private source.

including a new masthead, and associated up-grading of some parts of the printing operations, a decade after the installation of the newest press. This involved the installation of a new press for colour advertising.

The productivity deal, concluded early in 1969,[14] had two substantial benefits for the company. Wage differentials between different members of the case-room staff were reduced or eliminated, and case-room overtime was, from now on, to be restricted to circumstances in which late-breaking news demanded it. The workforce got, in return, an extended range of social benefits, and agreement on a basic 40–hour week, with a 36–hour week for those on night work. The significance of this can be gauged from the fact that in 1970 there were no fewer than 122 case-room staff members between compositors and lino-type operators alone, at a time when the journalistic staff for the three titles combined was approximately 147.[15] The total number of staff amounted to almost 1,400.

These elements all combined, in a sort of domino effect, to affect the quality of the paper itself. Deadlines were advanced, so that the paper had to be put to bed earlier. The size of the daily paper was reduced, which meant – given that advertising would not be reduced – that the amount of space available for news was being restricted. The combination of earlier deadlines and fewer column inches meant that the *Irish Independent* was now – as his deputies frequently complained to McRedmond – under-reporting some important stories, and missing others completely. Circulation was also falling: the 1969 average was down to 165,500, which, while within shouting distance of the figures for 1965 and 1966, marked a fall of some 6,500 since the previous year. The editor held the disruption and difficulties attendant on the re-organization (about which he had frequently complained to the board, without avail) responsible for the fall in circulation: the board of directors blamed the editor.

This was, effectively, a new situation. There had been only one occasion previously on which an editor had departed unwillingly, and that had been before Geary's time. This did not mean that the board was uninterested in editorial matters – rather, that its interest in editorial matters tended to the superficial. In Abbey Street, where the board met every week (a chef arrived beforehand, complete with white toque and apron, to prepare lunch), editors were occasionally summoned to the post-prandial boardroom to answer queries. Most of them were of a very insignificant nature, and dealt – as often as not – with minor editorial decisions about the placing of stories or photographs that had long been forgotten by the journalists concerned. After Michael Rooney had his first experience of this mini-ordeal, he asked his predecessor, Frank

14 *Ireland's Press and Print*, 1:5, May–June 1969, p. 17.   15 *Personnel 1970*, Independent News and Media archives.

Geary, what he ought to make of it. Geary replied gruffly that it had happened to him, too, and that he had learned not to pay any attention to it.[16]

The situation in late 1969 was, however, different. After one board meeting at the end of December 1969, Pitcher came into McRedmond's office and suggested that he sit down. As McRedmond did so, Pitcher informed him that, at its meeting earlier, the board had come to the conclusion that they had made a mistake in appointing him as editor: they were now going to undo that decision.

McRedmond was shocked – and doubly shocked by a subsequent television interview that implied his editorship had not been in the best interests of the shareholders.[17] He was allowed to come back the following day to clear out his office. This was a rash decision on the part of management, because by then the word had spread, and the journalistic staff was up in arms. A deputation from the NUJ chapel came to see McRedmond, saying that they had decided to go on strike to protest against his sacking. McRedmond dissuaded them from this course of action on the grounds that he did not want the end of his tenure of office to be marked by a day on which the paper failed to come out: the journalists compromised by staging a brief protest walk en masse around the block before returning to work. McRedmond, despite having taken over the editorship without having a formal contract, issued proceedings both for defamation and for wrongful dismissal, which were subsequently settled.[18] E.M. Murphy, the director deputed by the board to do the RTÉ interview about the sacking, famously remarked that the *Irish Independent* did not change policies – the newspaper just changed editors.[19]

McRedmond was succeeded by Aidan Pender. Pender had originally joined the *Evening Herald* advertising department, had graduated to the sub-editors' desk, and eventually became editor. It was an appointment that spoke volumes. The growth of the *Irish Times* circulation, even though it was at this stage still a massive 100,000 copies a day behind the *Irish Independent,* had been provoking some nervousness in the Abbey Street boardroom, which had heretofore seen the *Irish Press* as its main, and in effect its only, rival. It now had two rivals: which was the more dangerous? McRedmond was an editor of the old school. His concern for the quality of writing in his newspaper, and the general breadth of his education and tastes (he had been successfully nudging the *Irish Independent* away from its predilection for the crustier Catholic values in his reports on Vatican II from Rome) made him a good foil to the rising *Irish Times*. Within the Independent's management team, however, there was more scepticism. The rumour was that if a board member asked why the *Irish Independent* couldn't be

16 Private source.   17 The RTÉ recording does not survive, but there is a reference to it, and a quotation from it, in Tom O'Dea's contemporary television column, *Irish Press,* 10 Jan. 1970.   18 His barrister was Declan Costello, SC, later Attorney-General and subsequently a High Court judge.   19 See note 17.

more like the *Irish Times*, the stock management response was that the board could have a newspaper like the *Irish Times* if that was what they wanted – as long as they were prepared to accept an *Irish Times* level of circulation to go along with it.

Pender's appointment was a clear sign that the opposition most clearly in view was now the *Irish Press*. The goal was circulation. The means was news – and the display of news. Two of his deputies were integral to this purpose. One was Vincent Doyle, who had joined the *Irish Press* in the late 1950s, and had moved to the *Sunday Press* in 1962. He moved from there to work with the *Sunday Independent's* colour magazine, but lost his job when it folded, and did shifts and freelance work for some time before getting a job on the *Evening Herald* in 1966. He subsequently moved from the *Evening Herald* to become one of Pender's assistant editors. The other was Niall Hanley, the *Irish Independent's* assistant chief sub-editor, who went on to become editor of the *Evening Herald* and who died in an air crash along with a number of other journalists – Kevin Marron, Tony Heneghan and John Feeney – while taking part in a Beaujolais wine race in November 1984. Another key Pender appointee was Liam Shine, a tough, no-nonsense journalist from Co. Kerry, who had worked in London and was *au fait* with the ways of Fleet Street, including the ways in which news editors shouted at their reporters. His gruff exterior, nonetheless, concealed the proverbial soft interior: he also contributed a column to the *Evening Herald* called 'The Man on the Bridge', which generated a considerable quantity of gifts and money from Dublin readers for the hard-luck cases he wrote about.

The daily title was at this stage, according to Doyle, 'a powerful paper, steeped in tradition and staffed by righteous men, many of whom were slaves to what had been "politically correct" in the 1950s.' It was also, he thought, 'lifeless, without flair or style.'[20] However, it was not without younger firepower. Its leader writers included the young barrister Philip O'Sullivan, later a High Court judge. Its reporters included Michael Denieffe, who was to become editor of the *Evening Herald* and who later played a major part in management through the 1990s and into the new century; Aengus Fanning, who was to become editor of the *Sunday Independent*; James Farrelly, who was to become editor of the *Sunday Tribune*; Arthur Noonan, later political correspondent of the *Irish Independent* and of RTÉ; and John Walshe, later education editor. Walshe's appointment was in itself something of a novelty, as he was one of the first individuals to become a journalist at the *Irish Independent* straight from university. Most recruitment in Abbey Street still came from the provinces, at a time when the *Irish Times* was moving towards a policy of dividing its intake almost equally between provin-

---

20 I. Kenny, *Talking to ourselves: conversations with editors of the Irish news media* (Galway, 1994), p. 18.

cial journalists and university graduates. The features department included Joe MacAnthony, who had been among those hired by McRedmond and who was shortly to move to the *Sunday Independent* when Conor O'Brien succeeded Hector Legge. As these names indicate, it was also a virtually all-male environment. In 1970 Ita Mallon was still in her solitary glory as the 'Lady Correspondent'. There were only three female reporters, one of whom, Lorna Reid, was once brought into the news editor's office to be given a drop of poteen. The news editor concerned, according to *Irish Independent* lore, said that he was teaching her how to drink so that she could keep up with the men in the newsroom.[21]

The new regime generated a lot of excitement but not, initially, much by way of circulation gains. Indeed, in 1972/3 the circulation of the daily title, at 166,000, was below its 1970 figure. The *Irish Times* was still creeping up; the pace of the *Irish Press* decline was still gradual. At the same time, Pender's new, brash editorial style was alienating some traditional readers. One Catholic bishop, alarmed at the ways in which the old *Irish Independent* was being transformed, asked Pender what he was trying to do with the paper. 'Sell it, my lord', was the answer.[22] The difficulties were not confined to the daily. At the *Sunday Independent*, a rise in circulation from 330,000 in 1968 to 342,000 in 1972/3, though valid in itself, had to be read in its own context. This included the spurt in circulation by the *Sunday Press* to a new high of 432,900 in 1972/3 and – more problematically, from the *Sunday Independent*'s point of view – the launch of the *Sunday World* in March 1973. By the end of that year, this new kid on the block (which had been launched with an initial capital of £40,000 and a half-expectation that it might not last for longer than six weeks) was selling 200,000 copies a week. Nor was the *Evening Herald* out of trouble. Its circulation had slipped between 1968 and 1972/3 from 142,000 to 134,000: in the same period the circulation of the *Evening Press* had gone up from 147,000 to 150,000: the latter paper's small ads, in particular, were a huge selling point to which the *Evening Herald* had never found a satisfactory answer.

There was an air of considerable national economic optimism, partly generated by the successful conclusion of the negotiations surrounding Ireland's application to join the European Economic Community. The expansionary policy at Independent House embarked upon by Pitcher was moving into a higher gear. In March 1971, E.M. Murphy wrote to his son:

> I have been having talks with the proprietors of the weekly newspapers
> in Counties Wicklow and Wexford with a view to possible acquisition.
> If my bid succeeds I will have the whole of the East Coast of Ireland

---

21 The other two were Mary McGoris and Miss R. O'Donoghue.   22 Kenny, *Talking to ourselves*, p. 8.

wrapped up from the border at Dundalk right down to the Wexford-Waterford boundary. These local papers are quite small individually but could build up into quite a big group.[23]

In due course the *Wexford People* group was acquired for some £140,000, with the *Kerryman* following at a cost of £378,000. The group's annual profits, announced on 4 March 1973, showed annual profits up by 120 per cent to a total of £770,100,[24] partly fuelled by cover price increases on both the daily and Sunday titles. Advertising rates, the company announced, would be increased by 10 per cent to pay for the national wage agreement. One shareholder had already taken advantage of the rising tide and had sold his shares, purchased some years earlier, at a tidy profit: his name was Major T.B. McDowell, a director of the *Irish Times*.[25]

By that date, however, unknown to the readers and to most of the shareholders, other changes were in train, which would alter the trajectory of the group and its titles in ways that could not readily have been foreseen. A critical date in the process was 21 January 1973 when the editor of the *Sunday Independent*, Conor O'Brien, published a multi-page *exposé*, by Joe MacAnthony, on the Irish Sweepstakes. The decision was typical of O'Brien's courage as editor, and of his dedication to breaking exclusive stories, which he had carried with him to the *Sunday Independent* from his previous berth at the *Evening Press*. In MacAnthony he had a gifted reporter, who had come into journalism from the unlikely position of public relations and marketing, via a stint as a researcher on the *Late Late Show* before being hired by the *Irish Independent*. Uncomfortable with the new style being pioneered by Pender, he had moved over to the Sunday title, where O'Brien had given him his head.[26] The great advantage of working for the *Sunday Independent*, with a single weekly deadline, meant that reporters like MacAnthony who realized the importance of research were not continually distracted by the need to file large amounts of copy, and could be given extended periods to work on more detailed reports.

To say that MacAnthony's report on the Irish Sweepstakes was detailed would be a profound understatement. The piece ran to 8,000 words and was originally designed to be published in two separate parts. It posed huge questions, not just for the government, which had for years licensed the private Sweeps organization to run a highly successful lottery on behalf of Irish hospitals, but also for the Sweeps promoters themselves. The article suggested that the promoters made excessive profits and commissions and had broken the laws

23 E.M. Murphy to Gerry Murphy, 9 Mar. 1971. Gerry Murphy papers.   24 For comparison, the profits of the McInerney building group for the same period were approximately £1.5 million.   25 Private information.   26 Personal information from Joe MacAnthony.

of other countries in which the Sweeps tickets were sold in huge numbers.[27] The implications were serious for the McGrath family, one of the most powerful business families in the country and substantial advertisers in the Independent group papers as well as being one of the controlling interests in the whole Sweeps operation.

When O'Brien saw what the original article contained, he realized that if he published the first instalment on 21 January, the likelihood was that the second instalment would never be allowed to appear. So, at some risk to his own career, and, as it turned out, to that of his reporter, he published the report in its entirety.

At his home in Foxrock in south county Dublin, the chairman of the board, T.V. Murphy, was totally unaware of his editor's plans. The business, personal and economic consequences of what had been published were unimaginable. Murphy had an appointment that very Sunday morning with a young Irish businessman who, fuelled by energy, charm, and an apparent blithe disregard for the serious financial obstacles to be negotiated, plainly wanted to take the whole business off his hands. As he went out to greet Tony O'Reilly in his morning coat, Murphy was in a state of exasperation, anxiety, and shock. One chapter was ending, another beginning.

27 Some Independent Newspapers employees added to their income by acting as 'drops' – lending their names and addresses to the Sweeps organization, which directed ticket-sellers in the United States and elsewhere to use these addresses for the return to Ireland of money and counterfoils in ways that would not attract the attention of the US postal authorities.

# 12 / 'The sense of history': working at Independent House

## IDA MILNE

The home of Independent Newspapers from 1924 to 2004 was Independent House, a labyrinthine block of linked buildings stretching from Middle Abbey Street back to Prince's Street, where the vans queued to collect the newspapers for distribution. On the west side, it was bordered by Prince's Lane. The Middle Abbey Street facade was four stories high above street level, with the fourth floor housing senior management who were known as just that, the Fourth Floor, appropriately enough for heads of the main Fourth Estate institution in the country. Behind that facade the buildings ranged in height and style, built and altered as function demanded. At the centre of the structure was a small courtyard, the mishmash of exterior walls towering high overhead. Here too was the library, a long narrow building with an apex roof of glass, and a crudely carved wooden statue of the Virgin Mary at the end. Independent House's own moving statue, it whirled around on its base to face into the room, a relic of an earlier era when the staff would congregate to say the rosary. Behind the Abbey Street facade, the ground floor housed the machine hall, location of the printing presses; when each edition went to press, the building shook as the machinery clanked into action. The familiar rumble meant that all was well within the business; failure to start on time, a change in the noise, or a sudden stop caused a general alarm and a flurry of anxious discussion.

The labyrinthine and varied style of the buildings was mirrored in the composition of the staff, with new groups added on and removed or expanded as need required. Three groups of employees – journalists, clerks and printers – dominated trade and social relationships within the company. Each group zealously guarded their own areas of expertise, wary of encroachment into tasks under their control and from changes planned by management. They shared, however, the thrill of working for a newspaper group: the smell of the ink, the roar of the presses, the mad dash of the distribution vans, the feeling that your work was a small part of history, no matter what function you performed within the building. Rita Doyle, who started working in Independent House at the age of 16 in 1959, and stayed for the rest of her working life – moving from advertising to accounts, and finally personnel – was not untypical: 'I loved going into that building, going up the steps every day with the *Nation* sign on the wall, the sense of history when you would go up the steps that you were part of history.'[1] This chapter focuses on the employment profile of the Independent staff while also examining the terms and conditions of those whose combined efforts produced three national titles. The discussion in the narrative includes interview material from retired and current employees of the newspaper group.

## RECRUITMENT

Most Independent Newspapers employees were recruited until as recently as the 1980s through family and friendship networks. This was the case even for jobs requiring specialist training. Many clerical staff started working with the company as young teenagers, and stayed for their entire working lives. Harry Allen's long family history of employment with the newspaper group was not unusual. His grandfather, also Harry Allen, had been a journalist on the *Freeman's Journal* and then the *Irish Independent*; his father went to work in 1939 at the age of 15, and stayed with the company for almost fifty years, finishing as head of accounts. Harry Allen himself went in for the summer after leaving school in 1969, and was still there forty-two years later, having worked in circulation, personnel and managerial accounts.[2]

This was a typical experience. Other examples of such life-long association with Independent House include Michael Doran and Willie O'Connor who were both employed initially as messenger boys. Michael Doran's contact was an uncle who worked in the advertising department, while Willie O'Connor's connection was the company secretary, John O'Riordan. 'He got me a job as an office boy, as it would have been termed at the time. Most people would have come in that way – based on a recommendation. That was in 1945. In general there wasn't any advertising for recruitment,' Willie O'Connor recalled.[3] His first job involved bringing advertisements from the Carlisle Building on Burgh Quay to the offices on Middle Abbey Street, and then distributing responses to individual advertising companies around Dublin. By retirement Willie O'Connor had become the company's chief cashier while Michael Doran had become deputy personnel manager.

A list of the permanent staff shows that over 1,200 people worked for the company in 1966. There were 149 people on the editorial staff, including the quaintly titled 'Female Correspondent'. The *Sunday Independent* had a skeleton staff of thirteen, including the editor and eight sub-editors, and only one dedicated feature writer; as was company policy these reporters were rostered

1 Interview with Rita Doyle, 7 June 2011. The *Nation* had been based at 90 Middle Abbey Street.   2 Interview with Harry Allen, 6 June 2011.   3 Interview with Willie O'Connor, 18 May 2011.

across all three national titles. There were forty-three people working in the circulation department, including eight travellers (later called circulation reps.), thirteen typists and two addressograph operators. Seventy-four people were employed in the transport department, including sixty-two drivers. Seventy-one people were employed in the branch offices in London, Belfast, Kilkenny, Cork, Limerick, Waterford, Dundalk and Sligo; these offices are now closed, although the company still retains reporters in some regions.[4]

Some 265 people were employed in the caseroom including ten overseers, seventeen men working on the stone, twenty-four readers, forty-two copy-holders, two stone assistants, forty compositors, ten apprentices, eighty-seven linotype operators, eleven teletype operators, three monotype operators, three monotype casters, six lino engineers, and ten lino assistants.[5] Most of these printer jobs are now gone. New technologies, outsourcing of functions and rationalization of others have combined to take their toll on employment numbers. For example, in 1966 one hundred people worked in advertising and another thirty-six were employed in the accounts department; these functions are now largely outsourced. A series of redundancy measures from the 1980s onwards, but particularly in 2004, significantly reduced the company's workforce. By 2012 there were 360 employees working for the now renamed Independent News and Media at its new Talbot Street premises in Dublin and its print plant at Citywest on the outskirts of the capital.

In the earlier era the company was not just a place of employment but also part of the social life of staff. For example, those who had worked for Independent Newspapers in the 1950s and 1960s recall a social life that revolved around dinner dances and sports events – sometimes organized by the in-house credit union – although a drink culture, a feature of newspaper work, was also evident in these and subsequent years. The main Independent public house, the Oval, was conveniently located a couple of doors up from the main entrance to Independent House on Middle Abbey Street. For many years, its credentials as a newspaper establishment were underwritten by the Pyke cartoons of well-known journalists that line its walls.[6]

While the company remained in Middle Abbey Street, the Oval was the main haunt of not only the newspapers' staff but also those who wanted to network with them including people from the worlds of advertising, public relations and business. Individuals looking for a quiet drink went to the Sackville on Sackville Place while print staff favoured Madigans, on Moore Street, or the Bachelor, on Bachelor's Walk. Late night drinkers would gravitate after hours

4 Interview with David Halloran, 28 July 2011; communication with Claire Grady, 5 Aug. 2011.  5 List for 1966, courtesy of Tony O'Reilly, deputy group director human resources director, Independent Newspapers (Ireland) Ltd.  6 The caricaturist, Bobby Pyke, regularly contributed cartoons to Dublin newspapers.

to the Irish Times Club, while those with real stamina might make it through the night until the early houses opened, as recalled by journalist Liam Collins, who is today news editor at the *Sunday Independent*:

> The social network was probably the pub, the Oval first of all, which would be jam packed with people from all the departments. I knew people from the wire room, the journalists, some of the printers who we knew from the pub, but the Oval would be full on Friday night, everybody from the Independent, and then also down to Higgins. That was where the people who had been banned from the Oval would go.[7]

Those who worked for Independent Newspapers in the Abbey Street era tell stories of meeting colleagues staggering along Independent House's serpentine corridors having overindulged on alcohol at press receptions, business meetings, the early houses or the Oval itself. Usually, somewhere along those corridors a door would open, and helping hands would bring in the miscreant, ply them with coffee, clean them up and keep them out of sight until they had recovered. Even executives were awarded this courtesy. Heavy drinking that persistently prevented people from performing their jobs was a different matter, and would lead to intervention.

## TERMS AND CONDITIONS

Before the development of third-level journalism courses, there were two main training paths for employment as a journalist on the Dublin daily newspapers – working initially on the provincial papers, or coming in directly as a copyboy and then progressing to reporter or sub-editor status. Danny Thornton, who later held senior positions on the editorial production staff and on the business pages, was one of those who started out as a copyboy in the sub-editorial department: 'I was asked by the chief sub if I harboured any ambitions to become a journalist. I asked if it paid more. When he said it did, I replied that I was interested.'[8] Thornton worked as a copyboy at night and by day studied for the Leaving Certificate so that he could transfer to the editorial staff. The first journalism programme began in the Rathmines College of Commerce in 1963. Former *Sunday Independent* journalist, Martin Fitzpatrick, was one of the first to take the course, being released each Monday for one academic year:

7 Interview with Liam Collins, 26 July 2011.  8 Interview with Danny Thornton, 8 July 2011.

> Sometime in the early to middle sixties they decided that journalists needed training and they set up a system in the Independent for all three newspaper groups, a half day course in Rathmines ... training for young reporters and subeditors. It was curious to think half-a-day training a week was considered enough to turn people into good journalists.[9]

Despite the expansion of external journalism courses, on-the-job training remained part of the learning process. Liam Collins wrote for provincial newspapers before working as a freelance for the *Evening Herald* in the late 1970s. In his experience, photographers often gave guidance when on a marking with a rookie reporter; similarly, copytakers would sometimes make suggestions to help out a young reporter having trouble composing copy to file over the telephone.[10]

Training for the printers was also undertaken in-house, although with apprenticeships, the processes involved were more formal than for other positions. Des Macken secured his job in 1947 through a client of his father, a hairdresser in O'Connell Street. The client, a manager at Independent House, said there was some casual work available. Macken was first sent for a reading test, and with successful results he started working with the company:

> I was still only 14 years of age. My mother was delighted because I got paid on a Friday, I gave her the 17s. and she gave me back 2s. Her vegetable bill for the week was 5s., so that paid the vegetable bill for three weeks. It was big money to her. I got an extra half crown by the following week, because there had been an [in-house] agreement. I could go into the Wooteners [cinema] every night of the week, with those wages.[11]

After eighteen months in the reading room, he sat the annual examination for the twelve coveted places available as printers' apprentices. He came first:

> You were inducted in 35 Gardiner Street [the premises of the print union], you had to stand in front of a committee and swear allegiance to the society, your father had to come in, you had to do a medical and you had to sign indentures. They tied you to the firm for seven years; they could dictate what you did and how you did it and how much you were paid. The conditions were not rigorously enforced, but you could not gamble and you could not get married without permission.[12]

Macken and his former colleague Jimmy Tierney recalled many characters working in the printroom when they started in the late 1940s and early 1950s: 'The

9 Interview with Martin Fitzpatrick, 11 July 2011.  10 Interview with Liam Collins, 26 July 2011.  11 Interview with Des Macken, 8 June 2011.  12 Ibid.

older men were great, but they were all caught in this time warp, many of them were in their late sixties or older, they had been there forever.'[13] A review of the printing staff at Independent House was undertaken in the 1950s. The findings revealed that twelve of the printers were almost 80 years of age. All twelve were let go, as insurance only covered them up to 72 years of age. Jimmy Tierney recalled that people kept working beyond what is now viewed as the normal retirement age, as there was no formal pension, only an *ex gratia* payment, that could be stopped at any time.[14]

Both men and another Independent employee, Tony O'Reilly, who began as a printer before progressing to the human resources division, all testified to the colourful nature of some of their colleagues in the print room. Several had been in the British army or the Royal navy. Others had been involved in the war of independence including Billy McLean who had been a member of Michael Collins' 'hit squad'. 'He came in on the morning after Bloody Sunday, with a hole in his hand,' Des Macken recalled.[15] Of McLean, Jimmy Tierney added: 'He worked with us, his hand was all twisted. We used to sit near him, and every so often he would start to roar, with the pain in his hands'.[16] Another colleague, Mick Molloy, had helped set and print the Proclamation of the Republic in Liberty Hall, in April 1916.

Like the society in which it operated Independent Newspapers was a conservative workplace in the 1950s. The Murphy family and the redoubtable company manager, John J. Dunne, were part of a conservative religious elite, and the workplace reflected that. This conservative attitude impacted on the newspapers; company policy was that every illustration or cartoon had to be inspected before it appeared in print.[17] Maureen O'Connell was detailed to check whether illustrations passed the declared moral standards. If, for example, a cartoon contained a female figure wearing a bikini, it would be whisked off to the artist to turn the bikini into a more modest swimsuit. Underwear advertisements were subjected to similar treatment. When a new hotel opened and advertised itself as a 'roadhouse', one member of the advertising staff deemed the term unsuitable to appear in print as it was considered to have unsavory connotations.[18]

Management also kept a watching eye on the behaviour of the staff at Independent House. Each year, employees had to apply in writing for a pay rise; it was felt that those who were known not to attend church services and who frequented public houses were less likely to succeed in these applications. When Bartle Pitcher was appointed company manager in 1963, an incremental pay scale was introduced for the first time, ending the need for the annual letter. Some

13 Interview with Jimmy Tierney, 8 June 2011.  14 Ibid.  15 Interview with Des Macken, 8 June 2011.  16 Interview with Jimmy Tierney, 8 June 2011.  17 Interviews with Michael Doran and Willie O'Connor, 18 May 2011.  18 Interview with Willie O'Connor, 18 May 2011.

long-time members of staff received substantial pay increases which only confirmed a belief that Pitcher's predecessor had blocked their annual applications. 'Pitcher's era brought in massive improvements for staff,' Michael Doran recalled.[19] When some of the more conservative employees complained because the clerical staff planned to join the Workers' Union of Ireland, Willie O'Connor recalled that Pitcher responded: 'I'd rather deal with the WUI than with every member of staff in the place.'[20] The trade unions were powerful forces within Independent Newspapers. For many years nothing could happen without their permission. Pauline Maher, who joined the company in the late 1960s as a member of the clerical staff, recalled: 'The print union was the most powerful union in the house. If they stopped, there was no paper. After that, it was probably the journalists.'[21] Indeed, there were regular periods when industrial disputes meant the newspapers were not published; during the prolonged strike of 1965, all three titles were off the street from early July to mid-September.

New employment practices were introduced at Independent House as the Irish economy modernized with greater priority paid to the terms and conditions of employees and more focus on their legal rights. A marriage bar, whereby women were obliged to give up their jobs when they got married, ended in the 1970s. Under the marriage bar, women could be rehired on a temporary basis, losing pension rights, and going to the end of the holiday list. Some women remained employed in a temporary capacity for many years.[22] Equal pay for women was introduced in the 1970s, on foot of an EEC directive to eliminate pay discrimination on grounds of sex and the raising of some test cases by the clerical union.[23] Yet, even thirty years later women within the clerical staff accounted for a greater proportion of the lower pay grades than their male colleagues.

Like in other areas of employment in Ireland, women found they were confined to certain roles. Copy-taking, which involved the typing of reports read over the phone by journalists, was usually done by women. The printing staff was a male domain. Editorial jobs that offered the chance of overtime tended to be in areas where women journalists did not work and reporters were not paid overtime. The news subediting staff was exclusively male, and was so until 1982 even though there was no bar to women being appointed.[24] The antisocial hours that the night subeditors worked may have been viewed as being unsuitable for female workers; but that did not stop women filling most of the tele-ads positions that involved similar functions to the stone sub-editors. The appointment of women to execu-

19 Interview with Michael Doran, 18 May 2011.  20 Interview with Willie O'Connor, 18 May 2011.  21 Interview with Pauline Maher, 18 Apr. 2011.  22 Interviews with Rita Doyle and Eleanor Murphy, 7 June 2011.  23 EU Directive 75/117/EEC (Equal Pay), 10 Feb. 1975.  24 Interview with Martin Fitzpatrick, 11 July 2011. Also, communication with Paul Hopkins, 4 Aug. 2011, and with Claire Grady, 5 Aug. 2011.

tive positions within the editorial staff was slow, to say the least. A few women progressed in editorial positions including Anne Harris (as deputy editor at the *Sunday Independent* and from February 2012 as editor) and Noirin Hegarty (at the *Evening Herald*, and independent.ie) and Claire Grady (*Evening Herald*). Despite these advances, however, Grady, who is executive editor at the *Evening Herald*, observed that in her time with the group only one staff photographer was female while no woman worked on the newsdesk of the *Irish Independent* prior to 1998.[25]

The female staff members were pleasantly surprised when a free cervical smear scheme was introduced on a management initiative in the 1980s along with an eye test for all staff to deal with concerns about the increased use of computers. There were other perks: a four-day week – introduced in the 1970s, six weeks holidays – introduced in the 1980s and the possibility of being paid extra for working anti-social hours and public holidays. As Pauline Maher put it: 'The main reason people stayed in the Independent was wages, not job satisfaction; especially in the clerical end. We had no qualifications, and the terms and conditions were excellent. Where else would you have got a four-day week?'[26] Independent Newspapers may not have been the perfect employer but many of those interviewed for this chapter viewed their terms and conditions as relatively good. As David Halloran explained; 'I genuinely thought they were a great employer. After O'Reilly took over, we got a four-day week and shortly afterwards my salary jumped from thirty to seventy-two quid a week. That was huge. You had problems, but I always felt O'Reilly was a good employer.'[27]

## MANAGEMENT

When Tony O'Reilly took over Independent Newspapers in 1973, journalists at the company staged a sit-in that caused a production stoppage. One of the issues about which they sought assurances was editorial independence, an assurance the new owner duly provided.[28] O'Reilly's influence proved to be more subtle than crude according to many editorial staff. According to David Halloran, who was deputy news editor at the *Irish Independent* in the 1970s and 1980s, 'the owner didn't influence the news, but you would be influenced by the owner'.[29] Halloran noted that he never received a call from O'Reilly:

> He was never one to leave himself open to the charge that he would influence something. The thing about it is that if someone owns a news-

25 Communication with Claire Grady, 5 Aug. 2011.   26 Interview with Pauline Maher, 18 Apr. 2011.   27 Interview with David Halloran, 28 July 2011.   28 Interview with Danny Thornton, 8 July 2011.   29 Interview with David Halloran, 28 July 2011.

paper and their wife is the president of the Soroptimist Society you are going to cover that meeting. You are going to take a photograph, get the right side of her face, get everything right, and it will get on a prominent page. It's not going to be buried in a two-inch double column down on the bottom of page thirty-seven.[30]

Another retired journalist, Martin Fitzpatrick, offered the example of where an owner might ensure the appointment of a business editor, who would be likely to treat his business interests favourably, as a substitute for direct editorial interference. Fitzpatrick observed he had only one personal experience of editorial interference; that was when Michael Hand, then editor of the *Sunday Independent*, excised copy he [Fitzpatrick] had written about Atlantic Resources, a company in which O'Reilly had an interest. The action led to a threat of a work stoppage in June 1981. Fitzpatrick remembered that 'The Dublin newspaper management association cobbled together an agreement that whenever Tony O'Reilly's business interests were mentioned they would be treated without any favour. That is the only incident I can cite directly.'[31] From an earlier era, Willie O'Connor recalled a comment made by one of the Murphy family when pressed on whether the owner would try to influence the news: 'Murphy said that they would never try to change the news, but they might change the editor.'[32]

The business of Independent Newspapers was transformed following O'Reilly's arrival. The appointment of Joe Hayes as managing director for the Irish operations in July 1981 was credited by several interviewees for this chapter as bringing a new dynamism to the company. Hayes joined Independent Newspapers in 1978 from Gallagher Tobacco where he had been marketing manager and remained as managing director of Independent Newspapers until 1994. 'He was looking at newspapers in a different way, and was very influential in the way that the newspapers were moving at the time,' Liam Collins acknowledged.[33] Hayes was, Collins observed, very aware of the changing dynamic of media at that time and the appointment of Aengus Fanning as editor of the *Sunday Independent* in 1984 reflected that awareness: 'He started to move away from the idea that news is all important and got commentators. I think it was Aengus and Joe Hayes that made that fundamental change'.[34] Interestingly, until the latter part of the O'Reilly era few management appointments were made from outside the company – and some of the more dynamic trade union representatives were candidates for promotion. 'They promoted the union activists, because they were too good. Paddy MacMahon, Jack Gilroy, Michael Doran,

30 Ibid.   31 Interview with Martin Fitzpatrick, 11 July 2011. See also, chapter 14.   32 Interview with Willie O'Connor, 18 May 2011. See also, n17, chapter 11.   33 Interview with Liam Collins, 26 July 2011.   34 Ibid.

Declan Carlyle, all were promoted to management because they were such efficient union negotiators,' Pauline Maher recalled.[35] Three names from the latter
list subsequently worked in the personnel or human resources department.

With all the focus on the company's present and future little enough attention was paid to its past. Demands on storage space occasionally led to management instructions to destroy archival treasure. From time to time staff, acting
on their own initiative, rescued potential archival material designated for dumping. When an editorial executive ordered the destruction of an older section
of the library's chief research resource – the newspaper cuttings files – in the
1990s, the person designated to do the job tried to negate the effects of the
destruction of what she saw as valuable research material by delivering bun-
dles of cuttings specific to areas of interest to reporters. Other staff rescued
potential archival ephemera, designated for shredding when management was
trying to clear space in the basement (Harry Allen found an old *Irish Independent*
newsroom markings book from the 1920s, which carried details of the jobs his
grandfather and other reporters had been assigned).[36] Bound copies of *Sport*, the
weekly sports newspaper published by the *Freeman's Journal* were retrieved from
a skip and donated to the National Library, thus filling gaps in that institution's
still incomplete run, and making an invaluable contribution to the study of
sports history. Glass plate negatives were dumped almost en masse during a
mid-century cull when only some of the more obviously historic ones were kept.
Film negatives and a small selection from the vast hardcopy collection of the
photographic library, designated for dumping when new technology was introduced, were also ultimately preserved. The failure to treasure potentially valuable archival material was not confined to Independent Newspapers – similar
attitudes prevailed in other newspaper offices in Dublin.[37]

CONCLUSION

While Independent Newspapers may not have been the perfect employer, many
of those interviewed for this chapter viewed their terms and conditions as relatively good, and enjoyed the excitement of working in the newspaper industry
and the sense of collegiality that accompanied newspaper life. The relationship
between management and staff was generally cordial and respectful, a reflection
perhaps of the fact that many managers emerged from the staff.

By the time of the most recent major round of redundancies in October
2004, when the company moved its offices from Middle Abbey Street to Talbot

---

35 Interview with Pauline Maher, 18 Apr. 2011.　36 Interview with Harry Allen, 6 June 2011.　37 Interview with
Martin Fitzpatrick, 11 July 2011.

Street, that sense of collegiality had been damaged. Restructuring of the clerical and pre-press functions resulted in over 200 redundancies. Of the 360 jobs still extant in 2012, 180 are held by journalists, some because of functions the editorial staff took over from other sections of the print and clerical staff. Many of the staff closely involved with the 2004 round of redundancies found that period very traumatic. One interviewee from the clerical staff noted: 'An awful lot of bitterness came with those redundancies. All the letters came on the same day, who was going and who was to be kept, when it came to moving from Abbey Street to Talbot Street. It created an awful atmosphere.'[38]

While others recognized that long-term changes in the newspaper business, combined with greater competition, required radical measures, the 2004 process was confirmation that the golden era of plenty of jobs, high wages and a four-day week were over. The values and changes to the workforce in Independent Newspaper in the period reflected, if only gradually, the values and changes in the wider political world that the group's titles chronicled. When the pace of change, delayed by a strong union presence, accelerated dramatically as the unions saw their power bases annihilated and as other factors came into play, many staff members were nostalgic for what had passed. While they were busy chronicling the events that occurred outside the building, nobody took the trouble to record the fascinating story of what was happening within. The irony was not lost on many of the interviewees for this chapter.

38 Private information.

# 13 / Heavy lifter or great news-hound? The editorship of Vincent Doyle, 1981–2005

## JOE BREEN

On 22 September 2010, the day following the death of Vincent (Vinnie) Doyle at the age of 72, the *Irish Independent* united in tribute to a man variously described by his colleagues as 'probably one of the greatest of all editors', 'a true newspaper romantic', and a 'legend … a talisman, an iconic figure who guided the fortunes of the *Irish Independent* through some of Ireland's most turbulent years'.[1] This was predictable enough; newspapers are notoriously sentimental about their own and in death even the relatively successful journalist can expect a colourful send-off. However, the tributes that flowed for Doyle carried considerably more than a tinge of regret at his passing. For almost twenty-five years he had deftly steered the *Irish Independent* through a rapidly changing Ireland, critically maintaining its circulation dominance over the local and British competition by fair means and foul. In the process he helped to generate the money that funded the growth of Independent Newspapers, later to become Independent News and Media (INM), fuelled the global ambitions of Tony O'Reilly and consolidated the dominant position of INM in Ireland.

The glowing tributes to Doyle might have surprised the people he most ardently sought to serve – the *Independent*'s readership – because though a charismatic figure in the heat of a deadline-dominated newsroom, and a legend in the world of Irish journalism, he was generally unknown to the people who bought his newspaper every day. He liked it that way. One colleague remembered that 'he was uncomfortable away from his newspapers and seldom appeared on radio or TV. He was, essentially, an exceptionally private man. He used to say that editors are best heard through their own newspapers'.[2] Doyle was also different in that he was a sub-editor at heart. In newspapers there is traditionally a metaphorical wall between subs and reporters. Though both are described as journalists, each coterie views themselves as superior. In addition, editors are typically drawn from the reporting class, particularly in broadsheet newspapers. As such his appointment was unusual for a newspaper that saw itself as a 'quality' publication. This point was raised in the *Irish Times* obituary, which pointed out that many observers felt at the time of his appoint-

1 *Irish Independent*, 22 Sept. 2010.  2 Ibid.

157

ment that he was, by education and instinct, ill-suited for the task.[3] But Doyle would prove them wrong by increasing the pace of change begun under his predecessor Aidan Pender's editorship, revamping what was an ageing and staid publication into a dynamic Irish version of a newspaper Doyle greatly admired – the *Daily Mail*. That British newspaper controlled the middle market in Britain and Doyle was determined to do likewise with a similar diet of hard news and soft features, jettisoning the newspaper's traditional support for Fine Gael in favour of a more pragmatic approach to politics. In the process, over almost twenty-five years, he would bustle through controversy and criticism, savour much success and survive the most dramatic period of change in newspaper history.

EARLY DAYS

Vinnie Doyle's voice carried absolute authority in the newsroom of the *Irish Independent* but it was very rarely heard outside it – apart, that is, from late evening liquid debriefing sessions in the Oval pub, just down the street from the *Independent*'s Abbey Street offices. Doyle made an exception for *Talking to Ourselves*, Ivor Kenny's 1994 series of interviews with the editors of the island's main newspapers. This long interview covered much ground, from his humble beginnings to his belief in the primacy of news to deliver circulation, and from his formative influences to his way of working. It is essential reading to gain an insight into what drove Doyle throughout his career.

Born in Dublin on 9 February 1938, his parents were Ned Doyle, a labourer, and 'housewife' Kathleen Harris, and they lived on Fontenoy Street, on Dublin's northside. Within five years his father had died and his mother faced the daunting prospect of rearing her only child alone at a time of great deprivation for the working class. 'The late 40s and early 50s were difficult times in Dublin and we were poor,' he told Kenny. His mother tried dressmaking but was eventually forced, in order 'to keep body and soul together', to work as a cleaner.[4] By this stage he was in St Vincent's CBS in Glasnevin. This school traditionally catered for boys from both the working- and middle-class communities in the area. It was here that he learned hard lessons in the gulf between the two:

> There were things that they did not have to do. I would have to go to a local turf depot and bring free turf home on a hand-cart – we had no other way of heating our house. That was no big deal but it does take

3 *Irish Times*, 25 Sept. 2010.   4 I. Kenny, *Talking to ourselves: conversation with the editors of the Irish news media* (Galway, 1993), p. 13.

on a significance when you see your school pals wheeling by on new Raleigh bicycles, something you could never aspire to.[5]

The romantic story would have Doyle rising above these disadvantages, but it was not so simple nor so soon. By his own admission he was not an outstanding pupil; 'did all right in my Leaving Cert' – but he hoped his love of English, writing and books would help him avoid a dead-end job.[6] As a result of a 'lucky break' in 1958 he got a job in the library of the *Irish Press*, then a feisty Fianna Fáil supporting competitor to the market-leading, Fine Gael tending *Irish Independent*, the fast-declining, Protestant Big House eminence of the *Irish Times* and the restricted regional base of the *Cork Examiner*. Doyle felt at home: 'Instinctively I knew I was in the right place – I wanted to stay there.'[7]

Within six months he moved on when he applied successfully for the job of copyboy in the sub-editors department. The role of copyboy has long since disappeared into newspaper history – there is no scope these days for young men (and subsequently women, hence the later title copysorter) to make tea, run errands, sort wire agency copy and, occasionally, get the chance to learn subbing. A year later to his delight he was appointed a junior sub: 'There was a certain romanticism about the subs, a certain air of "we run the show" and a definite distaste for even the best of reporters.'[8] This empathy and association with the subs' lot never left him. He was determined to succeed. For example, after the senior subs had gone home he would stay behind so that he could go over any of their discarded work and learn from it. In his interview with Ivor Kenny he observed that 'If you're handed a story and you're nervous, the story tends to dominate you. You don't know how to handle it, what to cut out. In the end, you find yourself knowing instinctively what to do with a story'.[9]

He stayed with the *Irish Press* for two-and-a-half years, finessing his skills as a wordsmith, learning about layout and design and even becoming the person responsible for the show-business page of the *Sunday Press*. This involved him reviewing film and theatre as well as subbing copy. (According to a 1983 profile in *Magill* magazine he was fired by editor Matt Feehan for 'lifting' a story from *Time* magazine – but before his dismissal could take effect Feehan himself was dismissed).[10] The next stop on his journey of discovery was his first job of many in Independent Newspapers. In 1963, inspired by the success of the *Sunday Times* magazine in Britain, the *Sunday Independent* launched the country's first colour magazine and Doyle was asked to work on it. At the time, Independent Newspapers was going from strength to strength buoyed by its

5 Ibid. 6 Ibid. 7 Ibid., p. 14. 8 Ibid. 9 Ibid. 10 A. Murdoch, 'The cutting edge of the Indo', *Magill*, Nov. 1983, 35–41 at 36.

titles' 'confident appeal to the increasingly prosperous Catholic middle classes'.[11] However, the magazine was ahead of its time and, having lost the huge sum of £750,000, it closed after nine months. Doyle found himself jobless and in a pickle. He had met and married Gertie Leech – 'my wife, my lover, my best friend'[12] – and she was six months pregnant with their first child. He searched for work, getting some shifts on the *Evening Herald* and the *Sun* and then in 1966 he secured a staff post on the *Herald*. This time he would not leave Independent Newspapers until he retired.

His rise was steady from that point. When *Herald* editor Aidan Pender took over the *Irish Independent* editorship in 1970, he brought Doyle with him as assistant editor. In 1973 Doyle was promoted to night editor before taking over as *Herald* editor in 1977. In a two-horse race the paper, which had a circulation of 125,526 in 1980, was running a very poor second to the *Evening Press,* which had a circulation of 172,780.[13] The *Herald* was under-resourced and Doyle was under pressure. He responded in characteristic fashion. At an internal conference of senior managers and editors he made a direct plea for support and more resources to Tony O'Reilly who had taken over the Independent Group in March 1973. O'Reilly agreed and following intensive market research and the introduction of a weekly junior soccer supplement, the *Herald* began its ascent. In his report to the board in 1980, O'Reilly described the *Herald* as 'editorially the most improved paper in Ireland'.[14] Two years later, the *Herald* was published in tabloid format and began to attract a larger share of the under 35-year-old readership. By 1983 the gap between both evening newspapers had fallen to 26,400.[15] O'Reilly, the 'folk-hero of capitalism',[16] obviously saw in Doyle a man who could do good business for him. As O'Reilly sharpened the business side, we can surmise that he expected Doyle to do likewise with the group's editorial standard bearer. And so, in 1981, Vinnie Doyle, who only twenty-five years earlier would have been considered as one of society's disadvantaged, took over as editor of the most popular newspaper on the island.

## EDITING THE 'INDO'

The role of editor in any major newspaper requires a plethora of skills and a temperament to match them. You must lead and inspire staff, placate and cajole management (often at the same time), nurture and seduce readers and avoid offending the all-critical advertisers unless absolutely necessary; all this while

---

11 J. Horgan, *Irish media: a critical history since 1922* (London, 2001), p. 64.   12 Kenny, *Talking to ourselves,* p. 27.   13 *Business & Finance,* Oct. 1989, p. 15.   14 Murdoch, 'The cutting edge of the Indo', p. 36.   15 *Business & Finance,* Oct. 1989, p. 15.   16 F. O'Toole, 'Brand Leader', *Granta,* 53 (1996), 47–74 at 65.

critically retaining your independence and that of your publication. Harold Evans, the former London *Times* and *Sunday Times* editor whom many consider the greatest editor of his generation before he fell foul of Rupert Murdoch in 1981, once stated that, concerning the thorny issue of editorial control, the best results come from 'a marriage of an editor and an ownership/management where both agree on the core identity of the newspaper and its resources, and then leave the editor free to do his best, mistakes and all'.[17] Tony O'Reilly has always maintained that his editors are free to publish what they wish though commentators such as Fintan O'Toole and Roy Greenslade contest the validity of that oft-repeated statement.[18] Vinnie Doyle never strayed from that official line.

When he took over from Aidan Pender, Doyle diagnosed the *Irish Independent* as 'suffering from being out of touch with the new liberalism which had been growing in influence since the late 60s and early 70s'.[19] He brought a new team, a new ethos and a new vitality to the *Independent*. It was as if he had been rehearsing for the role throughout his whole life; it was, he said, his 'lifelong ambition' to edit the newspaper. Having been assistant editor and night editor there was nothing he did not know about how the newspaper functioned, the strengths and weaknesses of staff as he perceived them and the personal politics, egos and jealousies that are typical of any newsroom. From his time as *Evening Herald* editor, and as a close associate of Pender's, he would have been very aware of the taut dynamic between editorial management and general management and of the more subtle demands of the newspaper's owner. In addition, Doyle would have been aware, as no doubt O'Reilly was, that both were northside boys, albeit raised on different sides of the tracks, though O'Reilly's past, as Fintan O'Toole revealed, was not quite the soft middle-class upbringing of popular understanding.[20] It is safe to assume that both men understood each other, knew what was demanded of each other and knew what each aspired to. In Doyle's case it was to have the necessary support to get the job done, to crush all opposition, to make the *Independent* the undisputed voice of middle Ireland just as his hero David English had achieved with the *Daily Mail*.

O'Reilly needed Doyle to update the *Independent*, make it again central to the national conversation, consolidate and grow its circulation and ensure that it produced the money required to fund the company's global ambitions. It may be argued that each achieved their goal, though Doyle's vision of total editorial victory over his nearest and most mocked competitor, the *Irish Times* – 'I

think the *Irish Times* have shot their bolt', he said in 1993 – was very wide of
the mark.[21] While his editorship was notable for a pronounced sharpening of
the *Independent*'s editorial performance, many observers and competitors believe
that he went too far. John Horgan, now the press ombudsman, stated that Doyle
'brought to his position a tough – some would say ruthless – approach to news,
and a determination to beat the opposition on all major stories.'[22]

One of the first steps Doyle took as editor was to commission extensive
market research into how the paper was perceived by the public. Lansdowne
market research found that the public viewed the paper as 'dull, sensational,
parochial, rural, unreliable, lacking in appeal to females and that no one identified with it'.[23] The research resulted in the introduction of a news analysis section, a property section, more features and a modernized business section. Doyle
also pulled a core team around him. Journalists of the calibre of Michael
Brophy and Jim Farrelly were happy to join his cause. Many followed him from
the *Herald*. They were his gang and he was the undisputed leader. One former
senior executive remembers what it was like in those early days:

> In a word: exciting. Every day in the Indo was a blank page; you never
> knew what the final product would be like. Under Vinnie it was made
> much more uncertain because of his volatility and demanding news-
> driven energy. He had boundless energy. In at 9a.m., driven in by his wife
> Gertie in his company car – he didn't drive. When he took over from
> Aidan Pender everyone knew it was going to be a dramatic change in
> operations. Pender, a silver-haired, pipe smoker was very much the gen-
> tleman editor. He spoke through people, each evening he'd visit the news-
> room basically to say goodnight to the news editor and nod to the few
> reporters still working away. It was all very sedate. Doyler changed all
> that from day one. He mirrored himself on the *Mail*'s David English. He
> dressed well above everyone in the office. His uniform was to show he
> was in a different class. At the time the subs desk was manned in the
> main by an elderly bunch of cardigan-wearing eccentrics. They moved
> with that slow step of the night worker. Habits grown out of years of
> shift work meant the subs desk had another world quality. A monastic
> silence was the first thing that hit you. No TV or radio, loud talking or
> any talking was frowned upon by the subs themselves. Rituals abounded
> among them, like tea-making. They had an air of superiority. Doyler's
> arrival changed their world. He lined up a chief sub in Vinny Mahon

---

21 Kenny, *Talking to ourselves*, p. 22.   22 Horgan, *Irish media*, p. 107.   23 Doyle cited in M. O'Brien (2001) *De Valera, Fianna Fáil and the Irish Press* (Dublin, 2001), pp 158–9.

who exuded a brusque, no-nonsense air. He pushed story after story on subs. Now they didn't have time to talk.[24]

Doyle's insatiable appetite for breaking news meant that competition was everything, including against titles in his own group. The *Evening Press* had been the target when he was at the *Herald*, now it would be the *Irish Press* and the *Irish Times* and later the *Irish Examiner* when it dared publicly, and rather optimistically, to challenge the *Independent*'s control of the middle market. He also had a 'particular dislike' of RTÉ because he believed it cut into print advertising.[25] The former senior executive remembers:

> He was driven by news. If a reporter from the *Press* or the *Times* had a line we hadn't he took it personally … You were picked because you would do as Doyler would do. If the RTÉ 9p.m. news had a story you didn't have, you 'lifted' it. Forget the newsroom. If they couldn't provide in time you started banging it out straight from the notes taken from the TV and radio.[26]

This was also the era of the elevator shift, the late shift so called because when the first editions of the other newspapers arrived in the office they were to be combed for exclusives suitable for 'lifting'. Any and all would then be typeset and carried in the *Independent*'s second edition, most often without any attribution or perhaps with a line buried deep at the end of the story. He also arranged for the first editions of the Fleet Street dailies to be sent over to Abbey Street by fax, a crude but effective mechanism. London's Fleet Street exclusives were no safer from Doyle's clutches than those in Dublin. Doyle's changes had the desired effect – at least the effect desired by O'Reilly. Market research showed that under his editorship the paper was 'seen to display the common touch with authority, had a core audience right across the social spectrum, had an improved layout of content and was perceived to be trying harder'.[27] But for all this, the paper's circulation declined during the 1980s. In 1983 its circulation stood at 165,768 compared to 86,146 for the *Irish Times* and 94,295 for the *Irish Press*. In 1988 the *Independent* stood at 154,296, the *Times* at 86,227 and the *Press* at 79,108; in 1992 the figures stood at 149,065, 92,797 and 50,443 respectively. Annoyingly for Doyle, perhaps, in 1987 Independent Newspapers launched the *Daily Star* (with a 1988 circulation of 81,169) that damaged not only the *Irish Press*, but also soaked up readers, particular younger readers, that might otherwise have been attracted to the *Independent*.[28]

**24** Private source, interview with author, 12 Apr. 2011.   **25** J. Downey, *In my own time*, p. 237.   **26** Private source, interview with author, 12 Apr. 2011.   **27** Doyle cited in M. O'Brien, *De Valera*, pp 158–9.

James Downey, a former deputy editor of the *Irish Times*, changed his view of Doyle for the better after the *Independent* editor created space for him at the newspaper. While Downey undoubtedly carried baggage from his experience at the *Times*, where he lost a bitter battle for the editorship to Conor Brady in 1986, his observations of Doyle's strengths and his way of working are informative if contested. He found the *Independent* 'infinitely more professional and more news-conscious' [than the *Irish Times*] and that working for Doyle 'was exciting for an old-time newsman like myself':

> To be sure, he and his editorial executives might sometimes take their enthusiasm too far. As they said themselves, he would do 'anything for a story'. Having got hold of a good one, he and they would exert themselves to see how much they could 'firm it up'. Can we say this? Will the facts we know for sure support such and such a conclusion? Finally, will we go for it? Occasionally that ended in going too far, and perhaps falling foul of the libel laws or the NUJ code of practice. But old-timers who cling to the time-honoured belief that boundaries are there to be tested have the right attitude.[29]

Downey also states that Doyle's 'hands-on' working methods were extraordinary: 'I found it amazing when I first saw him, as was his custom on Friday nights, sitting at the back desk with his sleeves rolled up, performing the function of a night editor or chief sub-editor'.[30] Conor Brady, who edited the *Irish Times* from 1986 to 2002, understandably is less convinced of the *Independent*'s superiority in news gathering:

> 'News' can be viewed at two levels. There is the 'breaking' of news, the bringing for the first time into public knowledge of information that has hitherto been unknown. Then there is 'running news' in which an ongoing situation that is developing and changing over weeks, months and perhaps years, has to be reported. There were times when the *Irish Independent* beat the *Irish Times* in 'breaking news', but not as often as myth would have it. In reality, the *Irish Times* probably beat the *Independent* more often in breaking news stories. But when it came to 'running news' the *Irish Times* invariably left the *Independent* standing. Whether it related to the Northern Ireland Troubles, the development of the European Communities or the emergence of crises within the Catholic church, the *Irish Times* was so far ahead that comparisons with the *Independent* would not be fair.[31]

28 Circulation figures are from Kenny, *Talking to ourselves*, p. 9.   29 Downey, *In my own time*, p. 234.   30 Ibid., p. 235. 31 Interview with Conor Brady, 12 Apr. 2011.

This concept of 'running news' is echoed in comments made by the former senior *Independent* executive in response to a question about Doyle's most obvious shortcomings:

> His refusal to accept that some issues deserved to be covered. The North was a bore to him unless atrocities were capable of taking over the front page. Campaigning journalism was a bore. He couldn't accept running a series of articles on anything. Every day was a new day. The Birmingham Six were all guilty until the world recognized their innocence. The Maguires and Guildford Four never got support from the Indo Group. The poor and disadvantaged didn't sell papers, so there was no room for championing their cause.[32]

The word that surfaces repeatedly when journalists recount working with Doyle is excitement. He relished big breaking stories, particularly if they were exclusive; he was 'fearless', running stories when lawyers urged caution. Reporter Sam Smyth, who, in November 1996, wrote the story that led to the creation of the Moriarty Tribunal into payments to politicians, credited Doyle with bravely holding his nerve and supporting him. The story outlined how supermarket mogul Ben Dunne had arranged for Dunnes Stores to pay for the refurbishment and extension of politician Michael Lowry's house. Doyle's response to Smyth's story was 'Great story if you can stand it up'.[33] Once Smyth had secured copies of the cheque and invoices involved, Doyle decided to run the story under the headline 'The Minister, a tycoon and the £200,000 house bill'.[34]

## CONTROVERSIES

There was no shortage of controversies during Doyle's career. The furore over the already cited 'lifting' practice was a constant running sore. In 1975, while still night editor of the *Independent*, Doyle lifted an exclusive story from the *Irish Press* between editions. During the siege in which Dutch industrialist Tiede Herrema was held hostage in a house in Monasterevan, Co. Kildare, *Irish Press* photographer Cyril Byrne had gained access to the house next door and recorded the conversations and negotiations that were ongoing for a full thirty hours. This sensational *Press* exclusive did not last long: the *Independent*'s city edition printed the story almost verbatim and without attribution.[35] In 1981, Doyle was fined £500 by the National Union of Journalists for lifting a story by Frank

---

32 Private source, interview with author, 12 Apr. 2011.  33 S. Smyth, *Thanks a million, big fella* (Dublin, 1997), p. 126.
34 *Irish Independent*, 29 Nov. 1996.  35 *Irish Press*, 24 October 1975 and *Irish Independent*, 24 October 1975.

McDonald that had been published in the *Irish Times* and a story by Eamonn McCann that had been published in the *Sunday World*. McDonald's article, which established a link between the owners of Dublin's Stardust Club and the accountancy firm of which former Taoiseach Charles Haughey had been a partner, was 'lifted' word for word from the *Irish Times* and reprinted, without attribution, in the later city edition of the *Independent*. Similarly, the paper had reprinted an exclusive interview that Eamonn McCann had conducted with Bernadette McAliskey.[36] The coverage of refugee affairs in the 1990s by the Independent group's titles also proved controversial.[37]

However, arguably the most striking controversy concerned the 'Payback Time' editorial carried on the *Independent's* front page on 5 June, the eve of the 1997 general election. In the editorial the newspaper urged its readers to vote for Fianna Fáil and the Progressive Democrats. Irish taxpayers had, it contended, been 'bled white' by the outgoing rainbow coalition of Fine Gael, Labour and Democratic Left and now it was 'payback time'. In his memoir, James Downey records that he wrote most of the leader with some help from colleagues but that the phrases 'bled white' and 'payback time' were Doyle's.[38] However, it was not just the language that surprised many but the positioning of the editorial on the front page on the day before the election.

On 14 June 1997 the *Irish Times* ran a story claiming that senior representatives of Independent Newspapers had warned the ruling rainbow coalition some months before the editorial was published that it would lose Independent Newspapers 'as friends' unless illegal television deflector systems in the west of Ireland were closed down.[39] A subsidiary company of Independent Newspapers, Princes Holdings, had invested heavily in a television distribution system that was being illegally received, free of charge, by these deflector systems. This *Irish Times* account of the communications between government representatives and those of Independent Newspapers was contested by the company and a statement denying that any threat had been made was issued swiftly. It asserted that the statement 'was never made or the threat contained within it ever implied ... and ... at no time during the meeting was editorial policy in relation to the election discussed.'[40] Whatever the truth of the matter, there was a general belief that something had changed in Irish media, and not for the better. Chris Morash, in his *History of the media in Ireland*, concludes: 'After the heat had waned from the issue, it became clear that regardless of what had actually happened, the very possibility that influence in one medium might have been used to shape policy in another medium brought with it the real

---

36 *Irish Press*, 20 Sept. 1981. 37 A. Pollak, 'An invitation to racism? Irish daily newspaper coverage of the refugee issue' in D. Kiberd (ed.), *Media in Ireland and the search for ethical journalism* (Dublin, 1999), pp 33–46. 38 Downey, *In my own time*, p. 250. 39 *Irish Times*, 14 June 1997. 40 Ibid., 16 June 1997.

ization that Ireland had moved into a period in which large media conglomerates would have increasing power'.[41]

DOYLE'S ACHIEVEMENT

James Downey sums up Doyle's achievement thus: 'He accommodated the *Irish Independent* to the revolutionary social changes then occurring or about to occur, while maintaining its standing as the newspaper of Middle Ireland – which itself has changed beyond the recognition of his predecessors'.[42] He states that he never knew anyone more steeped in the craft of journalism or better informed about the newspaper business in general. 'He greatly admired the *Daily Mail* and in particular its long-serving and immensely successful editor David English'.[43] Interestingly, Downey states that the *Mail*'s politics chimed with Doyle's own. This contrasts with the general description of Doyle as apolitical. Michael Denieffe, the *Independent*'s managing editor and Doyle's close associate, stated after his death that 'apolitical to a fault, he called the paper's political slant broadly on the simple basis of what he perceived as being positive for the good of the country in social, economic and strategic terms'.[44] It is interesting to contrast what one commentator construes as *Mail* ideology with Doyle's *Independent* as described by an insider:

> *Mail* views can be characterized thus: for Britain and against Europe; against welfare (and what it describes as welfare scroungers) and for standing on your own feet; more concerned with punishment than the causes of crime; against public ownership and for the private sector; against liberal values and for traditional values, particularly marriage and family life. It puts achievement above equality of opportunity and self-reliance above dependence. The *Mail* celebrates achievement against the odds, particularly where no 'state help' has been involved. It believes that too often the taxpayer is being taken for a ride and that bureaucrats are invading areas of private responsibility.[45]

The comments of the previously quoted former senior *Independent* executive illustrate how much Doyle was in thrall to the *Mail* ideology:

> Ever the slave to the *Daily Mail*, his was an Irish society of 'classes'. Fianna Fáil of the mohair suits fitted perfectly into this view, a view that the rest of the Indo Group followed. In the Irish context there was

41 C. Morash, *A history of the media in Ireland* (Cambridge, 2010), p. 210.   42 Downey, *In my own time*, p. 234.   43 Ibid., p. 236.   44 *Irish Independent*, 22 Sept. 2010.   45 P. Cole, 'Why Middle England gets the Mail', *The Guardian*, 20 Aug. 2007.

the Charlie set, the Fianna Fáilers with money, living in the affluent areas of Dublin. There was the old money class; the Lords and Lady this and that who regularly appeared in the feature pages. He was very conscious of them. He was a royalist or, more importantly, vehemently opposed to the IRA. No discussion; they were beyond the Pale. He would talk of having been sent a bullet in the post by the Provos. He would outdo the *Daily Telegraph* in his hatred of them. Then there was the literary set, the Brendan Kennellys and John McGaherns and J.P. Donleavy and, of course, Edna O'Brien. And on top of all that there was Hollywood. His days as the *Sunday Press* film reviewer never left him, Elizabeth Taylor at 45; 50; 55; 60; 70; Marilyn – what she would look like at 55; 60; 65. There was no end to it ... On the downside the underclass didn't warrant coverage. Pictures of the aged and infirm and disabled were out, in the early days at least. It was glitz and glam and heaven help a photographer who came back with pictures of 'some oul dogs at the Horse Show'.[46]

As Downey asserts, and colleagues in appreciations agreed, Doyle did eventually put his newspaper behind much social change, the so-called liberal agenda.[47] On 25 June 1983 the *Independent* published a page one editorial calling for a 'yes' vote in the next day's divorce referendum.[48] As Doyle himself saw it, this was 'a daring and controversial decision by the newspaper of middle Ireland which offended many traditional readers'.[49] But his opposite number at the *Irish Times*, Conor Brady, viewed the *Independent*'s conversion to social liberalism as too little too late:

> The *Irish Times* was a liberal newspaper, committed to the 'liberal agenda'. It urged freedom of conscience. It supported the availability of divorce and contraception and, in certain limited circumstances, the right of a woman to avail of therapeutic abortion. It supported the decriminalization of homosexual acts. The *Irish Independent* either opposed these or sat on the fence. I think that stance cost it dear. It was not seen by very many serious people as playing a full role in national debate.[50]

Nonetheless, Brady is generous, with qualification, in his assessment of his great rival: 'Vinnie's greatest achievement was to make the *Irish Independent* appear to be more than it was ... He had huge energy, enthusiasm and an unshakeable

---

46 Private source, interview with author, 12 Apr. 2011.   47 Downey, *In my own time*, p. 234.   48 *Irish Independent*, 25 June 1986.   49 V. Doyle, 'A unique place in Irish society' in B. Brennan (ed.), *Irish Independent: 100 years in the news*, centenary supplement, Jan. 2005, p. 8.   50 Interview with Conor Brady, 12 Apr. 2011.

belief in the power of the "scoop". He states that Doyle endured tight editorial budgets and was short-changed in staff 'if one measured his resources
against what was available to comparable newspapers in other European countries'.[51] This is an important point and one that must have rankled with Doyle,
especially as he watched the parade of resources at the *Irish Times* and the ever-
tightening *Independent* purse. He delivered for O'Reilly but O'Reilly never
matched Doyle's faith in him. Unlike his great hero, Sir David English, who
served as chairman of the Associated Newspapers board, Doyle was never
appointed to the board of Independent Newspapers.

## CONCLUSION

The picture that emerges is of a man who was not a crusader, who had no particular ideology but who was driven by a relentless need to be first, to be top, to
be best. When the *Independent* heard the *Irish Times* was planning a Saturday magazine, what *Magill* magazine called his 'gut competitive instinct' enabled him to beat
his rivals to it.[52] He also oversaw the remarkable production of a compact format
*Independent* along with the broadsheet – a very cumbersome production task. He
distrusted what he perceived as the grandees of the *Irish Times* with their high
notions of values. They could be the 'historypaper', or the 'viewspaper' or the
'snoozepaper' – he was editor of the newspaper. It was dog eats dog and, as far
as he was concerned, his teeth would always be sharper. He was no less indulgent
of the *Irish Press* before it folded in 1995, regularly, and unapologetically, 'lifting' its
best stories to the point when, on 7 July 1986, the *Irish Press* carried a piece outlining the number of stories lifted by the *Independent* the previous week.[53]

He was conservative by nature, devoted to his newspaper, suspicious of lofty
discourse and had little patience for the politically correct. While he adapted
to the changing world around him – though both he and the *Independent* initially
struggled to come to terms with the challenge of the internet – his newspaper
never made the running for social change; the most innocent reading of
'Payback Time' is that it was about getting tax breaks for the middle class. Yet
he was truly a major figure in the history of the *Irish Independent* and Irish journalism generally, a 'one-off' who clearly relished every minute he sat in the
editor's chair. He had come a long way from the poor boy struggling with a
load of turf enviously watching classmates zip by on their new bicycles. But in
a way he had not come that far: until the day he retired in 2005 he remained the
one who believed that he always had to do it the hard way.

51 Ibid.  52 Murdoch, 'The cutting edge of the Indo', p. 35.  53 R. Burke, *Press delete* (Dublin, 2005), p. 338. See also
*Irish Press*, 7 July 1986.

# 14 / Independent Newspapers and Irish society, 1973–98

## MARK O'BRIEN

Writing in 1889 the legendary nationalist MP and newspaper editor, T.P. O'Connor, took a side-swipe at those publications that proclaimed their independence of all political and business interests. He declared that he liked 'an "independent" journal as little as the politician who assumes to himself the same adjective'. In his long experience of newspapers and politics, he had, he declared, ultimately found that 'independence' was simply 'a euphemism for personal vanity, personal interest, or mere crankiness of temper and opinion'.[1] As we have seen in chapter two, despite its declaration that 'The extravagances of partisanship will be unknown in its editorial columns', William Martin Murphy was not shy in using the *Irish Independent* to defend his commercial interests during the Great Lockout of 1913.[2] Similarly, the *Irish Press*, although declaring that it would not be 'the organ of an individual, or a group or a party', was the political organ of Eamon de Valera and, to a lesser extent, Fianna Fáil.[3] In contrast, the *Irish Times* was upfront about where it stood: its first edition had declared 'As Irishmen we shall think and speak; but it shall be as Irishmen loyal to the British connection …'[4]

As Ireland modernized in the 1960s and as RTÉ began television broadcasting that was, by statute, obliged to be fair and impartial in relation to news and current affairs, the role of the newspaper as an advocate or defender of its owner's political or commercial interests became outdated. Briefly put, the *Irish Press* gingerly attempted to distance itself from its Fianna Fáil roots through the adoption of the 'fair to all, friendly to Fianna Fáil' mantra. For its part, the *Irish Times* transformed itself into an ownerless trust, 'free from any form of personal or of party political, commercial, religious or other sectional control', in 1974.[5] That left the *Irish Independent*. In 1973 the Murphy and Chance families sold their voting shares in Independent Newspapers to Tony O'Reilly. What followed was the rise of a media magnate, the growth of Independent Newspapers and concerns about the dominant position the company came to hold, and, ultimately, debates about what all this meant for Irish society.

---

1 T.P. O'Connor, 'The New Journalism', *The New Review*, 1:5 (1889), 423–34 at 433.  2 *Irish Independent*, 2 Jan. 1905. See chapter 2.  3 *Irish Press*, 5 Sept. 1931.  4 *Irish Times*, 29 Mar. 1859.  5 Irish Times Trust Ltd, memorandum of association, article 2.d.ii.a.

## THE RISE OF A MEDIA MAGNATE

In the early months of 1973 rumours abounded that Independent Newspapers was set to undergo a change in ownership. At this time, the company published the *Irish Independent,* the *Sunday Independent,* the *Evening Herald,* the *Drogheda Independent,* the *Dundalk Argus,* the *Wexford People* and the *Kerryman.* When, on 22 February, the board confirmed that 'certain approaches have been made' the quoted share price jumped from 145p to 200p in the space of one day of trading. Among those mentioned as being behind a possible takeover were Tony O'Reilly, Rupert Murdoch (who, the *Irish Times* reported, had apparently been spotted at Dublin Airport), Michael Smurfit, and Patrick McGrath, who had been incensed at the *Sunday Independent's* exposé of the running of the Irish Hospital Sweepstakes.[6] The prospect of such a large number of newspapers passing into Murdoch's ownership prompted the then minister for industry and commerce, Patrick Lalor, to declare that 'a situation in which ownership or control of Irish newspapers passed into non-Irish hands would be unacceptable' to the government.[7]

However, it was not Murdoch, but Tony O'Reilly that was talking to the Murphy family about the purchase of their voting shares that controlled Independent Newspapers. Born in Dublin in May 1936, O'Reilly studied law at University College Dublin and in 1980 earned a PhD in marketing from the University of Bradford. A talented rugby player, he earned twenty-nine caps for Ireland between 1955 and 1970. He joined the Irish Dairy Board as its general manager in 1962 where he developed the hugely successful 'Kerrygold' brand for exported butter and in 1966 he became managing director of the Irish Sugar Company. Thereafter, he made his name in international business.[8]

In January 1973 O'Reilly approached Independent chairman T.V. Murphy after a rugby international at Lansdowne Road and offered to buy the company. Murphy 'showed enough reluctance to keep the price up and enough interest to keep him bidding'.[9] They agreed to meet at Murphy's house the following day: the day the *Sunday Independent* published the Sweepstakes exposé that ended Murphy's passion for newspaper ownership. As rumours of a takeover abounded, one editorial executive met with Murphy and expressed concerns about editorial freedom. Murphy admitted he was not sleeping well and was 'haunted' by having to decide the future of the newspapers.[10]

In early March the company's NUJ chapel held a meeting that resulted in the non-appearance of the *Irish Independent.* In a statement, the chapel noted that the 180 journalists had been given no information about the impending takeover

6 *Irish Times,* 23 Feb. 1973.   7 Ibid., 24 Feb. 1973.   8 For more on O'Reilly's business life, see, C.H. Walsh, *Oh really O'Reilly* (Dublin, 1992), I. Fallon, *The Player* (London, 1994), or F. O'Toole, 'Brand Leader', *Granta,* 53 (1996), 47–74.   9 Private source.   10 Ibid.

or any guarantees about their continued employment. It noted that 'a group of faceless men is buying an important newspaper chain [and] its workers are being sold as if they were bonded slaves'. It also called for journalists to be represented on the board of directors.[11] The board of directors responded by sacking all 180 journalists.[12] The *Independent* remained off the streets for five days and several journalists staged a sit-in at Independent House. Although the board gave a written assurance that there would be no redundancies, that the newspapers would 'maintain their character', and that these conditions would be written into any takeover contract, the NUJ rejected it on the grounds that it had not been made by the new owners.[13] The union eventually received the same assurances from Tony O'Reilly and the employment of the journalists was deemed not to have been terminated. However, the request for journalistic representation on the board was rejected.[14]

In a radio interview, O'Reilly stated that his takeover of the company was 'primarily commercial'. His ambition for the company was for it to 'continue its aggressive commercial standards and for reasonable commercial expansion, whether in Ireland or indeed abroad'. The concerns expressed by the journalists, were, he observed, 'legitimate' and he had given them 'specific assurances in relation to editorial freedom [and] quality of employment'. He declared his intention to be a hands-off proprietor and noted that he 'drew a specific difference between ownership and management'. Asked whether the *Independent* would become a Fianna Fáil newspaper, he re-stated his point that editorial freedom had been assured. Asked whether he supported Fianna Fáil, he noted that he had been variously described as a supporter of 'all three parties' though he had never declared which political party he supported. When questioned on the power that control of so many newspapers might bestow on one person, O'Reilly was forthright in his view:

> That concern is legitimate. Each man in his own way has to show that he means what he says in terms of the commercial and editorial freedom of his papers. If he abuses that decision, the concern expressed will be shown to be legitimate.[15]

At least one newspaper expressed concern about the concentration of such a large number of newspaper titles in one pair of hands. The *Anglo-Celt* noted that Independent Newspapers held 'a commanding position in Irish newspapers [and] such power should not be transferred to one company never mind one person'.[16]

In late March 1973 the chairman of Independent Newspapers, T.V. Murphy, wrote to its shareholders to inform them that the holders of 'over 80%' of the

11 *Irish Times*, 13 Mar. 1973. 12 Ibid., 14 Mar. 1973. 13 Ibid., 16 Mar. 1973. 14 Ibid., 19 Mar. 1973. 15 Ibid., 19 Mar. 1973. 16 Ibid., 5 Mar. 1973.

company's 100,000 'A' voting shares (owned mostly by the Murphy and Chance families) had agreed to sell their shares to O'Reilly for a price of £10.95 per share.[17] While O'Reilly had been fortuitous in his timing of his offer to the two families (both of whom wanted out of the newspaper business) he was less fortunate with the regulators. The stock market rules had recently changed and since O'Reilly was gaining control of the company, he was now obliged to make a bid for the 2.3 million non-voting 'B' shares. This had not been the original plan. According to O'Reilly's biographer, Ivan Fallon, 'he [O'Reilly] and the bankers argued furiously with the takeover authorities, who refused to yield'.[18]

Ultimately the 'B' shareholders were offered £2.00 per share and several companies, including Fitzwilton and New Ireland Assurance (O'Reilly was a director of both companies), purchased over 900,000 'B' shares.[19] The holders of the 'B' shares were later given voting rights, with O'Reilly receiving additional shares, depending on the profitability of the company, to compensate for the loss of the exclusive voting rights of the 'A' shares. After all these manoeuvres O'Reilly's shareholding was estimated at 30 per cent.[20] In August 1973 O'Reilly wrote to the shareholders and informed them of his vision of the company expanding into the fields of advertising, publicity and commercial radio and television. Such activity would not, he maintained, be confined to Ireland: the company would, in due course, become 'an international communications group'. It was, by any standards, a prophetic letter.

## THE GROWTH OF INDEPENDENT NEWSPAPERS

Once in control of the company O'Reilly remained true to his word and kept an eye out for expansion opportunities. One of his first acquisitions was the *Sunday World*. Launched by Hugh McLoughlin and Gerry McGuinness of the Creation Group as a brash tabloid, the *Sunday World* literally exploded onto the staid Sunday newspaper market in March 1973. As pointed out by John Horgan, the *Sunday World* 'absorbed many insights from its UK competitors, notably a cheeky willingness to engage in sexual innuendo ... occasionally delivered tough and fearless journalism ... adopted a campaigning mode ... [and] ... specialized in short paragraphs, screaming headlines, and huge by-lines for journalists'.[21] It was an instant success; by December 1973 its circulation stood at 200,000 and its annual profit was £100,000. O'Reilly could not resist making an offer: in 1978 Independent Newspapers purchased 54 per cent of the *Sunday World* and bought the remainder of the shareholding in 1983. By 1984, Horgan

17 Ibid., 29 Mar. 1973.  18 Fallon, *The Player*, p. 201.  19 *Irish Times*, 29 Mar. 1973.  20 See *Irish Times*, 14 & 15 Sept. 1973.  21 J. Horgan, *Irish media: a critical history since 1922* (London, 2001), pp 108–9.

notes, the newspaper was contributing £1m per annum to the profits of Independent Newspapers and was a significant cash generator for the group.[22]

O'Reilly's next attempt at an acquisition did not go quite as smoothly. Established by Hugh McLoughlin and John Mulcahy, the *Sunday Tribune* made its debut in October 1980. The following year, it had a circulation of 110,000. The initial success of the newspaper was, however, effectively gambled on the launch of a daily tabloid, the *Daily News*, launched in October 1982.[23] The gamble did not pay off and the tabloid dragged the *Sunday Tribune* down with it. Purchased by Vincent Browne and Tony Ryan, the Sunday title survived but encountered severe financial difficulties in the late 1980s, during which approaches were made to the *Irish Times* for investment. Instead, a large tranche of its shares was put on the market and in late 1990 Independent Newspapers purchased 29.9 per cent of the title. As Horgan has pointed out, given the lacklustre financial performance of the *Tribune*, the purchase was most likely a defensive move to prevent any other investor from taking an interest in the title and challenging the position of the *Sunday Independent*, which had, the year before, finally overtaken the *Sunday Press* as the biggest selling Sunday newspaper.[24]

In 1992 Independent Newspapers proposed to increase its shareholding to 53.09 per cent in return for an investment of £1.9m. To protect the independence of the title, an editorial charter was agreed upon.[25] However, under new legislation, the Competition Act 1991, the move was referred to the Competition Authority, the report of which declined to sanction the increase by concluding that it would 'be likely to prevent or restrict competition ... and ... would be likely to operate against the common good'.[26] The then minister for industry and commerce, Des O'Malley, agreed. From then on, Independent Newspapers simply maintained the *Tribune* on a hugely expensive financial life support machine, most likely to prevent any inroads being made by the expanding *Sunday Times* or the newly established *Sunday Business Post*, until it finally pulled the plug in January 2011. One estimate put the value of Independent Newspapers' loans to the *Tribune* at €40m.[27]

### TAKING ON THE PRESS GROUP

It was, however, the targeting of the Press Group by Independent Newspapers that is most illustrative of the company's aggressive expansionist policy. Effective control of the Press Group had passed down through three genera-

22 Ibid., pp 109–10.  23 Ibid., pp 111–13.  24 Ibid., pp 138–9.  25 Ibid., p. 141.  26 *Competition Authority report of investigation of the proposal whereby Independent Newspapers plc would increase its shareholding in the Tribune Group from 29.9% to a possible 53.09%* (Dublin, 1992), 6:17.  27 *Irish Times*, 2 Feb. 2011.

tions of the de Valera family, and from the early 1980s the Group seemed to be in permanent crisis mode. The introduction of computerized production resulted in a three-week gap in production in 1983 and a twelve-week gap in 1985. The transformation of the *Irish Press* to tabloid format in April 1988 was countered by a joint venture between Independent Newspapers and Express Newspapers that launched a cheaper colour tabloid, the *Star,* in February 1988. As losses mounted at the Press, Independent Newspapers upped the ante for market share by launching a series of promotional games – 'Fortuna' in 1988 and 'Scoop' in 1989 – that forced the Press Group to react. The loss of 20,000 readers a day to the *Irish Independent* during the first week of 'Fortuna' forced the *Irish Press* to launch its own promotional game that cost in the region of £250,000. It responded to 'Scoop' by highlighting the 5p price increase of the *Irish Independent* through the use of a promotional tagline – 'Our scoop is no price increase'.[28]

The endless disputes over who controlled the Press Group were also manna from heaven to Independent Newspapers. The much-feted partnership with Ingersoll Publications in July 1989, which had promised to give Independent Newspapers 'a contest they did not expect', led to nothing other than acrimony and prolonged litigation.[29] According to the then *Irish Independent* editor, Vinnie Doyle, senior Independent executives were only too well aware of the infighting between the various board factions that were tussling for control of the Press Group. This presented Independent Newspapers with an ideal opportunity to increase the marketing of its own titles and put further pressure on the ailing Press Group. According to Doyle, a decision was taken 'to attack the Press on three fronts':

> The Independent Group's response then, was to put a trickle of money into the *Irish Independent* to fight the *Irish Press* which we were ahead of anyway, but we poured money into the *Herald* to attack the *Evening Press* and poured money into the *Sunday Independent* to attack the *Sunday Press.*[30]

The strategy paid off: as the infighting within the Press Group worsened and the circulation of its titles continued to decline, the benefactor, in circulation and advertising revenue, was Independent Newspapers. In December 1994 the unthinkable happened: Independent Newspapers purchased 24.9 per cent of Irish Press Newspapers and Irish Press Publications for £1m and a loan of £2m secured on the three newspaper titles. The move was condemned by the

28 M. O'Brien, *De Valera, Fianna Fáil and the* Irish Press (Dublin, 2001), pp 189–93. See also E. McCann, 'Scoop!', *Magill,* Feb. 1990, p. 46.  29 *Irish Press,* 8 July 1989. See also R. Burke, *Press delete* (Dublin, 2005).  30 Interview with Vincent Doyle.

National Union of Journalists as being 'designed to drip feed the only real source of competition to the Independent Newspaper Group'.[31]

Having investigated the deal, the Competition Authority found that the acquisition represented both an abuse of a dominant position contrary to section 5 of the Competition Act and an anti-competitive agreement, contrary to section 4 of the Act.[32] It also found that the purchase would further strengthen Independent Newspapers' dominance in the various markets for newspapers and advertising and that it was designed to prevent a rival of Independent Newspapers acquiring control of the Press titles. In a strong rebuff to the growing might of the company the Authority unsuccessfully recommended that the then minister for enterprise and employment, Richard Bruton, seek a High Court order to void the purchase.[33] At the AGM of Independent Newspapers, O'Reilly denied that the company held a dominant position or had abused its position in its acquisition of a minority share in the Press Group.[34]

In May 1995 the *Irish Press*, the *Evening Press* and the *Sunday Press* ceased publication and the scramble for their readers produced an interesting example of the market power that Independent Newspapers now yielded. When, in 1996, the *Cork Examiner* re-launched itself as the *Examiner*, the price of the *Irish Independent* was reduced from 85p to 15p for three weeks in Co. Cork, the main market for the *Examiner* title.[35] All of these moves – the blocking tactics and the predatory pricing – were, of course, motivated by commercial logic. But where does commercial logic end and press freedom begin? It was this issue that the Newspaper Commission attempted to address in 1995 as it examined how best a society might structure its newspaper industry so that it represented as many viewpoints as possible.

In its deliberations the commission considered two options; plurality of ownership (the idea that ownership and control needs to be dispersed among a wide number of companies and owners, each with their own viewpoint) and plurality of titles (the belief that ownership and control do not matter, as editorial diversity is ensured in large newspaper groups by journalistic and editorial integrity and competition for readers). After much debate about whether the position of Independent Newspapers hindered diversity or acted as a bulwark against imported British newspapers, the commission simply concluded that 'any further reduction of titles or increase in concentration of ownership

31 *Irish Times*, 23 Dec. 1994. IPN was the publisher and IPP was the owner of the Press titles.  32 *Competition Authority interim report of study of the newspaper industry* (Dublin, 1995).  33 Ibid. Section 6 of the Competition Act allowed for the enforcement of the regulations of the Competition Act by way of High Court action on behalf of the minister for enterprise and employment if the case were believed to be of 'especial public importance'.  34 *Irish Press*, 28 Apr. 1995, cited in Burke, *Press delete*, p. 196.  35 See *Phoenix* annual, 1996, p. 34. When, in 2000, the *Examiner* changed its title to the *Irish Examiner* the *Irish Independent* warned it about it 'straying outside their market'. See *Irish Independent*, 16 Aug. 2000.

in the indigenous industry could severely curtail the diversity required to maintain a vigorous democracy'.[36]

While plurality of ownership might involve state regulation of ownership and control, the adoption of editorial charters and the cross-subsidization of different newspaper companies,[37] journalistic and editorial integrity very much depends on the political or commercial interests of an owner not being allowed to influence the content of their titles. It also depends on owners not seeking to influence coverage or using their titles to advance or defend their interests. Upon taking over Independent Newspapers in 1973, Tony O'Reilly gave an emphatic assurance that he would not interfere with what journalists wrote. While there is no evidence that he has not kept his word, from the early 1980s concerns began to be expressed about the commercial and political power that Independent Newspapers appeared to yield.

## COMMERCE, POLITICS AND INDEPENDENT NEWSPAPERS – 1

Of primary concern was how the Independent titles would report on O'Reilly's other business interests. One such interest was Atlantic Resources, an oil exploration company that was publicly floated in April 1981. On its first day of trading its share price quadrupled and many commentators expressed surprise as the company had no oil, only a 10 per cent stake in an American company that was due to begin drilling off the west coast.[38] The following June a dispute arose between Independent Newspapers and the NUJ after the then editor of the *Sunday Independent*, Michael Hand, removed part of an interview that a journalist, Martin Fitzpatrick, had conducted with the president of the stock exchange. The excised piece referred to 'dealings on the exchange in shares of the oil exploration company, Atlantic Resources'. After a mandatory chapel meeting that disrupted production, the NUJ received 'assurances from management that they had freedom to write about companies in which the newspapers' directors had interests on the same basis as any other company'.[39]

The links between Atlantic Resources and Independent Newspapers did not stop there, however. In an interview in September 1983, O'Reilly told *Forbes* magazine that the geologist hired by Atlantic Resources had chosen six blocks of seabed for exploration and that 'Since I own thirty-five per cent of the newspapers in Ireland I have close contact with the politicians. I got the blocks he

**36** *Report of the commission on the newspaper industry* (Dublin, 1996), p. 30 (1.10). **37** See C. Rapple, 'Newspapers are being squeezed by pressures of commercialization', *Irish Times*, 24 May 1995. **38** *Irish Times*, 7 Apr. 1981. **39** Ibid., 1 June 1981. Hand also spiked Kevin O'Connor's story on the Sean Doherty affair; see J. Joyce and P. Murtagh, *The boss* (Dublin, 1983), pp 268–71.

[the geologist] wanted'. The perception of the then Taoiseach, Garret FitzGerald, was that while O'Reilly received the blocks he wanted he was unhappy with the terms attached to the exploration licences. As remembered by FitzGerald, after the government refused to amend the terms 'the *Independent* swung somewhat' in its support for his government. It was FitzGerald's belief that 'the oil thing was a major factor' in this.[40]

In the late 1990s the relationship between Independent Newspapers and O'Reilly's other business interests came under sustained scrutiny. In May 1998 *Magill* magazine revealed that in June 1989 the then minister for communications, Ray Burke, had received a cheque for £30,000 from Rennicks Manufacturing, a subsidiary of Fitzwilton, a company in which O'Reilly had a stake.[41] The cheque had been, Fitzwilton explained, intended as a political donation to Fianna Fáil.[42] In September 1989, Burke, as minister for communications and justice, announced that an Independent Newspapers subsidiary, Princes Holdings, had been awarded the bulk of the contracts to supply a multi-channel television service around the country.[43] This company operated a microwave system called MMDS to deliver TV channels, but many areas already operated their own, albeit illegal, deflector systems to receive British channels. In February 1991 Burke wrote a letter of comfort to Independent Newspapers, stating that once the MMDS system was available in any franchise region, his department would apply 'the full rigours of the law to illegal operations affecting that franchise region'.[44]

Some years later, in August 1996, the then Taoiseach John Bruton met with O'Reilly. In his recollection of the meeting, Bruton observed that O'Reilly had 'expressed a general dissatisfaction about the way he and his interests were being recognized by the government'.[45] Among the issues raised by O'Reilly was the inaction on the part of the government against the illegal deflector operators. By then the deflector systems had become a political hot potato with huge pressure being put on politicians to legalize the systems.[46] Nonetheless, Bruton asked his senior advisor, Sean Donlon, to follow up on O'Reilly's concerns. At a meeting with Independent Newspapers executives in September 1996, Donlon was left, he recalled, 'in no doubt about Independent Newspapers' hostility to the government parties if outstanding issues were not resolved to their satisfaction'.[47] Bruton later recalled that he subsequently felt that Independent Newspapers 'did take a negative view, both towards the government and towards me personally'.[48]

---

40 O'Toole, 'Brand Leader', pp 64–5.  41 V. Browne, 'O'Reilly's Fitzwilton gave a £30,000 cash cheque to Ray Burke in June 1989', *Magill*, 28 May 1998, pp 16–22.  42 Ibid.  43 *Irish Times*, 5 Oct. 1989.  44 Ibid., 14 June 1997.  45 V. Browne, 'Challenging a Taoiseach', *Village*, July 2007, p. 28.  46 One deflector activist, Tom Gildea, was elected in the 1997 general election for Donegal South West.  47 *Irish Times*, 31 Mar. 2004.  48 Ibid., 24 Mar. 2004.

In May 1997 O'Reilly informed the Independent Group's AGM that Princes Holdings had accumulated losses of £21m. 'Various governments', he noted, 'did not police the enforcement of their licences in an effective way'.[49] As outlined in a previous chapter, in June 1997, on the eve of polling day for a general election, the *Irish Independent* published a front page editorial entitled 'Payback Time' that strongly criticized the economic policies of Bruton's outgoing Fine Gael, Labour and Democratic Left government and urged readers to vote for Fianna Fáil and Progressive Democrats (PD) alternative.[50] The decision to run the editorial was made by the paper's editor, Vinnie Doyle, who also directed its general thrust, although the bulk of the content was written by editorial writer, James Downey.[51] Doyle's reasoning for the editorial was, according to Downey, based on a memorandum from finance editor Brendan Keenan that postulated that the country could afford tax cuts if the government restrained public spending. The view taken by the editorial was that a Fianna Fáil and PD government would cut taxes and restrain public spending.[52] As Fianna Fáil returned to power, the reaction was swift; the leader of the Labour Party, Dick Spring, labelled the editorial as 'disgraceful and despicable, a new low in Irish journalism'.[53]

When the *Irish Times* revealed what had transpired at the Donlon / Independent Newspapers meeting, the latter company clarified that there was no connection between the meeting and the editorial. Editorial policy was, it noted, 'a matter for editors, not senior executives'. It asserted that, as a commercial organization, it had a legitimate right to meet with government representatives and to encourage them to enforce the law. It also explained that when the representatives of Independent Newspapers had told Donlon that the government 'would lose Independent Newspapers as friends' they were referring solely to the mediating role that the newspaper company was playing between Princes Holdings and the government.[54] For his part, O'Reilly denied having any input into the editorial and declared that he was 'absolutely unequivocal' that the reference to the government losing Independent Newspapers as friends was a reference to potential litigation (in relation to the government's refusal to shut down the deflector systems) rather than editorial content.[55] While the event left a sour taste in many mouths, there, for some time at least, the matter rested.

---

49 Ibid., 14 June 1997.  50 *Irish Independent*, 5 June 1997.  51 J. Downey, *In my own time* (Dublin, 2009), pp 250–1.  52 Ibid. While the Fianna Fáil & PD coalition did cut taxes it also allowed public spending to soar.  53 *Irish Times*, 14 June 1997. Whether the editorial had any real impact on the election result is debatable. Bertie Ahern was a popular leader and Fianna Fáil ran a campaign based on thorough vote management. Fine Gael actually increased its number of seats. The Labour Party was hardest hit; a result, perhaps, of having campaigned strongly against Fianna Fáil during the 1992 election and then forming a coalition with it.  54 *Irish Times*, 16 June 1997.  55 Ibid., 1 Apr. 2004.

COMMERCE, POLITICS AND INDEPENDENT NEWSPAPERS — 2

The debate about the commercial or political power of Independent Newspapers reignited dramatically in May 1998 when *Magill* revealed the payment from Fitzwilton to Ray Burke in 1989. In the Dáil, former Taoiseach John Bruton observed that the chairman of Fitzwilton was Tony O'Reilly whose many business interests included 'the television transmission system, MMDS, which was a source of considerable controversy in the lead up to and aftermath of the general election of June 1997. Mr Burke was linked to that controversy. Dr O'Reilly's newspapers took an unprecedented interest in the result of that election'.[56] Deputy Pat Rabbitte pointedly asked:

> When huge donations like this are transferred to politicians most people ask *cui bono*? Who benefits and profits from it? Does it support democracy or are there other reasons for it? We are assured that Tony O'Reilly knew nothing of this £30,000 donation. However, as Minister for Communications ... Mr Burke would have been well aware through Dr O'Reilly of the connections of the Rennicks subsidiary to Princes Holdings, to whom he granted 19 of the 29 licences awarded from the MMDS system.[57]

Independent Newspapers came out fighting. In a front page editorial, the *Irish Independent* declared that the company had 'been the subject of a vicious, calculated and damaging smear campaign which has sought to suggest that the company was linked in some way with improper payments to a politician'. It was a campaign of 'malicious denigration' and the company had, it asserted, 'been attacked on the flimsiest of evidence'.[58] Fitzwilton, it noted, had no business connections with Princes Holdings. This riposte, however, only fanned the flames of controversy. In a rancorous Dáil debate, Pat Rabbitte roundly criticized what he called 'the frenetic four day campaign by Independent Newspapers to defend the economic interests of their proprietor':

> 'Lying letters, phantom meetings and calculated smears' screamed yet another front page editorial in the *Irish Independent*. As the tirade continued, one conclusion is inescapable: if ever there was a doubt about the undesirability of a dominant position in such a sensitive industry then the conduct of Independent Newspapers over the weekend removed that doubt. Journalists and columnists were used in such an overkill to defend the economic interests of their proprietor that the public were given a glimpse of what abuse of dominant position means in practice.[59]

56 Dáil Éireann Debates, vol. 491, col. 998 (28 May 1998). 57 Ibid., col. 1004. 58 *Irish Independent*, 30 May 1998. 59 Dáil Éireann Debates, vol. 491, cols. 1153–5 (3 June 1998).

The affair prompted at least one *Irish Independent* journalist to write an article that was mildly critical of the whole affair but it was spiked by the editor Vinnie Doyle. After the NUJ made representations to him, Doyle claimed he had acted on legal advice. Who or what entity might have sued the newspaper was never made clear.[60] Ultimately, the government referred the Burke payment to the Mahon Tribunal of Inquiry into certain planning matters and payments. In July 2007 Fitzwilton won a Supreme Court case that prevented the Tribunal from holding public hearings into the payment. The Tribunal had investigated the affair in private, but had, the Supreme Court ruled, not followed proper procedure in its attempts to initiate a public hearing.[61]

CONCLUSION

By the beginning of the twenty-first century Independent Newspapers, under O'Reilly's tutelage, had come a long way. Having taken control of the company, he shook the titles out of their 1950s slumber and, on the back of them, built a powerful, world-wide, media empire. But for all the titles in all the lands that the company owns, the dominant role that it plays in Ireland's newspaper market and its power to set the news agenda is still what preoccupies policy makers and commentators concerned about the existence of a diverse and free press. As O'Reilly himself acknowledged in 1973, such concerns are always legitimate. Amid the rapidly changing media industry and greater regulation of media cross-ownership it is unclear what the future holds for Ireland's largest media organization. As the first decade of the new century ended, the power of Tony O'Reilly to control the company had been effectively ended by another rising media mogul, Denis O'Brien.

60 Private information.  61 *Irish Times*, 5 July 2007.

# 15 / Global players: Tony O'Reilly and Independent News & Media

## GAVIN ELLIS

After he took control of an under-performing Dublin-based newspaper group beset with industrial problems in 1973, Tony O'Reilly re-assured staff by telling them he planned to make Independent Newspapers the centre of an international communications group. He was as good as his word: two decades later the company, which had been worth £IR5m and published only seven titles when O'Reilly bought the Murphy family's controlling shareholding, had grown into a media operation with a market capitalization of almost £IR600m that published more than 120 newspapers and magazines in Europe, Africa and Australasia.

Three decades after he first walked into the Abbey Street offices, the business had a market capitalization of €1.9bn, and India had been added to the O'Reilly imperial map. The proprietor compared his empire favourably with that of the New York Times Company (market capitalization, €3.6bn) and the Times Mirror Group (€2.8bn). Shareholders were told that, in assessing the performance of the re-branded Independent News & Media (INM), 'the figures speak for themselves'. Indeed, the figures spoke volumes: a non-voting share was worth the equivalent of €1.59 when O'Reilly bought the company in 1973; by mid–2007 the share price had peaked at more than €16.

Like all empires, however, decline was part of the ultimate destiny. By early 2012 INM's market capitalization had shrunk to €145m, the share price languished at €0.25, and the 'colonies' had either gone, were asserting their independence or showing signs of neglect. And the emperor himself had been toppled from the throne now occupied by a son wrestling with compounding woes and threatening foes.[1] No single factor accounted for the turmoil and decline. Like Rome before it, O'Reilly's media organization was the victim of multiple forces, some of its own making, others visited upon it. The audacity that characterized the early expansion carried high risk, manageable while O'Reilly's luck, and the international markets, held good. But when fates turned, an empire founded on high debt and low costs lacked the strategies to stop the thread unravelling. It was, nonetheless, a business story that made Tony O'Reilly the stuff of modern Irish legend.

1 In May 2009, amid a vigorous takeover bid by Denis O'Brien, O'Reilly stepped down as CEO and was succeeded by his son Gavin.

## THE BEGINNING

O'Reilly laid the foundations for his business career while he was a rugby international in the 1950s. He was the star of the Lions tours of the southern hemisphere where, as Rupert Bates wrote in the *Sunday Times,* he turned the toes of defenders and the heads of women with equal facility.[2] This fame ensured a degree of familiarity when he went looking for media acquisitions 'down under' in the 1980s and 1990s. He once said that the Australian-born Rupert Murdoch was one of the three most outstanding businessmen he ever met.[3] Murdoch gave O'Reilly his first significant opportunity to build a global media company. In 1986 the Australian Labor Government enacted a policy change that precipitated what has been described as the 'carve-up' of the country's media. In exchange for restrictions on cross-media ownership, proprietors were allowed to establish unprecedented levels of concentration within a medium. Murdoch went on a buying spree and the jewel in the crown was Australia's largest newspaper publisher, the Herald & Weekly Times group (HWT), which had been managed by his father, the late Sir Keith Murdoch. He did so with the blessing of a government that had regarded the existing HWT owners as its enemy.[4] There were, however, some niceties to be observed: the Trade Practices Commission ruled that the concentration of ownership created when Murdoch's existing interests in Queensland were combined with those of HWT, which also owned newspapers in the state, required divestiture.

O'Reilly became aware of the forced sale of a subsidiary that published a number of small but profitable regional dailies and weeklies with unlikely titles like the *Chincilla News, Tweed Daily* and the *Coral Coaster.* Murdoch, who wanted a quick sale, agreed to sell his interest in Provincial Newspapers (Queensland) Ltd to the Irishman he had met socially in his role as president of the H.J. Heinz Company.[5] O'Reilly had to overcome foreign ownership rules that limited his company to a 15 per cent maximum holding. Here luck played a part. O'Reilly had married an Australian, Susan Cameron, after the 1959 British Lions tour and their six children were entitled to Australian passports. A trust was established in their names and O'Reilly used his own money to acquire the 85 per cent that Independent Newspapers was precluded from purchasing.

The financing of this first major international media foray was leveraged to the limit and stretched Independent Newspapers, and O'Reilly, in spite of the fact that Murdoch had agreed to leave a substantial amount in the company as a subordinated five-year loan. Two men were, however, largely responsible for turn-

2 Quoted in K. Quinn, *A century of rugby greats* (Auckland, 1999), p. 225.  3 N. Coleridge, *Paper tigers* (London, 1994), p. 461.  4 P. Chadwick, *Media mates: carving up Australia's media* (Melbourne, 1989).  5 I. Fallon, *The Player: the life of Tony O'Reilly* (London, 1995), p. 323.

ing what appeared to be a high-risk venture into a highly profitable investment in
a remarkably short space of time. The first was Liam Healy, the quietly-spoken
accountant who was head of Independent Newspapers' fledgling international
division and who would become chief executive in 1991. The other was O'Reilly's
self-directed eldest son, Cameron. Between them Healy and Cameron O'Reilly
rationalized costs and management structures in Provincial's far-flung operations
– Queensland is nearly twenty-five times the size of Ireland. Within four years
profits had tripled and in 1992 a public share flotation created Australian
Provincial Newspapers (APN). Independent Newspapers, and O'Reilly himself,
had initially put $A10 million cash into the deal – an investment which, after
the float, was worth $A138. O'Reilly later conceded it was 'an *unreasonable* reward'.[6]
The float reduced Independent Newspapers' ownership in APN to 21 per cent
(with the O'Reilly family trust holding 35 per cent) but the Australian investment
had already whetted O'Reilly's appetite for further expansion.

O'Reilly next turned his attention to Fairfax, publisher of the *Sydney Morning
Herald* and the Melbourne *Age* which had run into trouble following a highly
leveraged buyout. In 1991, after months of acrimonious jousting between contenders, Independent Newspapers made a $A1.49bn bid for Fairfax that was
rejected in favour of a lower (but arguably better financed) offer from a consortium that included Australian media magnate Kerry Packer and the Canadian
newspaper owner Conrad Black (through London's *Daily Telegraph* group).
O'Reilly unsuccessfully attempted to block the consortium's bid. Black labelled
the litigation 'frivolous and totally without legal foundation'.[7] Although Black
secured a dispensation from Australia's foreign ownership rules that took his
company's holding in Fairfax to 25 per cent he wanted the investment to be
'transformed into one of unquestionable control or liquidated'.[8] Unable to over-
turn the foreign ownership rules, he sold to a New Zealand corporate raider,
Ron Brierley, who played a pivotal role in a drama that ultimately placed a jewel
in APN's crown. In the meantime, O'Reilly saw new opportunities – a continent away.

## INTO SOUTH AFRICA

While the battle for Fairfax raged in Australia, a revolution was taking place
in South Africa where post-apartheid elections swept Nelson Mandela and the
African National Congress (ANC) to power. The country's newspaper market
had been anything but open: the powerful mining interests that were central to

6 Coleridge, *Paper tigers*, p. 469.   7 *Financial Post* (Toronto), 19 Dec. 1991.   8 G. Tombs, *Robber Baron* (Toronto, 2007),
p. 290.

South Africa's economy also owned the vast majority of its English-language newspapers. Fifty-eight per cent of daily newspaper circulation was controlled by Argus Printing & Publishing, which was in turn ultimately controlled by the Anglo American Corporation, which was described as 'a major force in the economic, political and social life of South Africa'.[9] Anglo American's senior executives had met with ANC representatives in exile in 1985 and began preparing for an eventual move towards democracy. However, as the likelihood of an ANC-led government became more apparent the corporation began to worry about possible nationalization of some of its assets to address its strong hold on the South African economy. By one reckoning Anglo American had an interest in 40 per cent of the stocks listed on the South African exchange. It began planning for an infusion of foreign capital and divestiture of non-core assets to forestall such a move. One of those assets was the Argus group.

For an outlay of $US32m in 1994, Independent Newspapers received a 31 per cent interest in the Argus group. Within a year the shareholding was raised to 60 per cent and by 1999 O'Reilly had achieved full ownership. Much has been made of the relationship between Mandela and O'Reilly in sealing the fortunes of the Argus group and its internationally recognized mastheads including the *Star* in Johannesburg and the *Cape Times*. In his biography of O'Reilly, Ivan Fallon stated that 'a great deal hung on Nelson Mandela's reaction'.[10] While it is undoubtedly true that opposition from Mandela would have weighed against the Independent Newspapers bid, the ANC leader's role may have been less than presented. Mandela had little interest in business and his much-touted stays at O'Reilly's holiday home in the Bahamas in 1993 were not occasions for doing deals – apart from a butler, the Mandelas were alone.

Indeed, the ANC was not overly happy at the Irish presence in the South African media landscape. Congress officials – not Mandela – met on numerous occasions with INM executives after the Argus group invited the Irish takeover and they attempted, without success, to persuade Independent Newspapers to accept local black shareholding. A former consultant to the ANC newspaper project, Moeletsi Mbeki, made it plain that by the end of 1994 the dialogue had ended.[11] This suggests that O'Reilly's on-going friendship with Mandela was personal, not commercial.

O'Reilly installed the former deputy editor of the *Sunday Times*, Ivan Fallon (who had just completed the O'Reilly biography, *The Player*) to mastermind the redevelopment of the Argus group. It ushered in what one former editorial director of the South African group, Shaun Johnson, describes as 'a golden age'.[12]

9 D. Innes, *Anglo American and the rise of modern South Africa* (New York, 1984), p. 13. 10 Fallon, *The Player*, p. 349. 11 *Mail & Guardian*, 8 Dec. 1995. 12 Telephone interview, 31 May 2011. Johnson was an outspoken political journalist

In his first year in the position Fallon launched three new publications, re-launched the *Cape Argus* and paved the way for increasing INM's ownership of the South African group.

## NEW ZEALAND

On a quiet day in November 1994 an Air New Zealand aircraft carrying the managing director of the country's largest newspaper left Auckland International Airport. Inside the terminal was a man whose sole task that day was to make a telephone call once the jet's wheels had left the ground. The call was made to Brierley Investments Ltd and set in train a share raid carefully planned to be executed within the eight-to-twelve-hour 'window' that managing director Michael Horton would be in the air, incommunicado, and unable to counter-attack. A radio message from the company secretary was eventually relayed to Horton via the pilot and he arranged an immediate return to New Zealand as soon as the aircraft touched down in the United States. But it was too late: the corporate raider had acquired a 28 per cent stake in Wilson & Horton Ltd, publisher of the *New Zealand Herald* and a string of regional titles.[13]

Ron Brierley's company, Brierley Investments Limited (BIL), was regarded as an asset stripper. It had taken over the third-largest newspaper group in the country, NZ News Limited, in 1986 only to break it up and sell off the assets after a share market crash a year later. The board of Wilson & Horton (W&H) did not regard it as a fitting cornerstone shareholder for New Zealand's most influential newspaper group. The board's fears were realized when a BIL representative arrived in the boardroom and behaved, as John Maasland (then a recently appointed executive director) recalls, 'like the new gauleiter'.[14]

Negotiations with BIL produced an agreement that the investment company would sell its shares if W&H had a buyer willing to offer 20 per cent more than BIL had paid. A search for a white knight commenced and at Horton's invitation, Liam Healy led a team to New Zealand to carry out a detailed examination of W&H. He found a company with a new state-of-the-art press hall that had been bought from financial reserves that stood at $NZ93m. The flagship *New Zealand Herald* was the country's largest selling newspaper by a sizeable margin. O'Reilly was not present during the negotiations. In a telephone conversation with Healy, he asked what the W&H executives were like. Healy said

and editor in the Argus group who became a close associate of Nelson Mandela.  13 BIL accumulated a small holding in W&H prior to the raid, which took its holding to 28%.  14 Interview, 20 June 2011. Maasland was at the time managing director of the print division of W&H. He would later become W&H group managing director and then a director of APN.

he thought W&H were 'people we could do business with', to which O'Reilly replied: 'If that's the case, then that's fine.'

Brierley Investments had paid $NZ9.50 a share for its holding. Six months later, having contributed nothing to the running of the company, it received $NZ10.50 a share from Independent Newspapers plus a $NZ1.50 a share special dividend – a profit of about $NZ70m. Within two months, Independent Newspapers increased its holding to 32.9 per cent and by the end of 1995 this had grown to 45 per cent. In October 1996 it launched a full market bid for Wilson & Horton at a cost of $NZ1.1bn. In this period there were also profitable moves into the radio market in both Australia and New Zealand. A partnership between APN and Clear Channel Communications of the United States purchased a significant number of radio stations in Australia. The partnership, Australian Radio Network, was joined by the Independent-controlled Wilson & Horton, to successfully tender $NZ86 million in 1996 for the loss making commercial networks that the New Zealand government had decided to sell. The profitable venture is now the largest radio owner on both sides of the Tasman Sea.

Elsewhere, a further opportunity arose for INM when the Indian government relaxed foreign ownership rules in 2002 to allow up to 26 per cent foreign ownership in newspapers and periodicals. In 2005 INM paid €28.5m for a stake in Jagran Prakashan Limited (JPL), publisher of *Dainik Jagran*, which had been credited by the World Association of Newspapers with the largest daily readership in the world. However, India's ownership restrictions meant INM was never likely to draw JPL fully into the group and, faced with mounting financial woes, it progressively sold the stake five years later for €95m – almost three-and-a-half times what it had originally paid.

## AN INDEPENDENT EXISTENCE

In Australia, South Africa and New Zealand the media companies that were now part of the Independent group operated with traditional business conservatism. South Africa's English-language press had been burdened by sanctions that created technological deficiencies and also by repressive laws that even courageous journalism found difficult to overcome.[15] Australia's rural press was a collection of small, inefficient and intensely local titles while in New Zealand, the largest newspaper, the *New Zealand Herald*, was known as 'Granny Herald' for its staid appearance and style.

Change came quickly. In Australia, Independent Newspapers hired management consultants, the Collins Hill Group, to assess its provincial newspaper

15 See W.A. Hachten & C.A. Giffard, *The press and apartheid: repression and propaganda in South Africa* (Madison, WI, 1984).

acquisition. The consultancy would subsequently be used in a similar exercise in New Zealand. One manager at the Australian group told the consultants of his frustration in having to refer even minor financial matters to a 'bloated' head office of almost forty people. He recalled how in a single afternoon Liam Healy reduced head office to four or five people and the business was split into four regions under separate managers:

> Liam's central focus was on lifting financial performance by eliminating waste, off-loading or closing non-core assets but also encouraging us to press ahead with initiatives that lifted revenue … He pushed a policy of people, products, profits. Get the first two right and the third would happen. But there was an unrelenting focus on achieving the bottom line as contained in the agreed budget.[16]

In South Africa, the *Cape Times* was redesigned, its editorial system upgraded and, most significantly, Moegsien Williams became the first 'man of colour' to edit the newspaper.[17] A former staffer stated that Williams' elevation signaled that the 'colonial era was over and its social attitudes would not be part of Independent's operating style and approach to appointments'.[18] Under Ivan Fallon's guidance a new business section was inserted into three of the group's dailies and a new weekend paper, the *Sunday Independent* was launched. Its first editor, Shaun Johnson, is convinced that he would not have been able to create and edit the newspaper had INM not bought the Argus group. The group also showed its commitment to the new South Africa by appearing before the Truth and Reconciliation Commission in 1997 to apologise for shortcomings during the apartheid era, with Fallon telling the commission: 'Tony O'Reilly and Independent Newspapers have, from the very beginning, indeed, from before the beginning, been significant friends, internationally, of the new South Africa and, as a company, we remain so.'

In New Zealand, the *Herald* underwent a complete redesign and re-launch. Among the developments were the introduction of a *Business Herald* on which Fallon (a former financial journalist) acted as a consultant and a new *Weekend Herald* to replace the Saturday editions. In line with O'Reilly's view that newspapers in New Zealand were under-priced, the company instituted a 20 cent cover price increase that was the first of a succession of rises. Several of the group's regional dailies were also redesigned and printing plants were rationalized.

A pattern emerged in the way the South African and Australasian businesses operated. Three words came to dominate the way they were expected to do busi-

16 Email correspondence, 3 July 2011 in which anonymity was requested.   17 Williams, the son of a painter and a seamstress, is now editor-in-chief of the group's South African flagship, the *Johannesburg Star*.   18 G. Shaw, *The Cape Times: an informal history* (Cape Town, 1999), p. 342.

ness. They were the 3Bs: brand, budget and bottom line. The southern hemisphere divisions came to understand the meaning of a series of phrases that emphasized the 3Bs; '*the* brand leader', '*the* weekly forecast' and '*the* low cost operator'. O'Reilly liked to see fresh new looks that newly enlarged marketing departments could promote. He was in his comfort zone when talking about brands. Healy's comfort zone was in numbers and he moved all divisions to a weekly financial reporting cycle that included forecasts of the coming week's revenues. Both men believed that if profit could not be made from increased revenue, it was to be achieved by cutting costs. O'Reilly had built an impressive reputation in Heinz when he radically rationalized its cost-base and coined the 'low cost operator' mantra that was applied to his newspaper interests with equal gusto.

Australia had felt the full force of cost-cutting early in Independent Newspapers' ownership with head office rationalization. The provincial press outlets had, however, traditionally run on meager rations so budgets and staffing were not subject to further dramatic cuts. Instead, there was a stringent process of justification for every line in income and expenditure budgets. The management consultants' report suggested that a 'Big Mac' approach could be taken on the provincial newspapers and common content would reduce the number of journalists required. The McDonald's concept of uniformity was debunked internally because regional readers wanted local content but, although there was no reduction in staff, the newspapers did begin a page pooling arrangement (on racing form, television listings and world news) to move 'backroom' journalists to fill an acute shortage of reporters. An attempt at centralized sub-editing had little success. It was resurrected in New Zealand in more recent times when seventy-two sub-editors and paginators were replaced by an out-sourcing agreement with Pagemasters (a subsidiary of the Australian Associated Press news agency) that improved the finances but not, it is argued, the journalism.

At the *New Zealand Herald* the first of a succession of redundancy rounds was imposed in 1998 and created a climate in the editorial department – which had in the past been subject to no more than occasional freezes on new hiring – that led to strike action by union members in 2001. O'Reilly was present during one of the rolling stoppages and did not appreciate the sight of placard-waving union members outside his hotel.[19] A similar wave of redundancies took place in South Africa when the group cut 440 staff in 1999, prompting Fallon to tell shareholders that, 'as a result the cost base of the operation is now considerably leaner'.[20] The moves were typical of the reaction to economic downturns: any shortfall in budgeted revenue growth was redressed by cost

19 Union members were on strike during 9/11, when the *Herald* produced five special editions including its first midday paper.   20 Independent News & Media annual report 1999, p. 35.

reductions. Editors learned not to rely on budgets set at the end of the previous year and, while there was short-term investment in new sections or 'products' aimed at attracting advertisers, there was little new investment in core journalism in the group's antipodean newspapers.

Editors were, however, given editorial control and there is no evidence that O'Reilly or Healy interfered in the content of their newspapers in the southern hemisphere. When this author was appointed editor of the *New Zealand Herald*, Healy placed only one editorial requirement on him: that he 'will not advocate the use of violence as a legitimate means to a political end'. No explanation by the Irishman was needed and the undertaking was readily given. The only other instance of 'head office interference' during almost a decade of running the newspaper was a request from O'Reilly (and he was at pains to couch it in those terms) to promote the distribution of generic Aids drugs in Africa.

The regional editors in Australia enjoyed similar editorial independence and Shaun Johnson recalls no attempts in his time as editor and editorial director in South Africa to interfere with editorial freedom. In fact, INM was at pains to protect it. Johnson and Maasland both recall a meeting of its International Advisory Board[21] in Capetown, at which a representative of President Thabo Mbeki (Mandela's successor) had berated the board over the group's political coverage in South Africa and demanded it intercede. Mbeki had come under attack on a number of fronts including his attitude toward the Aids epidemic. The advisory board's reaction was to seek an audience with Mbeki himself at which the newspapers' editorial independence was robustly reaffirmed. O'Reilly subscribed to the principles of editorial independence but he also saw his newspapers as products, and his abiding interest was in their bottom lines. Divisions were pitted against each other at annual meetings at O'Reilly Castlemartin residence in Co. Kildare or his French chateau at Deauville. He had perfected the strategy at Heinz where executives had to account for their operating income in a challenging gathering of their peers over which he presided.[22] However, one former executive noted that the INM gatherings were not only about 'the numbers':

> I don't think you can overlook the forelock-tugging aspect of the carnival. It was at least partly about paying homage to the emperor and the emperor responded by applauding and rewarding the efforts of all, how-

21 A group of influential people from Europe, North America and South Africa (including former US ambassador to the United Nations, Andrew Young; *Washington Post* editor, Ben Bradlee; former Canadian prime minister, Brian Mulroney; and author Anthony Sampson) that met twice yearly to advise O'Reilly and INM on international affairs. Initially the group concentrated on Southern Africa in fulfilment of an undertaking to Nelson Mandela. 22 David Irving was subjected to what he called 'the special pressures of group accountability for business success' while working for Heinz. See D. Irving & K. Inkson *It must be Wattie's! From Kiwi icon to global player* (Auckland, 1998), p. 149.

ever insignificant. This was undoubtedly a highly motivating experience for some and regarded as a depressing waste of time by others.[23]

## THE AFTERNOON OF EMPIRE

The dedicated pursuit of the 3Bs had provided INM with impressive profit growth. Australia and New Zealand showed consistent year-on-year increases in operating profit from 1992 to 2005. South Africa was less consistent but there was a six-fold increase in annual operating profits over the same period. The Irish operation had an even more impressive record of sustained profit growth from 1992 to 2007. But there were two sides to the ledger and group debt was also rising – to peak at $US2.1bn in 2007, the year that the international credit crisis began. In the same year APN's debt peaked at $US832m.

APN, like its Irish shareholder, had been an acquisitive company. Cameron O'Reilly had overseen thirty-eight acquisitions before resigning as chief executive in 2000 amid rumours that he had fallen out with his father, and brother Gavin, over succession strategies.[24] He had gone by the time APN made its most significant acquisition – buying Wilson & Horton from its Irish parent in 2001, a move that allowed INM to pay down debt. The deal involved a payment of $A809m in cash and the assumption of $A429m in W&H debt.[25] It doubled the size of APN and was funded partly by borrowing and partly by a share issue. It was a win-win strategy for INM, which raised its holding in APN to 45 per cent while at the same time extracting what it had originally paid for W&H. However, INM would find that, like most colonies, APN would eventually want independence.

Perhaps O'Reilly sensed this natural inclination because in 2006 he made a bold bid to buy out the Australasian group's other shareholders. He teamed up with two private equity groups to make a surprise offer worth $A3.8bn for APN. Major institutional investors in APN, however, rejected the offer, as did more than 50 per cent of the votes in a shareholders' ballot. The rejection in 2007 led INM to put its stake in APN on the market but in spite of 'several unsolicited expressions of interest' no sale took place. In 2009 APN initiated a share issue as a solution to its debt problem; as a result, INM's shareholding was reduced to 31.6 per cent. The appointment of Brett Chenoweth, an Australian-born telecommunications executive and merchant banker, as CEO in 2010 was seen as further evidence of a separate course from the Irish group. Chenoweth had no previous connections with INM and since his appointment

---

23 Email correspondence, May 2011. Identity withheld.  24 *Sydney Morning Herald*, 27 Oct. 1999. Cameron O'Reilly remained on the APN board until 2010.  25 Imposed on the W&H balance sheet by the group's sale to INM.

he has been at pains to treat the Irish group as no different to other share-holders. Dublin receives the same weekly financial report that is circulated to all directors. The business is clearly on an independent course that takes advantage of Chenoweth's background in digital communications. He says that he can benefit from INM's media experience and philosophy of cost containment 'but it stops there'. He sees a future for APN in which it is no longer a manufacturer (owning and running its own presses) but a 'content creator' across a range of delivery systems.

In South Africa, the INM bottom line focus saw optimism replaced by disquiet. In a column in *Business Day* in 2009, a former editor of the *Mail & Guardian*, Professor Anton Harber, said that after a good start in reorganizing and redeveloping the old Argus group, O'Reilly for a number of years 'has treated it like an extractive industry' (a pointed reference to the Argus group's former mining associations) by putting profit ahead of all else.[26] Harber said that its flagship *Sunday Independent* had been reduced to a shadow of its former self. In 2011 he told this author that the group had lost its position as premier newspaper publisher in South Africa, and 'has become a miserable, depressed place with more rats and cockroaches than journos in their newsrooms'.[27]

Full-ownership of the South African group shielded INM from shareholder agitation. INM shareholder Denis O'Brien unsuccessfully opposed the €100m sale of the group's outdoor advertising interests there, figuring they could be as successful as APN-owned counterparts in Australasia and Hong Kong. O'Brien remained on the offensive (over directorships) at the 2011 INM annual general meeting in Dublin but equally embarrassing was the presence of a South African shareholder activist, Theo Botha, who questioned the group's failure to allow black economic empowerment by opening up the South African group's ownership. Gavin O'Reilly's subsequent criticism of the track record of equity empowerment in the republic and unequivocal rejection of the sale of the South African group also scotched the ambitions of local journalists who had hoped to establish a trust fund to buy a stake.[28]

CONCLUSION

Independent News & Media grew in a remarkably short space of time from a relatively small local player to a recognized presence on the international media

26 *Business Day*, 28 July 2009. Harber is professor of journalism and media studies at the University of the Witwatersrand, Johannesburg. Email correspondence, May 2011. 27 Although it launched a tabloid (*Daily Voice*) to satisfy a growing market among the black population, INM failed to gain a lead over rival group Media24. The latter's *Daily Sun* became South Africa's largest circulation newspaper after its 2002 launch. 28 P. Mabandu, *Mail & Guardian*, 13 Aug. 2009; A. Cotty, *Business Report*, 6 June 2011.

scene. By 2001 it published more than 200 newspaper and magazine titles with weekly circulations in excess of 15m copies in Europe, Africa and Australasia. It employed more than 12,100 people, had a turnover of €1.5bn and gross assets of €3.5bn. Yet in December 2010, the company's revenue was less than half that of a decade earlier (€626.4m) while its assets were valued at €841.2m. In comparison, APN — by now de-coupled from the INM empire — had revenue of €808m ($A1.06bn) and assets of €1.65bn ($A2.162bn). The causes of the dramatic transformation in INM's fortunes amount to a cautionary tale.

Independent News & Media made a success of its international operations by buying companies that had become inefficient through decades of benign ownership. O'Reilly demanded a hard-headed approach to costs and managerial efficiency, and Healy and his successors ensured that this was delivered. A willingness to allow broad 'product development' unlocked dormant editorial creativity, particularly in the flagship newspapers in each region. This in turn led to rapid increases in both turnover and profit. As time went by, however, new 'products' were to be created by doing more with less. The formula was successful in all of INM's newspaper markets except the United Kingdom where the London *Independent* failed to achieve critical circulation levels, although the acquisition of the *Belfast Telegraph* improved the division's financial position.

The strategy of identifying assets that could rapidly be made leaner and more profitable was inherently opportunistic. With each opportunity the company was stretched and never more so than when it paid 'top dollar' for its New Zealand acquisitions. Debt was to be the biggest threat to INM's future and ultimately to the hold that O'Reilly had on the company. In the same year that its share price peaked (2007), INM had total debt amounting to €2.1bn. Strong cash flow made interest repayments and refinancing manageable in good times but the exposure was too high to be sustainable when the global economy went into a tail-spin in 2008. In the normal ebb and flow of business INM had been able to compensate for revenue fluctuations by selling physical assets and cutting operating costs. There is hardly an annual report that does not include the phrase 'the industry low cost operator'. Over time, however, cost cutting has its limits, and INM went beyond the expeditious trimming of expenditure to compromise core, particularly editorial, resources. Editorial quality and coverage suffered and, although INM was not alone in experiencing the 'state of flux' that has engulfed news media, particular vulnerabilities made it fall further and faster.[29]

There are questions over the group's strategic management. Although the *Irish Independent* had existed for more than seventy years before O'Reilly's involvement, INM has displayed many of the characteristics of the family firm in

---

29 See P. Preston, *Making the news: journalism and news cultures in Europe* (Routledge, 2009).

which there is a dominant founder whose persona pervades the business. Did Tony O'Reilly's larger-than-life personality and business success on both sides of the Atlantic create a culture in which commercial decisions were not open to the level of critique that would prevail in a more egalitarian environment? And was this exacerbated by his desire for dynastic succession? Certainly, his executives were invariably deferential and when O'Reilly handed over control, his 42-year-old son Gavin was left with a challenging legacy. In April 2012, amid a deteriorating business environment, Gavin O'Reilly resigned his executive position at INM.

Tony O'Reilly has been a risk-taker throughout his life but that does not always equate with consistently sound business judgment. The failed attempt to buy APN through a highly geared private equity partnership (which may have foundered in the post-2008 credit crisis) and INM's decision then to put its stake in the Australasian group up for sale (only to withdraw it), sent to an already nervous market extremely negative signals about long-term commitment. By the time INM's stake was diluted by its inability to take up a share offer, it was obvious that APN would assert its independence and break a hold that had always seemed disproportionate to O'Reilly's shareholding and which was now demonstrably the case. The push for constant growth led the group into growing debt and it was, quite literally, living on borrowed time. The operations in South Africa and Australasia would have been a proud legacy for INM had they been allowed to stay in the form that took them to the top of their game but the focus on brand, budget and bottom line was taken beyond its logical limit. Print and broadcasting assets were stripped of muscle as well as fat, and brand marketing became a substitute for substance. And, always, the group sought newer and greener pastures.

It was a process that ultimately calls into question the depth of INM's commitment to journalism. The company and O'Reilly had a commendable record of non-interference in editorial policy. However, was this symptomatic of a more general lack of interest in journalism and, therefore, a greater readiness to endorse newsroom cuts? There may be a clue in the 2007 annual report. After O'Reilly listed that year's journalistic awards he noted that 'running a media business is not like making cement blocks, widgets or ketchup: It is something where you produce a new product in its many forms every day'. He then went on to state: 'More important, indeed, than awards are the circulation and advertising revenues of all our papers.'[30] INM was, in fact, interested in editorial content for its marketing and sales potential, and the journalistic awards and accolades lauded in annual reports owed little to a corporate philosophy that kept editorial budgets to a minimum as group finances were stretched tighter and tighter.

30 Independent News & Media annual report 2007, pp 8 & 9.

# 16 / Profits, politics and personal position: the role of the proprietor

## KEVIN RAFTER

Two individuals dominate the history of Independent Newspapers – William Martin Murphy and Tony O'Reilly. As several contributors to this volume have shown these two men defined the newspaper business that was relaunched in 1905 with the new *Irish Independent*. If William Martin Murphy was Ireland's first press baron then Tony O'Reilly was the country's first – and in many respects until very recent times, only – media baron. The media baron has been described by one authority as someone who controls a media outlet, who oversees it with a distinctive personal style, who takes entrepreneurial risks and who is not motivated exclusively by profit.[1] In respect of this definition both Murphy and O'Reilly, to varying degrees, fulfil the first three criteria. They assumed and held the lead role in their newspaper business. They were risk-takers and not afraid of investment in pursuit of expanding market share – in Murphy's case in the local market; in O'Reilly's both domestically and internationally. With a more out-going personality O'Reilly never feared public oratory as Murphy did. Nevertheless, both men enjoyed colourful and controversial careers.

They became newspaper proprietors through different routes – Murphy established a new business, his family then inherited one; O'Reilly bought one while also seeking to ensure family control passed to a second generation. The Murphys enjoyed outright ownership. The O'Reillys showed that in the modern era it was possible, at least for a time, to control a media organization without owning a majority stake in the business. Where they parted from the defined characteristics of the media baron was in relation to profit. Owing newspapers – and in O'Reilly's case, other media operations – was not pursued as a hobby or as a loss-making activity tolerated because of indirect rewards arising from personal elevation or political access. Profit was not something either man dismissed lightly. Despite subsidising the loss-making *Sunday Tribune* and London *Independent* from wider group profits O'Reilly was not wealthy enough to run his overall newspaper business at a loss – profitability was essential, as it was for the Murphy family in the pre-1973 period. This chapter examines the role of the proprietor from Murphy to O'Reilly while casting an eye to

---

1 C. Seymour-Ure, *Prime ministers and the media: issues of power and control* (London, 2003), p. 98.

the future with the emergence of a third dominant individual in the history of the Independent group, Denis O'Brien.


### THE MEDIA BARON

In the first half of the twentieth century in the United Kingdom there was considerable cross-over between the political elite and newspaper proprietors like Beaverbrook, Northcliffe and Rothermere. These press barons – as they were known in the world of print – used their newspaper ownership to shape political debate, influence policy and, on occasion, to make or break political careers. They even used their press power to become directly involved in the party political process. For example, Beaverbrook – who controlled the *Sunday Express*, the *Daily Express*, and the London *Evening Standard* – openly admitted to being motivated by power. In explaining Beaverbrook's interest in the newspaper business Cudlipp argued that, 'the new proprietor's object was solely to use the Press for political propaganda to influence the political leaders: the quest was for power.'[2] In this regard, Beaverbrook used his titles to promote a new political lobby group, to contest elections with his own candidates and to back other candidates sympathetic to his views.[3] Greenslade has written about Beaverbrook's 'ubiquitous roles as political fixer, advisor to prime ministers and confidants of the business and political elite.'[4] He was not alone in seeking to use the press to shape political opinion and elevate his own role. On the other side of the Atlantic it has been written of another press baron from this era, William Randolph Hearst, that 'his reporters sought out causes he could espouse and political scandals he could expose. They also investigated the activities and backgrounds of his opponents.'[5]

Newspaper ownership changed dramatically in the United Kingdom during the twentieth century. In the 1920s eleven different owners controlled the twelve leading daily newspapers whereas in the aftermath of the Second World War nine of these newspapers were still being published but each was owned by a separate individual or business. Concentration of ownership became a feature of later decades as new players arrived, among them Rupert Murdoch, Conrad Black and Robert Maxwell. The power of the contemporary baron remained considerable. Having left office former British prime minister Tony Blair openly admitted that, 'politicians are scared of the consequences of challenging powerful media interests'.[6] When accepting an invitation to address a News

2 H. Cudlipp, *The prerogative of the harlot: press barons & power* (London, 1980), p. 250.   3 Ibid., p. 265.   4 R. Greenslade, *Press gang: how newspapers make profits from propaganda* (London, 2004), p. 7.   5 H. Cudlipp, *Press barons*, p. 66.   6 T. Blair, *A journey* (London, 2010), p. 687.

Corporation conference in Australia in 1995 Blair remarked: 'You go, don't you?'[7] There was apparently no other option in light of the authoritative position acquired by Murdoch during the Thatcher era. Moreover, Blair also conceded that the support of Murdoch's newspapers (and the *Daily Mail*) was important for Gordon Browne winning the Labour Party leadership unopposed: 'any likely contenders didn't get a look-in; they got squashed.'[8]

Another British Labour Party figure – but from a different position on the party's political spectrum to Blair, Tony Benn, was more explicit in outlining what he thought these businessmen got for their media investments. According to Benn proprietors can use their ownership to promote their commercial inter- ests as well as to promote political parties, which would protect those same interests.[9] Indeed, there is sufficient evidence over several decades to show that some members of this British proprietor class expect their editors to do their bidding.[10] Proprietors have benefited from political patronage through, for example, elevation to the House of Lords or indeed, even direct participation in public life with ministerial appointment. More informally, the position allows the proprietor access – and the company of politicians at social occasions and private dinners – although it is difficult to determine the real measure of these interactions. Nevertheless, the 'behind the scenes' nature of much of this activ- ity undoubtedly raises the issue of public accountability.

Unlike in the United Kingdom where the profile of the proprietor class continued to change during the twentieth century – an indication that news- papers were worth owning even with their precarious records in terms of delivering a financial return – ownership in the Irish market remained remark- ably stable. The four leading daily titles after 1932 – the *Irish Independent,* the *Irish Press,* the *Cork Examiner* and the *Irish Times* – enjoyed a prolonged period of proprietorship stability. The de Valera family effectively controlled the Press group of newspapers until they ceased publication; the *Irish Times* altered its ownership structure to ensure it could not be a newspaper in play for those interested in developing media interests; the Crosbie family continue to run the *Examiner* to this day. There was somewhat more drama at Middle Abbey Street as the titles at Independent House saw a significant ownership change in 1973. The Murphy family had overseen the group in the era of the press baron – their media world was that of newspapers. Television and radio as competitors to print emerged in the final years of the Murphy ownership but interestingly even after O'Reilly's arrival as the dominant force in Independent Newspapers the defining 'product' – and source of profit – has remained the newspaper.

7 Ibid., p. 96.  8 Ibid., p. 655.  9 Quoted in R. Greenslade, *Press gang,* p. 375.  10 Greenslade, *Press gang,* p. 375.

There are varying ownership arrangements in the Irish newspaper market – from privately owned to publicly quoted to trust structures. In reality, however, all these publications share the common characteristic of being privately owned. They are motivated by varying degrees of commercial focus but they are all profit orientated. Survival is determined by profit – if they do not sell enough newspapers these businesses ultimately close. In this regard, owners have a key interest in ensuring that the editorial direction of the title attracts readers. After all, without readers there is insufficient advertising, the absence of which in sufficient quantities ultimately serves to undermine viability. Yet, irrespective of their private ownership and profit orientation these newspapers, to varying degrees, play a role in facilitating – and shaping – public debate. As such there are democratic issues at stake in the determination of their editorial positions. In the absence of the type of legal obligations governing public service broadcast companies newspapers are free to determine their own editorial direction. In an earlier era the leading newspapers had political preferences, most particularly the Press titles as the voice of Fianna Fáil and the Independent publications showing varying degrees of loyalty to Fine Gael. By way of contrast, today the editorial policies of Irish newspapers remain free of any one political party. In this environment, given their business focus, the challenge for newspapers is to strike a healthy – and transparent – balance between being a commercial enterprise alongside delivering a public interest ethos.

At the Leveson Inquiry into the British press in early 2012 Richard Desmond – owner of the Express group of newspapers – was asked about this very issue. His primary motivation, he declared, was profit.[11] It is understandable that proprietors would maintain a watchful eye on their investments. But newspapers – inevitably not all titles in a given market but certainly those that aspire to quality news and current affairs coverage – have a vital democratic role alongside delivering a return for their proprietors. The newspaper proprietor is a key player in delivering on this dual function. Concern rightly emerges where a proprietor might use a newspaper to pursue exclusively private agendas or to influence the political system in a manner that usurps public accountability. In this world profits and propaganda are very much linked and in Greenslade's words, 'the pair marched hand in hand.'[12] Much consideration has been devoted to determining to what extent proprietors do [mis]use their position for private gain. Central to ensuring that newspapers properly fulfil their democratic role is an understanding of what the proper role of the newspaper proprietor is, a role that is not always clearly defined or widely understood.

11 *Guardian*, 12 January 2012.  12 Greenslade, *Press gang*, p. 8.

## THE INDEPENDENT BARONS

At the turn of the nineteenth century William Martin Murphy, who had enjoyed considerable business success, was a rare breed in Ireland: 'a highly successful Catholic businessman.'[13] His interests ranged from railways and tramways to the Imperial Hotel in Dublin and Clery's, the largest department store in the capital. A stalwart of the Irish Parliamentary Party, Murphy had a history with newspapers but the decision to launch a new publication in early 1905 marked a significant departure from previous ventures. The *Irish Independent*, while nationalist in its outlook, was a non-partisan newspaper and intended as a purely commercial enterprise. Murphy had invested significantly in previous publications with little return. Nevertheless, more money was provided for the new *Irish Independent* – new printing presses arrived from Chicago – although in truth there was 'seemingly little assurance of a profitable return.'[14]

But Murphy was nothing if not a shrewd businessman. He was attracted by the success of the *Daily Mail* – launched by Northcliffe in 1896 – and several features of that title were incorporated into the new publication including better design, greater use of photographs, and signed articles with an attractive mix of content to win a wider readership. The newspaper sold at a halfpenny a copy and shook up the Irish newspaper market. According to one authority, 'This skilful blend of popular advertising and popular newssheet showed Murphy to be one of the most successful communicators in the country.'[15] The first issue appeared on 2 January 1905. The daily newspaper was soon joined by an evening title and a Sunday publication. Profits hit £15,000 in 1915 and three years later reached £40,000.[16]

Like many of his proprietor counterparts in the United Kingdom Murphy got more than a financial return on his investment. The risk of backing the new publication also brought a dividend in terms of editorial influence. Murphy appointed Tim Harrington as editor of the new *Irish Independent*. As Felix Larkin has shown in an earlier chapter Harrington was not afraid to argue with his boss over editorial autonomy. Nevertheless, the proprietor did not confine himself to being a mere bystander in editorial matters, keeping 'a very close eye on his paper'.[17] For instance Murphy's hostility towards the Irish Parliamentary Party was reflected on the pages and, while he was not responsible for the notorious Easter Rising editorials, he was said to have written editorials favouring home rule over partition in 1917. As Morrissey noted:

13 T. Morrissey, *William Martin Murphy* (Dundalk, 2011), p. 13.  14 Ibid., p. 37.  15 D. McCartney, 'William Martin Murphy: an Irish press baron and the rise of the popular press' in B. Farrell (ed.), *Communications and community in Ireland* (Dublin, 1984), p. 35.  16 Morrissey, *William Martin Murphy*, p. 38.  17 McCartney, 'William Martin Murphy', p. 36.

It is clear that Murphy did intervene from time to time on issues of particular interest to him, and was then likely to send notes and comments,
enclose letters or articles from friends, request that a favourite leader-
writer be set to work on his suggestions, and specify parliamentary figures and policies to be supported or attacked.[18]

William Martin Murphy died in June 1919 but his newspaper group remained
in the control of the Murphy family for another half century. His successors
retained the objective of delivering profit from the newspaper titles. They would
proudly proclaim in 1967 that their main national title, the *Irish Independent*, had
'been invariably included in every major Advertising campaign relating to new
and established commodities for more than six decades'.[19] But in achieving this
commercial outcome the proprietors were not passive bystanders from the
editorial process. The owners set the tone of the newspaper titles – to varying
degrees – they were Fine Gael-leaning and Catholic church conscious. In later
years under Tony O'Reilly the proprietor's editorial tone could be described as
favouring free market enterprise combined with outright hostility to paramili-
tary or terrorist violence. As mentioned previously, leading newspapers are
privately owned entities combining a commercial drive with a public interest
objective. Given the investment involved it is, however, not unreasonable to
expect a proprietor to want to protect their commercial interests – and to see
a profit on their investment. But due care is obviously needed in ensuring that
setting an editorial tone for a title does not become a means for promoting personal interests and undemocratically shaping wider political debate.

The diaries of Hector Legge – the long-time editor of the *Sunday Independent*
– record numerous instances where the Murphy family board of directors
kept a watchful eye on editorial matters. Two examples from 1960 testify to this
role. On Wednesday 17 February 1960 Legge wrote, 'Board discuss Kenneth
Deale murder series. Also pictures. Did not like last Sunday Independent's pic
on back page', while a fortnight later on Wednesday 2 March 1960 he recorded
the outcome of another board meeting, 'Chairman very keen to know what's
coming. Keen on money scandals'.[20] Legge, however, baulked at the idea that
this interaction between the commercial side of the company and his steward-
ship of the editorial domain amounted to interference: 'In my editorship of 30
years and two weeks, never once did they interfere editorially.'[21]

The Murphys and the O'Reillys shared, as mentioned previously, a drive for
commercial success. They were two wealthy families defined by dominant fig-

---

18 Morrissey, *William Martin Murphy*, p. 39.   19 Independent Newspapers, pocket diary 1967.   20 Diary entry, Hector
Legge (HL) papers.   21 Notes for draft memoir (unpublished), p. 92. HL papers.

ures with considerable professional career achievements and a taste for power. Labelled 'the most influential non-elected figure' in Ireland Tony O'Reilly has been described as a man interested in the wealth and social standing that power provides.[22] Murphy was a one-time public representative – although his political career was far from successful – and he enjoyed the company of, and had contacts with, leading nationalist politicians in the Irish Parliamentary Party. He does not seem to have cultivated connections with the emerging Sinn Féin constituency although his national daily newspaper was generous in its editorial stance in the post-1916 period.

O'Reilly toyed with the idea of a party political career in Ireland. He established 'political friendships', writing of Jack Lynch, who he first met in 1960, 'there was no better man in this century…'[23] The two families holidayed in west Cork, and Lynch was apparently prepared to parachute O'Reilly directly into cabinet as a Taoiseach's nominee to Seanad Eireann.[24] But O'Reilly opted for commercial success and in truth he built relationships in the two largest political parties in Ireland. Interestingly, despite claims of close friendships with leading political figures – Cooper made reference to a photograph of O'Reilly and Bertie Ahern having prominent place on the businessman's office desk – neither Ahern, nor Garret FitzGerald for that matter, mention O'Reilly in their respective memoirs. Still, being a media baron opened political doors. There are numerous published records of contact and meetings between O'Reilly and a succession of taoisigh. But O'Reilly has claimed he 'never sought to exercise any personal political power.'[25] Moreover, guarantees of editorial independence were features of takeover bids in Ireland, Australia and the United Kingdom. Matt Cooper – who worked as a journalist and editor in O'Reilly titles – points to a number of political decisions which were to O'Reilly's benefit although at no stage does he show direct intervention by the proprietor or the introduction of public policy measures that were exclusively to O'Reilly's benefit.

When there were editorial interventions – and Cooper provides a handful of episodes in a decade working on O'Reilly titles – they came from O'Reilly's proxies although it is not clear if these proxies were working on direct instruction of the proprietor or acting on their own initiative. On one occasion a senior independent executive contacted Copper to record his fury at a particular story and wanted action taken against the reporter involved. Yet when Cooper next met O'Reilly there was no mention of the story.[26] Moreover, an editorial in the *Sunday Tribune* in 2001 that called for the telecom company Eircom not to be sold to O'Reilly – or to two other leading Irish businessmen

22 M. Cooper, *Who really runs Ireland: the story of the elite who led Ireland from bust to boom … and back again* (Dublin, 2009), p. 3 and p. 9. 23 Quoted in D. Keogh, *Jack Lynch: a biography* (Dublin, 2008). 24 I. Fallen, *The player* (London, 1994), pp 164-5. 25 F. O'Toole, 'Brand leader', *Granta*, 53 (1996), 47–74 at 62. 26 Cooper, *Who really runs Ireland*, p. 23.

– accompanied by front page photographs of the three men, was met with a frosty reception by some Independent Group executives. But again Cooper records that when the editorial was discussed at a meeting with the proprietor 'it was O'Reilly who defended my independence'.[27]

The strongest evidence of the blurring of lines between editorial influence and personal-commercial position is offered in the case of Atlantic Resources, an exploration company backed by O'Reilly in the 1980s. O'Toole highlighted what he described as 'a rare moment of genuine indiscretion' in a 1983 interview with Forbes when O'Reilly remarked: 'since I own thirty-five per cent of the newspapers in Ireland I have close contact with the politicians. I got the blocks he [geologist] wanted.'[28] But for all the bravado about the power of the proprietor O'Reilly was actually left frustrated with the terms of the exploration license. His views were made very clear to then Taoiseach Garret FitzGerald but ultimately to no avail, and FitzGerald believed the editorial line of O'Reilly's newspapers 'swung somewhat' as a result (although the fact that he led a deeply unpopular government at a time of national economic crisis may also have been a contributing factor in the newspaper coverage). Regardless, the interesting outcome here is that despite his powerful position the proprietor did not automatically get his own way and was frequently left frustrated by government decisions. Indeed, Atlantic Resources has been described as 'one of the many expensive disappointments that he has endured in investing in Ireland.'[29] Moreover, in the case of Waterford Wedgewood in late 2008 O'Reilly was able to enlist the help of then Taoiseach Brian Cowen to try to convince the company's banks to extend credit facilities. The intervention was ultimately a fruitless exercise and O'Reilly and his wider family lost €400m on the failed investment.

When discussion turns to O'Reilly's editorial influence reference is inevitably made to the infamous 'Payback Time' editorial on the front page of the *Irish Independent* on the eve of polling day in the 1997 general election. In this instance the influence of the owner was seen as a means of penalizing an incumbent government for decisions taken, or not taken, that had a negative impact on O'Reilly's commercial interests in the television reception business. Those involved in writing the editorial denied any external intervention[30] but the episode stands uniquely in O'Reilly's forty-year tenure as the dominant force at Independent Newspapers, which depending on one's viewpoint can be taken as a positive or a negative fact. O'Reilly's response was to note that, 'government always feel they are being maligned by it [Independent Newspapers], whatever government, and opposition feel that they are being ignored.'[31]

27 Ibid., p. 27.  28 O'Toole, 'Brand leader', p. 64.  29 Cooper, *Who really runs Ireland*, p. 15.  30 Downey, *In my own time* (Dublin, 2009), p. 251.  31 Tony O'Reilly quoted in Colm Keena, 'On the paper trail', *Irish Times*, 3 April 2004.

Undoubtedly, since 1973 the broad parameters of O'Reilly's worldview were reflected on the pages of his newspapers, most specifically a healthy respect for private enterprise and in an Irish context distain for the activities of the militant republicans in Northern Ireland. When Cooper was appointed editor he was told by O'Reilly that the newspaper was not to offer support for the IRA – an instruction he deemed 'more than fair and reasonable'.[32] At the same time, 'another Independent executive' demanded that three journalists who O'Reilly did not like be sacked. Cooper resisted but two years later was forced to dismiss one of the three.

In a sense, however, the need for a proprietor like O'Reilly to pursue an interventionist editorial activity is abated through the editor selection process. It is unlikely that Cooper – or any of the other individuals who succeeded to editorial positions at newspapers controlled by Independent Newspapers – would have been selected for editorial promotion should their worldviews have been diametrically opposed to that of the owner. In his history of British journalism Martin Conboy noted how 'sympathetic editorial appointments' was one means by which Rupert Murdoch maintained his policy of arm's length proprietorial control.[33] This is, however, hardly a unique situation. Former *Irish Times* editor Conor Brady has observed that, 'Editors are generally chosen because they broadly share or reflect the proprietors'/publishers' values… there should be no need for crude interventions in the form of late night telephone calls.'[34] This view was shared from within Independent Newspapers by one of the main editorial writers over the last quarter of a century at the *Irish Independent*. James Downey recorded meeting O'Reilly socially but rejected the proposition that the owner directed editorial content: '… newspaper editors know what proprietors want, usually without being told, but I have no personal knowledge of any instance of proprietorial interference in the *Irish Independent*.'[35] In this respect, editors and journalists work within a framework laid down by the owner but that does not mean they work simply to do their master's bidding or that a newspaper operates exclusively as his mouthpiece. Indeed, it is likely that such a publication in the Irish news market would ultimately be rejected by readers and journalists alike.

## Conclusion

Media barons – or the press barons as they were in an earlier era – attract considerable hostility. The close proximity of the United Kingdom inevitably brings comparisons between the dominant individuals in the British media and their

32 Cooper, *Who really runs Ireland*, p. 24.   33 M. Conboy, *Journalism in Britain* (London, 2011), p. 54.   34 C. Brady, *Up with the Times* (Dublin, 2005), p. 29.   35 Downey, *In my own time*, p. 251.

counterparts in Ireland. In the Irish context, however, the only individuals to qualify as genuine media barons have been those associated with Independent Newspapers. So what can we conclude about the role of these owners?

First, in terms of editorial impact the influence of O'Reilly – and the Murphys before him – has been extensive at Independent Newspapers. As is their right as owner – or controlling owner – proprietors establish the editorial stance of their titles. In these privately owned newspapers there is a complicated and complex relationship involving editorial, profit and politics. Still, the examples of undue direct proprietorial interference at the Independent titles have been relatively few – and are probably no more, or no less, than examples at other privately and publicly owned media organisations in Ireland. Moreover, a study prepared by the independent think tank, tasc, noted that editorial interference by Irish media owners 'with the publication of stories of public concern very rarely occurs.'[36] Nevertheless, as has been mentioned previously, with the right editor in situ, and an established editorial ethos in place, the need for overt interference may be reduced, and this outcome has most certainly been achieved by the various Independent owners.

Second, there is evidence that media ownership provides political access. It is hard not to conclude that the Murphy and the O'Reilly motivation for the newspaper titles was primarily driven by commercial considerations. Yet, ownership of these media assets opened political doors. The negative consequences of the close nexus between barons and politicians was clearly demonstrated in evidence at the Leveson Inquiry in the United Kingdom throughout 2012. But the scale and extent of proprietorial and political influence on editorial matters for individual gain within Ireland would seem, on the available evidence, to be far less than that which has prevailed – and continues to exist – in the United Kingdom. And it is worth recalling that it is not just the media barons who seek access; there is ample evidence to conclude that politicians, and not just Irish ones, are cautiously eager to befriend members of the media mogul class. Transparency over such meetings and engagements is the best means of ensuring that these contacts are not reflected on the editorial pages or to the detriment of the public good in the policy formation process.

Third, alongside the specific position of an individual dominant owner/proprietor concerns have been expressed about the dominant market position attained by INM as O'Reilly expanded the range of titles in the Independent stable (see chapter 14). Seamus Dooley of the National Union of Journalists has suggested that INM's position provides the business with the ability to influence public, and ultimately, political opinion.[37] A contrasting view, however,

36 I. Hughes, P. Clancy, C. Harris and D. Beetham, *Power to the people: assessing democracy in Ireland* (Dublin, 2007), p. 409.   37 Seamus Dooley in I. Hughes et al., *Power to the people*, p. 424.

emerged in the aforementioned study prepared by the independent think tank, tasc, which concluded that, 'despite this concentration, there is enough variety of outlets and voices in the Irish media to facilitate democratic debate'.[38] So while the Independent titles attained – and over many years have successfully held – a dominant place in the Irish newspaper market the same market is sufficiently well supplied by other titles to ensure a diversity of opinion in the public sphere.

The early years of the twentieth-first century saw the emergence of a third dominant individual in a period in which the centre of power shifted at the now renamed Independent News and Media. Businessman Denis O'Brien invested some €500m in acquiring a stake in INM, eventually becoming the largest individual shareholder and vying with the O'Reilly family to shape the future direction of the business. The bitter war of words between the two sides saw O'Brien complain that he had been unfairly treated by the Independent titles: 'the hostile reaction to my shareholding in INM has been seamlessly executed through the editorial pages of all their publications'.[39] In the initial months of 2012 as the battle between the two camps further intensified O'Brien – against whom a government appointed tribunal of inquiry had made hostile criticisms over the awarding of a national mobile phone licence – was on the receiving end of repeated critical news stories and comment articles in a variety of Independent titles.

Unlike the O'Reillys whose media interests in Ireland were primarily in the newspaper sector, O'Brien had built a formidable presence in the Irish broadcast market. The potential emergence of cross-media ownership as a matter of public concern reopened consideration of the role of the proprietor in privately owned media, and also the complex relationship between control, commerce and public interest. Eoghan Harris – a columnist with the *Sunday Independent* – questioned O'Brien's intentions and whether his dominant position was having 'an inhibiting influence'.[40] And yet while the issue of cross-media ownership was a new consideration the fact that a dominant individual was seeking to direct the business was merely a continuation of a century-old pattern at the Independent titles. The media operation had moved from Murphy to O'Reilly, and now in 2012, to O'Brien. Presenting the news of the day 'without colouring or prejudice' was the task laid down in the *Irish Independent*'s first edition on 2 January 1905. That objective – however difficult to achieve – remains over a century later for William Martin Murphy's business, transformed by Tony O'Reilly into an international media organization and now embarking upon the next stage in its history.

38 I. Hughes et al., *Power to the people*, p. 409.   39 *Irish Times*, 15 Nov. 2011.   40 *Sunday Independent*, 1 Apr. 2012.

# Index

Page numbers in italics refer to figures or tables and those including 'n' refer to notes.